Grierson on the Movies

Also by Forsyth Hardy

JOHN GRIERSON: A DOCUMENTARY BIOGRAPHY
GRIERSON ON DOCUMENTARY
(Edited by)

Grierson on the Movies

Edited with an Introduction by
FORSYTH HARDY

FABER AND FABER
London · Boston

First published in 1981
by Faber and Faber Limited
3 Queen Square London WC1N 3AU
Filmset in Monophoto Times by
Latimer Trend & Company Ltd, Plymouth
Printed in Great Britain by
Redwood Burn Ltd, Trowbridge and Esher

British Library Cataloguing in Publication Data

Grierson, John
    Grierson on the movies.
    1. Moving pictures — Reviews
    I. Title   II. Hardy, Forsyth
    791.43′09′04   PN1995

    ISBN 0–571–11665–5

The publication of this book would not have been possible without the generous assistance of the John Grierson Archive, University of Stirling

Contents

Introduction

There was never any nonsense about Grierson; no one could fool him; neither the small, undeveloped talent, nor the big, meretricious bluff escaped him. Apart from his work as a film producer, he has written some of the most sensible and penetrating comments on films ever committed to British journalism, and it is my hope that some day some publisher will make it his business to collect them.　　　　C. A. Lejeune, *Observer*, 18 March 1945

John Grierson's first contact with the movies was as a subject for social analysis. In the United States in 1924–6 on a Rockefeller research grant, he went to Hollywood on the suggestion of Walter Lippmann who thought it would be helpful for him to add the cinema to the study he had been making of the popular press. In Hollywood, Jesse Lasky at Paramount gave him access to the studio files and he produced an analysis of the relationship between film content and box-office returns which subsequently formed the basis for a series of articles in the *Motion Picture News*.

For Grierson the movies had a fascination he could not resist. He was, of course, attracted to the cinema as a means of reaching and influencing a mass audience; but just as strong was his interest in the craft of film-making and in the men who were contributing creatively to it. Kindred spirits he found quickly in the studios and in the cafés on Hollywood Boulevard. At the Mark Twain Hotel he stayed with a group of writers who included Marc Connelly, Robert Benchley and Donald Ogden Stewart. Through Stewart he met Chaplin and through Chaplin, Josef von Sternberg. Others with whom he formed close and continuing friendships were Walter Wanger, King Vidor and Raymond Griffith.

Grierson drew on this background when he moved to New York and began to write regularly about the movies. His first articles appeared in the New York *Sun* whose film critic, Jack Cohen, soon realized that the young Scotsman who had joined him was a writer of exceptional quality. Grierson was encouraged both to write expansively about the nature of the film medium, still in a fluid and malleable state, and to seek out the directors whose work was opening out horizons wider than the commercial norm. Thus he met Robert Flaherty, and became directly involved in preparing Eisenstein's *Potemkin* for showing in America.

The cinema was in its transitional stage. Like other contemporary critics, Grierson was conscious that the technique developed since the turn of the century had reached a stage when the film had potential, if still limited achievement, as an art form. In his first article he wrote that, 'It is the very silence of the screen which gives it its magic', and his examination of the virtues of the 'unnaturalness' of the silent film is well founded and penetrating. What the cinema was losing by adopting sound was very much in his mind when he returned to Britain in 1928. In his first articles for British publication he was still much concerned with what he saw as the limitations of the talkie. These pieces show how he scorned the conversational picture and was apprehensive about the survival of the visual cinema. In time, the man who was to produce *Night Mail* acknowledged what sound could add to a film.

In Britain, Grierson began to write regularly about the movies. Given his devotion to social reform, it is not surprising that his articles appeared first in the Socialist monthly, the *Clarion*. Later he wrote weekly reviews for *Everyman*, a lively journal with a literary rather than a political emphasis. He wrote simultaneously for the quarterly *Artwork* and, still in the early thirties, for the *New Clarion* and *New Britain*. Later came *World Film News*. In addition to this regular film reviewing he was writing on film politics and documentary for a wide range of publications. In retrospect the volume of writing he produced seems enough to keep one man fully occupied. In fact it represented only a small part of his activity.

Grierson's reviews were individual and distinctive. He had gone to Hollywood knowing more about philosophy than film-making, and when he acquired his knowledge of the cinema and wrote about the movies, that mental enrichment was there to give a unique (at the time at least) breadth and depth to his writing. There were not many other critics so steeped in philosophy or so well read. This intellectual equipment he carried lightly, however, and it in no way inhibited his style: jaunty, witty, spirited and perceptive. In one devastating phrase he could destroy a film or expose a film-maker's inadequacy. Or he could write about a film in a way which doubled the reward of seeing it.

As one would expect from a man intent on achieving change, Grierson was an activist critic. His analyses always had a positive point. He found more American films to approve of than British because in general they seemed much nearer the workaday life of the nation. Most English films of the thirties, with their narrow, class-conscious reflection of the country, he found intolerable. He consistently attacked the film-makers for their shortcomings and their blinkered lack of courage in recognizing the drama on their doorstep. Had more producers in Britain listened to him, there might have been a British cinema to write about sooner than there was. Such films as *Millions Like Us*, *Waterloo Road* and *The Way Ahead*, meeting Grierson's demand for films closer to life in Britain, had still to be made.

But Grierson would not have caught and held the attention of his readers if all his critical writing had been in one key. He enjoyed writing about the work of the directors he had known in Hollywood. His friendship with von Sternberg did not blunt his criticism: 'When a director dies, he becomes a photographer!' His analysis of DeMille vividly conveyed his response to both the director's delight in spectacle and his craftsmanship. Indeed, examination of content and appreciation of craft are combined in most of the reviews. These are the judgements of a film-maker as well as a critic.

Grierson sensibly acknowledged that, 'We scribblers in cinema wander about for the most part making the best of second-class jobs.' Like others before and after him, he was sometimes obliged to write about the trivial and the forgettable. When a film of quality — *Kameradschaft* or *Earth* — did appear, his analysis of it imaginatively matched its achievement. In taking the measure of *All Quiet on the Western Front* he could convincingly argue that it was a braver and bigger, though not necessarily a better, piece of work than the original novel.

In a postscript he wrote for a collection I edited of his writings on documentary, Grierson upbraided me for presenting him as 'a pretty serious character', and I shall not make that mistake again here. As he said, the best things for him in films were the clowns and the comedians. His pieces on Chaplin, Harry Langdon, Laurel and Hardy, Keaton and the Marx Brothers hold his finest film writing and they have pride of place in this volume. He has his fun with Garbo and Dietrich, the worshipped ladies of the screen, and puts inimitably on record his delight in the great Mae West. His reaction to the bubbling vigour of the cinema was never narrow nor confined.

A word about the arrangement of the pieces in this collection. I have placed first an essay in general terms he wrote in 1968 for the *Critic*. As this was within four years of his death it was as near as possible a summing-up. From his writings in New York I have selected three representative pieces, including his review of *Moana* in which he first used the word 'documentary' in a film sense. The bulk of his critical writing on the movies was done within the years 1929–33. These reviews I have grouped under subjects where they have a natural co-relation or continuity. During the fifties Grierson was an occasional contributor to B.B.C. Scotland's *Arts Review* programme and from these contributions, with their understandable Scottish emphasis, I have made a small selection. It should be remembered that Grierson wrote them for radio and he was wise enough to know the different demands of the spoken and the written word. The concluding pieces on Flaherty, Eisenstein and Chaplin are tributes to three of the men who drew him most deeply into the cinema.

Here is the record of one man's affection for 'the living quicksilver' of the movies.

FORSYTH HARDY

Edinburgh
1 January 1980

1 · On Criticism

On critics and criticism I am out of the twenties, the earliest twenties, and as a point of vantage it is as good as any. I made my declaration of faith with the appearance of *A Dog's Life* and not only the world was young. The cinema was young; there was no body of criticism; we were creating it. In a more activist sense than critics could say today, the critics of the twenties were creating the cinema itself. I have heard a major national critic get proud in public and say the less the critic knew about production personnel and the production process, the better for criticism. In these days of first fine careless raptures, you couldn't keep critics away from production personnel and the production process. In America, if your stuff dealt with technical developments observed in French, German or Russian films, it was on the line to Hollywood immediately. It was also a heyday for the *a priori* boys, of whom I was the most hopeful. Perhaps it was that Hollywood wanted *a priori* respectability, but that stuff went on the line too and into the trade journals and at prices forty-five years ago our present host, the *Critic*, hasn't caught up with yet.

There are a lot of pluses and minuses in taking it that way from the top. In my time I have seen critics in the other media miss by a mile. I saw some highly respected gents miss by a mile on Joyce and even on Eliot, as others were mournfully struggling to get in the good word for Cézanne. For that matter, *Long Day's Journey into Night* was separating the men from the boys not so long ago. Maybe the cinema was easier; but we lived on 'firsts' and I don't think missed any. We even had one or two of our own, for the frontier was so wide open that we critics were sooner or later into making films, as writers or directors or producers. So very wide open was the frontier that my own 'first' was as a critic and in the way-out field of social analysis in a journal of sociology. I defined the need for a *nouvelle vague* in stars and story-lines which would reflect the high spirits I noted on the Chicago campus. Hollywood took me up on it. No, I didn't find Clara Bow. My one was Thelma Todd. Is there any critic around who can match me on Thelma Todd?

I don't mean to imply by this that film criticism is a deeper world of discourse because of its growth alongside the growth of movies themselves. Far from it. Depth is where it was in the beginning: with whatever Ghost it is necessary to call Holy. I have just been reminded by Peter Wollen that Gabo's Constructivist Manifesto in 1920 said that art was dead, that there was no room for it in the human work apparatus. 'Work, technique and organization! Let us tear ourselves away from our speculative activity and find the way to real work, applying our knowledge and skills to real, live and expedient work . . . replacing art which by its very nature cannot be disentangled from religion and philosophy and is not capable of pulling itself out of the closed circle of abstract, speculative activity'. We were full of that sort of thing at the time but many of us took the point without sharing the conclusion. We went with Trotsky, saying that art was a hammer, not a mirror; but we noted that he of all the Marxists allowed the antinomy of the Sublime and left a space for Tragedy. In all aesthetic it is the most important of spaces and, to be frank, the cinema has not been very good at tragedy nor very deep about anything. The theatre critics of my time, even if they sometimes miss on all six cylinders, have had bigger stuff to deal with: bigger in its engagement on both classical and social levels; and it is no miracle at all that the best criticism of my time has been in theatre criticism. Only, I think, in the field of comedy, has cinema come away with something of its own and something memorable by any standard in time.

Where film criticism has had the advantage is in the range of the cinema's manifestations. It has had a lot of windows opening on the world, which itself is a phrase pinched by the B.B.C. from one of the earliest film critics. On the richer papers in these days there was so much to get excited about that we divided up the territory. Someone did the stardust, but don't think we thought of this as only chit-chat. We were, we thought, finding them, confirming them, creating them and even—at the Rialto, Broadway, and to paper—making them our measure. Someone else did the day-to-day film criticism, and there was fighting for that too when we had purposes to serve. But, especially important, there was enough advertising to carry the more far-reaching observations on the importance of the medium itself; and these observations were sought and welcomed and for the same reason that Hollywood itself sought and welcomed every presence which would add to its sense of importance. Even the grubbiest of moguls could be occasionally conned into decency and they most deliberately were.

But sometimes we didn't do so well. It was probably not for the better but the worse that we critics loosed the European greats from their roots and delivered Lubitsch and Dupont and Murnau and Stiller and Lang and Jannings and Garbo and so many others to the Hollywood melting pot. The cinema was then, as now, an inter-national playground and no doubt the critics still conceive it to be part of their job to influence international exchange, but I wonder if producers still look to them and believe in them as they once did. It is a simple fact that I was once financed by Hollywood to wander over America and report on new audience reactions and over Europe to report on new faces coming up.

The coming of sound best illustrates the dilemma of the film critic. At first sight a drama was a drama was a drama; and the cinema could, it seemed, proceed to the depths of theatrical observation and the film critic with it. In fact there were losses to the critic without any compensation in kind. But begin first with the things that were taken over, so that they don't get in the way. The 'Western' was and the so-called 'epic' and the spectacle and the comedy. The out-and-about wanderings and intensities of the camera came over too, but with less conviction, now that everyone was wording away. What was lost mainly in the illusion that we were all boys together in the good old first division of dramatic criticism, was the original sense of pioneering a new medium, the original warm sense of having been one-and-all together on the ships at Mylae. Greatest loss of all was that activist approach to criticism I have emphasized.

But I said it was an illusion. Film criticism was not now in the first division of dramatic criticism: it was still where it was in a mass entertainment, strictly controlled by the requirements of mass appeal and mass profit and often cynically so — and with Government bless-ing — by thoroughly amoral men. Depth was as difficult as ever, if not impossible. Theoretically it was possible in the Socialist countries but there the imaginative permissives were, to say the least, dis-heartening.

I think that, after sound, the critics got mixed up in their analysis of the possibilities of their trade. I think that consciously or un-consciously they felt disappointed, frustrated and even impotent. I think that film criticism lost critical status by not remembering its limitations and working intensively within them. Just think: we had only just begun making a visual art. No doubt the people who wanted to do something about it got into production direct but, still, an un-ambitious, non-activist body of criticism is a sorrow for any medium.

I imagine there is something significant in the fact that the longest loyalties in film criticism these days are female loyalties and that some of the best criticism of the contemporary sort has come from females. Of course one of the greatest ever was a lady: that one on *Variety* who, on Costumes in general and Robert Taylor's night-gown in particular, managed a devastating account of the hairs on

Hollywood's chest. It was said that Robert Taylor never recovered from that particular activist specimen. Something else: now that the fashion in story-lines goes for the various deviations in domestic and personal derangement, it may be best to leave women to deal with it. It is their business. Whatever the reason, the fact that so much of the best criticism is coming from women, is worth a special adventure in social, not to say aesthetic, analysis.

But where I am bound to be respectful of criticism today is in this very effort to find a place *sub specie aeternitatis* for the many current species of personal disintegration. I have had reason to respect the academic distinction of André Bazin and his followers on the *Cahiers du Cinema* but I would feel muddled if I did not think that there is not one *nouvelle vague* but many—and on very different shores. What I have missed in the film criticism of *nouvelles vagues* has been a root in political philosophy which could give reality—in the true sense 'reality'—to each particular species of *vague*. I except Lindsay Anderson's critical approaches which I regard as the most impressive in this country and which I associate, I hope rightly, with Sartre's. Clive James has just been quoting a relevant passage from Sartre on Dos Passos. 'Fermez les yeux, essayez de vous rappeler votre propre vie, essayez de vous la rappeler ainsi: vous étoufferez. C'est cet étouffement sans secours que Dos Passos a voulu exprimer. Dans la société capitaliste les hommes n'ont pas de vies, ils n'ont que des destins: cela, il ne le dit nulle part, mais partout il le fait sentir; il insiste discrètement, prudemment, jusqu'à nous donner un désir de briser nos destins. Nous voici des révoltés; son but est atteint.' In the issue, some will say that Dos Passos hardly justified Sartre's attention but the Sartre argument gives a lead to the present-day clashes of force and the present-day potentials of drama and much justification to an activist cinema and an activist film criticism. I doubt if John Davis is listening. But I notice that the world's film festivals increasingly are.

When Anderson came out for his neo-realism, I noted at the time the unlikelihood of creating a movement without access to the means of production and distribution. Seeing the widespread revolt against the established patterns of political, financial and bureaucratic control, the divine discontent growing everywhere at the poverty of life (of all kinds) in a world of plenty, I am inclined to change my mind. I begin actually to believe that Anderson will win his argument in the streets. In the meantime, I hope we do not mistake the disintegration which has political implications with the sort which, in our time, has attended the American melting pot, and has been associated with melting pots from the very earliest dislocations in custom.

One rich prospect I am hopeless about and of another more hopeful. We have developed rich new ways of describing the many-faceted nature of truth in the complex present and Joyce's *Ulysses* is one of the aesthetic lighthouses of our time. I believe the cinema could do that sort of thing. I think we were playing with possibilities of the same kind in the silent days; I am sure we were deliberately doing so in two or three of the documentary films of the thirties. But this is a path for the cinema I see no money for, nor young people in the streets to urge it. When that night mail crossed the border it was on a sort of last journey.

But the revolt that has social and political implications is quite another matter and I believe that with a sufficient show of public disturbance all sorts of critical neo-realistic films can be promoted. The activist critic, if he wants to help, should rely blatantly on the thought that this is a time not for words but against words and for acts and the brisk encouragement thereof. I would like to hear Syd Newman saying one of these days: '*Nous voici des révoltés; mon but est atteint*'; for if ever a man wanted to know what is critically right it is he, the best guarantee of unrest in high places we possess. Sad to say, when the fields of criticism are drowsy, I look to the producers. With our lot up there — ex-critics or whatever, Syd Newman, Joe Losey and all — the prospect can't be all that bad.

Consider another, and one very dear to me. The B.B.C. has an excellent record, better than any in the world, in many fields of observation by camera: in journalism-in-depth not least. But it has been poor, poor, quite surprisingly poor, in the matter of poetic observation by camera. It doesn't even seem to be aware of the possibilities in so simple a theme as 'I remember, I remember, the house where I was born'. I just can't think why the critics have not stirred it up in the matter of visual poetry nor urged it to do something more aesthetically creative with television's genius for the intimate. These are prospects I hope to see fulfilled with no bother at all and in no time at all, if the critics see to their duty.

I don't want to leave the impression that I think we were superior as critics in these early days. I just think we were better educated politically, had more nerve, and were less sensitive about pushing people around. And we were lucky. We were lucky because we had a new medium to observe and we had, more obviously than today, new emerging aesthetic shapes to define. We were lucky because, in a world where everyone was starting at scratch, there was a special inter-dependence between the critic and the creator. We were lucky because it was an international world which made us think accordingly. We were even lucky that it was a world of mass entertainment;

for, within its strict and quite beastly terms of reference, we could still define much that was both possible and good and on a large scale.

So we were more self-consciously active in the making of the medium and the deepening of its influence than critics today normally try to be. They are, so many of them, just writers, word people. Whatever we were, we were active servants in the making of the people's images. We contributed to the development of visual spectacle and visual impact; we developed the exploratory powers of the camera and the rich associations of image at the cutting bench; we hailed the visual expansion of comedy and the especial genius of the cinema as a medium for clowns; we brought the working people to the screen.

But we failed too and on many important fronts. Working within the terms of reference of mass entertainment, coldly and vulgarly conceived, we could do so much but no more. We promoted the Western to the notion of epic; we got the cinema closer to the social democratic actuality of American life; but I have to remember that we couldn't get the last great Langdons on to Broadway and failed miserably to get the documentary notion into Hollywood's head, even though it was presented in the romantic formula of Flaherty. In fact we had to take it away from the normal film world altogether and give it other auspices. But, however you take it, our exercise in creative criticism was exciting and effective because it was ambitious about getting things done. The political and social influence of cinema as a mass medium and the present dynamic phase of political and social change make it more important than ever that the critics today should be active in getting things done.

(The *Critic*, 15 March 1968)

An Appreciation of the Silence of the Silent Drama

Today these columns are turned over to an essay written at my request by John Grierson of Scotland who is in this country on a mission that need not be described. He has studied the screen and knows whereof he speaks. In this essay he gives illuminating ideas on the possibilities of the cinema as an art medium, starting with the recent development of the phonofilm.

In my opinion the essay might be read with profit by any would-be motion picture critics (are there any?) as well as by those already practising. Motion picture criticism is, like the movies, largely a hit and miss proposition, there being no interchangeable, readily understandable terms wherewith to call attention to the many items that go to make up a given photoplay. At any rate, according to Mr Grierson, motion picture criticism isn't as bad here as it is in England. God help it over there!   The Moviegoer [Jack Cohen]

Mr Grierson speaking:

The phonofilm is the latest invention in these days of superthings. Already, as at the demonstration in the Selwyn Theater last Sunday, it has reached a point of development where orchestras can play recognizable jazz and the dancers can beat a recognizable clog-tattoo straight from the surface of the once silent screen. But even though the phonofilm progresses beyond the empty metallic tone of its present-day stage, even though its soprano notes become really soprano and not just bad phonograph soprano, it is doubtful if the future will look for the thin voice of Chaplin or the presumable bass of Wallace Beery. The screen has a value of its own as art, and that value would disappear if its silence were violated.

My meaning is, of course, the opposite of the dramatic critic's when he remarked that 'by the grace of God the movies have hitherto been dumb.' It is true that because of its dumbness the screen's possibilities in hokum have been limited. It is even true that, because of its dumbness, it has been able to avoid the intellectual inanities of the average modern drama. But the great thing about the dumbness of the screen is that it gives the movies a positive start where art is concerned. It is the very silence of the screen which gives it its magic.

The truth is that all art has been built on the unnatural. When the drama was really dramatic it was made up of poetry. In Shakespeare,

Corneille and the rest, the action went through in blank verse or rhyme as the case might be. The declaration of a lover and the protests of a mistress were in faultless feet. It was unnatural, perhaps, from a superficial point of view, but it gave a rhythm, a tempo, a power of expression to the drama which caught reality itself. Silence means the same thing to the screen. It, too, is unnatural, but it ensures that psychical distance, that magical and mysterious quality, which all art places between itself and the actual.

Only very slowly has the cinema world become conscious of this. It has progressed from those primitive days when it thought all it had to do was to turn the movie handle on the legitimate drama. But it has been content for the most part to follow a story in much the same sequence as it might occur in the pages of the *Saturday Evening Post*, with subtitles where the medium failed. The notion of a purely visual art (an art possibly far more akin to music than to drama), with its own technique and its own laws, is only beginning to be grasped.

Chaplin and Fairbanks are very distinct figures in this development. They, at least, developed cinema art on the side of pantomime. The broad and simple gestures of Fairbanks, the joyous spread of his arms, were an event in cinema history. The more subtle and, at times, uncanny pantomime of Chaplin was an achievement. But Chaplin did something more. It was in him that there developed the most powerful mask since the days of images and the gods. Perhaps Mack Sennett and the old Keystones are due some credit for this, but it was Chaplin that carried forward the mask's possibilities and brought it into the realm of tragedy. Like all great masks, he has made it talk into the depths, and always in silence.

But pantomime and the slow pungency of the mask (you may remember Chaplin's face when he walks into the dance hall as the stranger in *The Gold Rush*) — these were only a beginning. There the visual became conscious, and disciplined itself. The rest, to date, lies with men like Stroheim and men like Murnau, the director of *The Last Laugh*. The power of Stroheim, put simply, has been his use of the movie equivalent of the figure of speech. This thing which was so magical in the Shakespearean poetry, this throwing of the imagination to the ends of the earth to illumine a point, has been chained to the screen by Stroheim. Only in this case the things of the earth which illumine the point are brought into visual proximity with the point itself.

When the lovers in *Greed* go picnicking, the sewer pipe on which they sit is so brutally present that it might be the shadow of their fate. It is certainly a stroke of tragic irony as vivid as anything out of

Lear. The advertisement for Pluto Water which stands back of the lovers in the railroad station, or the incident in von Sternberg's *Salvation Hunters* where the satyr becomes identified with the horns on the wall, are perhaps more primitive examples. A flight of pigeons in one picture is made coincident with the handkerchief waving of a mob. It is, if you like, a more delicate example of how the environment can be set for the illumination of the action.

The Last Laugh has almost more lessons to teach than all the other pictures together. It has perfect examples of these figures of 'movie', and more. To the intoxicated brain of the old doorkeeper, and to us, the world really goes round. When, after the mad race with the stolen uniform the old man goes faint, the building over him really swoons. At one tragic moment a black and empty shadow flashes down the screen like an unearthly thing, as one might say 'Out, out, brief candle' to the figure of man. And so it goes. The revolving door, like the bucket chain in *The Salvation Hunters*, is charged with significance and repeated and repeated like a recurring theme, till it becomes the living symbol of Fate. A box is emphasized till it becomes as weighty as the world on the shoulders of Atlas. The earlier efforts of Chaplin are carried to new heights. The fateful qualities of public elevators and moving stairways, the sinister hostility of street cars in the rain, become weapons of poetic expression.

The limitations of silence, in fact, can be swept to the winds and kicked to the stars. The screen may use its camera-born capacity for miracle and for magic and achieve a vividness of imagery all its own. 'We lose half our quality if we lose our limitations', says Chaplin in a recent utterance. 'Motion, two planes, and a suggestion of depth: that is the chaos from which we will fashion our universe.' Chaplin is right. The screen may create within its own world a power of expression — a visual rhythm, a dramatic tempo — distinct from anything the other arts have been able to give us.

(New York *Sun*, 22 September 1925)

The Circus: Chaplin Tells the Story

Chaplin has a hut on his Hollywood lot where he retires of an afternoon to remember that he is an Englishman. The Californian sun filters through yellow shades into a cool interior and there are white tablecloths and rocking-chairs and tea to remind one of that primeval and not unwise laziness which Americans have forgotten.

But Chaplin is as vital in his lazy moments as in his occupied ones, and to sit with him for the first time is to sit and watch an amazing body, which is its own ceaseless commentary on everything its strange occupant happens to think of. As he told the story of *The Circus*, one looked, rather than listened, and to all intents and purposes Chaplin's mind was not engaged for a moment. The face and eyes articulated, and here if anything was the lost example of the Behaviourists, one whose body was his entire process of thought. Syllogisms rippled over his face and logic was a subtle affair of arms and legs that sought and found their conclusions of themselves.

The picture, it seems, opens with a hoop and a girl crashing through it. With a circle, and through it dimly the further circles of the ring itself. By emphasis the perfect figure becomes a rather sad affair. Chaplin wrote it on air. Again the crash, but the people under the big top bored to death. The pretty little lady being twisted into a shabby corner by the man with the whip.

Ya missed it again, didn't ya? Chaplin's face does a quick change from the Toulouse-Lautrec leer of the tough guy, and becomes innocent, sensitive and very frightened. I tried . . . only the horse . . . Hint of infinite Cinderella labours behind equestrienne frills. Gawd look at 'em . . . they're bored as hell . . . Chaplin pushes roughly but sinks immediately with the little lady . . . crash . . . through another hoop that lies discarded and shabby in the corner. First sequence.

Then my entry, Chaplin indicates. A bum mooching around among the concessions. A thief, a roll of bills slipped into the bum's pocket; discovery by a cop. A chase in the ancient manner . . . slap-bang into the ring of the circus. But on a revolving table places become changed and the hobo finds himself pursuing the cop . . . the bum pursuing the cop . . . they hug themselves in the ecstasy of magic.

Things straighten themselves out. Will the hobo consent to appear, etc.? A thousand dollars a week, he asks. The grand gesture of bums the world over. Four and four are nine . . . count it up, put a tick for the verification. Chaplin chuckles over it. A thousand dollars, and never been in a circus before. He gets seven, and seven only. Even then he is not worth it. He makes a poor student of tricks and is thrown into the streets till the crowd howl and howl for their bum again. Something must be done . . . the hobo comes back. Try him shifting the props. The very sight of him is enough. He can do nothing, absolutely nothing, right. The crowd yells approval of nothing, absolutely nothing, done right. His name goes into electric lights: he is the big hit. But *le comique est inconscient*; Charlot only thinks of himself as a propman, a very bad propman, at whom the people laugh; he can't read.

The little girl tells him and the director moves down with his whip. Charlot takes a long last chance. 'Hit her and I quit,' he says with a grand gesture. Chaplin likes that situation. It is the hobo asking his thousand dollars again and by a miracle getting it. It is Charlot become a millionaire again, with a tall hat and two fur coats, walking majestically up the gangplank. He goes on. Charlot is in love with the girl, but the girl is in love with the handsome tightrope walker. Inevitably. She looks up at him from the wings, and Charlot looks up, envying his magnificence. The beautiful body, the scarlet tights — he thinks if I could once get there. He practises secretly.

The tightrope walker falls sick. Try me — yeah, I can do that. But in a last moment of stagefright he compromises and a safety wire is fastened to his belt. So on the rope, wire full in view of the audience, deceiving nobody, he does his stunts. His tights are wrong, his body is wrong, but balances and tiptoe runs, he does them all and makes skill comic with certainty. It is so far a good average comedy premise. It develops. With the yells of the crowd and not knowing the reason of it, Charlot grows more certain of himself every second; there is nothing, it seems, that he can't do. The safety wire slips, but he doesn't notice; he breaks into a Charleston. The crowd goes wild as mimicry passes suddenly into magnificence. Chaplin illustrates it all on a plank line on the floor.

After? The stage hands grow fearful and point and Charlot notices and there comes over him the fear that makes havoc of all Charlestons. Bathos, and because of it, more laughter.

No, he doesn't get the girl at the end. He prays for the girl in a church on the simple word of the girl that she always got what she wanted there, but as he returns he is knocked down by an automobile and is only instrumental in bringing the doctor who will save the tightrope walker's life. So one resumes the proper logic of the puppet after his brief and foolish matrimonial venture in *The Gold Rush*. The fade out is of the ring where the picture began. It is deserted and shabby, and the stalls are empty, and there are no onlookers in shirt-fronts and diamonds even to be bored. Chaplin picks up something from the floor and with a shrug of his shoulders back-kicks it into space.

(New York *Sun*)

Flaherty's Poetic *Moana*

The golden beauty of primitive beings, of a South Sea island that is an earthly paradise, is caught and imprisoned in Robert J. Flaherty's

Moana, which is being shown at the Rialto this week. The film is un-
questionably a great one, a poetic record of Polynesian tribal life, its
ease and beauty and its salvation through a painful rite. *Moana*
deserves to rank with those few works of the screen that have the
right to last, to live. It could only have been produced by a man with
an artistic conscience and an intense poetic feeling which, in this
case, finds an outlet through nature worship.

Of course *Moana*, being a visual account of events in the daily life
of a Polynesian youth, has documentary value. But that, I believe, is
secondary to its value as a soft breath from a sunlit island, washed by
a marvellous sea, as warm as the balmy air. *Moana* is first of all
beautiful as nature is beautiful. It is beautiful for the reason that the
movements of the youth Moana and the other Polynesians are
beautiful, and for the reason that trees and spraying surf and soft
billowy clouds and distant horizons are beautiful.

And therefore I think *Moana* achieves greatness primarily through
its poetic feeling for natural elements. It should be placed on the
idyllic shelf that includes all those poems which sing of the loveliness
of sea and land and air — and of man when he is a part of beautiful
surroundings, a figment of nature, an innocent primitive rather than
a so-called intelligent being cooped up in the mire of so-called
intelligent civilization.

Surely the writer was not the only member of the crowd that
jammed the Rialto to the bursting point yesterday afternoon who,
as *Moana* shed its mellow, soft overtones, grew impatient with the
grime of modern civilization and longed for a South Sea island on
the leafy shores of which to fritter away a life in what 'civilized'
people would call childish pursuits.

Moana, which was photographed over a period of some twenty
months, reveals a far greater mastery of cinema technique than Mr
Flaherty's previous photoplay, *Nanook of the North*. In the first
place, it follows a better natural outline — that of Moana's daily
pursuits, which culminate in the tattooing episode — and, in the
second, its camera angles, its composition, the design of almost every
scene, are superb. The new panchromatic film used gives tonal
values, lights and shadings which have not been equalled.

The film traces pictorially the capture of a wild boar by the youth
Moana and his family, the capture of a giant turtle, surf-riding, the
preparation of a native meal (made fascinating by clever cinema
technique), and finally winds into the already talked-of tattooing
episode. Here, as a tribal dance proceeds, a fantastic design is
pricked by a needle into Moana's glossy epidermis. It is a period of
intense pain for him, but as the sweat pours off his face he bravely

bears it, for, as the subtitle has it, 'the deepest wisdom of his race has decreed that manhood shall be won through pain.'

Possibly I should become pedantic about this symbolizing of the attainment of manhood. Perhaps I should draw diagrams in an effort to prove that it is simply another tribal manifestation of the coming of age? It is not necessary, for the episode is in itself a dramatic, truthful thing. And if we regard the tattooing as a cruel procedure to which the Polynesians subject their young men — before they may take their place beside manhood — then let us reflect that perhaps it summons a bravery which is healthful to the race.

The film, time and time again, induces a philosophic attitude on the part of the spectator. It is real, that is why. The people, these easy, natural, childlike primitives, are enjoying themselves or suffering as the case may be before the camera. Moana, whom we begin to like during the first reel, is really tortured and it affects us as no acting could. Moana's life is dramatic in its primitive simplicity, its innocent pleasure, and its equally innocent pain.

Lacking in the film is the pictorial transcription of the sex life of these people. It is rarely referred to. Its absence mars its completeness.

The most beautiful scenes that Mr Flaherty conjures up are (1) Moana's little brother in the act of climbing a tall, bending tree flung across the clear sky; (2) the vista showing the natives returning after the deer hunt; (3) Moana dancing the Siva; (4) all the scenes in the surf and underwater; and (5) the tribal dance.

I should not, perhaps, say that any group of scenes is any more beautiful than any other; for all are beautiful. . . . and true.

Moana is lovely beyond compare.

(New York *Sun*, 8 February 1926)

3 · The Coming of the Talkies

The coming of the talkies has given the cinema magnates what they wanted. An occasion for boosting, bally-hoo, and all the gentle arts of selling nothing in particular. They are showmen, impresarios of the sidewalks, capitalists exploiting the bedraggled leisure of a rather less than emancipated democracy. Capitalists with profits to build — socially or anti-socially as the case may be.

And business was getting difficult for the poor devils. The shadow of art was creeping down on the movie joints, disturbing them immensely. The novelty of cinema silent was over. Its laws were beginning to be comprehended: its possibilities to be realized. The pace of production was getting harder and harder as critical judgement was being built up outside. The days in which the public goat unquestioning ate up all the rags, bones and bottles in the movie backyard were as dead as Barnum.

But now Talkie. With a yell of relief the impresarios are back at the old stand, selling the latest miracle to the everlasting hick. More rags, more bones and more bottles for the goggle-eyed goat. The soul of Barnum — who was ever their prophet — goes marching on.

'You ain't seen nothing yet.' 'The silent was a good old horse, but this is an automobile.' 'Take an earful.' 'THEY TALK. THEY TALK.'

A generation ago they were standing outside their nickelodeons shouting 'They move, they move!' and the silent was billed between the Fat Lady and The Latest from Paris. In the new style the touting is done at public luncheons and by the banner-heads of the newspapers. But the accent is identical. You have the firm and fulsome promise that when the shadow of art creeps in on the talkie, the talkie in its good turn will be sabotaged for another novelty.

In defence of this policy of novelty-mongering the showman will refer you to the Man from Wigan — for the Man from Wigan is the little god he keeps on the mantel-piece of his conscience. If there be such a mass figure of dumbness, you may trust the showman to keep him in all benightedness. He is easier that way.

Life certainly will be tough for a while. The production dollars will be going into talkie-Western, talkie-society drama, talkie-musical comedy. The big majority of them will be bastards, with a snatch of song here, and a dash of footling conversation there. They will be turned out at top speed (with the decencies nowhere) to meet the novelty market. Visuals will be the Ugly Sister. The critical cinema-goer will see no more of serious cinema for the present, unless people like Murnau and Flaherty—now gone on an expedition to the South Seas—send their masters to perdition and come through with something.

Always, of course, there is the solid hope represented by Russian cinema, and the persons of Eisenstein and Pudovkin. Pudovkin, they say, is to make a miners' film in England. There is mention of Eisenstein making that epic in Canada, which producers in the provincial fastnesses of Piccadilly have forgotten to do.

And there are still some films which may help to while away the time for the first year of the new dispensation: films like Taritch's *Ivan the Terrible*, Lubitsch's *The Patriot*, Seastrom's *The Wind*, May's *Homecoming*, Dreyer's *Joan of Arc*, Preobrajenskaia's *The Village of Sin*. *Ivan*, terribly cut since I saw it in Berlin, has its flax-spinning sequence more or less intact. *The Patriot* has Emil Jannings at his best and Lewis Stone better than that. *The Wind* is Swedish, in spite of a western setting, and is clearly as good as Seastrom's earlier work, with Lon Chaney, in the *Emperor of Portugalia*. *Homecoming*, which comes presently, is by Germany's best director after Lubitsch. It begins against a Russian horizon, but tails off against a German interior, and is all in all not so good as readers of the novel and the admirers of May expected. But it has something, and something is a good deal in the movie world.

The other two I saw in Paris, and they may or may not come over. *Joan of Arc*, French by a Danish director; *The Village of Sin*, Russian by a woman director who learned her job from Pudovkin. *Joan* is all, or very nearly all, in close-up against a white background. It has the subtlest and strongest camera work ever done in cinema, and is by all odds the most new and individual movie since *Potemkin*. Warm, one of the men who made *Caligari*, was art director; Mati and Katula were behind the camera. *The Village of Sin* is a tale of Russian peasants, with a rhythmic harvest scene so beautiful that it takes your breath away. The story of rape which goes with it is not so beautiful.

With which gossip, I shall return to this matter of Talkies. It cannot and will not kill the cinema we know, because it is a different thing.

You see, it is not a question of a single art having an essential development forced upon it. Cinema is not an art and never was. It is one way of writing—picture writing—and it is the raw material of any number of arts. Yes, and of near-arts and not-anywhere-near arts as well. It has no obligation to concentrate in one direction. In writing you may novelize or dramatize or poetize or journalize or musical comedize, as the spirit takes you. Each form has its own laws and its own satisfactions.

So with cinema. On the strength of the new line of best sellers, cinema publishers may clear their shops of everything else. But it is obvious that the forms of cinema which produced *Caligari* (masque macabre), *Joan of Arc* (masque tragic), Chaplin and Langdon (masque comic) and the epic activism of *Nanook*, *Potemkin* and *The End of St Petersburg* — cannot be pushed out of existence by the nit-wit pee-wee conversationalism of this new face-stuff. Society drama and other subtitular conversational forms will be, but they were only halfheartedly visual from the beginning.

The cinema of epic skylines and mass energies and the cinema of significant mask and significant gesture will, in fact, harness synchronization to their original purpose without sacrificing one iota of that rhythmic beauty and visual poetry for which some of us serve them. They will use an undercurrent of musical, choral and natural sound effects wherever such undercurrent helps them on their way. But this they have always done.

I am afraid only of one thing. It is that the cinema of this nature (with the visuals all on, so to speak) will find itself a poor competitor in the market place with the conversational and singsong varieties. With the visuals all on (the problems of rhythm, imagery, significant gesture, etc.) the silent cinema are great arts, but they are also difficult ones. They are properly — and will be increasingly — in a world with poetry, music and painting. And it may appear presently, with the conversational opposition at its height, that their place in the programme will be occasional and for variety's sake only. The pathos of distance which comes with skylines may prove too tense — the abstraction which comes with silence may prove too remote — especially for the women audiences who hang like a millstone round the aesthetic neck of democracy. Living and thinking, as they do perforce, in a world of petty horizons and only too personal satisfactions, they will fall for the chit-chat.

That precisely is the field for the talkie proper: the world of petty intimacies in which people love each other, hate each other, get jealous of each other, and otherwise take each other's little selves quite seriously. The Talkie takes over from the silent cinema the personal story of bourgeois ideology.

The silent cinema is well rid of it.

(*The Clarion*, June 1929)

I write this article from a sheep-station in the Highlands of Scotland.

Around me are the glens and corries and hills on which generation after generation of peasants have broken their wintry livings. There have been tragedies in these parts as grave as ever inspired the cameras of Sovkino. In the blessed reign of Queen Victoria one village of twenty crofts and a hundred souls vanished almost overnight into the wilderness. The fronts of the cottages were torn out, the furniture thrown into the road, and the people themselves left to find what way they could to the factories and Canada. Bracken has grown over the foundations, yellow broom sweeps madly over the fields, obliterating a century of men's labour. It is one story among ten thousand stories of the people, which the cinema will never touch.

Nor would I recommend it. It is of the past and goes nowhere; and I am very content to let the broom and the bracken have the last word on the subject. Yet, I find myself wondering—at the very distance of the theme—whether the cameras will ever come to the people, to the work they do, to the lives they in all actuality lead. Will we ever, while Wardour Street and Hollywood reign, unshackle the cameras from their studio foundations and take them into the open? Will we ever be able to yank these Piccadilly actors by their lily-white pants into the dramatic realities of the workaday world?

For I am convinced of this, that there are bigger stories to be taken out of the factories, the fields and the mines, than can ever be taken by studio out of Mayfair and the night clubs.

Some years ago Douglas Fairbanks remarked that if ever the cinema went indoors, it would perish. The point was a fairly solid one, for the cinema freed from the studio acquires the powers which take it a million miles away from the theatre and make it unique as a medium. It can come to the life and, by picking and choosing, build from the life. It was no Hollywood actor who hunted for Flaherty, but Nanook, of the North, with centuries of killing in the poise and thrust of his harpoon. And the camera's command over the genuine, over the spontaneous, over the thing-in-itself is not a power to be thrown lightly away. I can understand Eisenstein's chuckle when the American critics commended the superb acting of the Moscow Art Theatre players in *Potemkin*. There was not one professional in the film. For sailors Eisenstein uses sailors, for peasants, peasants. The camera never forgets and never forgives the difference.

Apart from the work of the Russians, the cinema has done very little for the world of the genuine. There was Flaherty with *Nanook* and *Moana*. Then Schoedsack and Cooper with *Chang*, and in between some excellent travel films like *Arctic Skies*, *Stella Polaris* and

Voyage au Congo. But in all these natural films the cinema has, for the sake of an easy romance, gone primitive. No one, to my knowledge, has gone forth on a wild expedition to the coal mines of Durham, or adventured under banners of publicity to Wolverhampton. No one for that matter has taken a tuppenny ride to Silvertown.

Yet, in a way, I cannot say clearly what I am seeking in this cinema of the actual. I do know definitely what I am not. I am not proposing for a moment to play the old triangular romance against the coalfaces and the steel furnaces. First National did that in *Men of Steel*, and Asquith — less ambitiously — did it in *Underground*. They imposed an unreal and stupid story on a magnificent background. It seems to me rather that out of the steel mills, out of the mines, out of the London docks, might be built the life-stories of steel and steelmen, coal and colliers, docks and shipmen: of things and men as they in all dramatic reality are, with the world living and moving as in truth it does, to the roar of furnaces, the hacking of picks and the clatter of derricks.

This I know is not a simple matter, and I will bear personal witness to the infinite labour of bringing such worlds of epic activity and mass labour to a point in drama which does a vestige of justice to them. But in so far as the cinematic mind has not in this country or in America been even faintly directed to the job, there is no great reason why it should be easy. A vast amount of capital and a vaster amount of creative thought will have to be diverted from stars and theatrical effects before anything considerable can be achieved in so virgin a field.

When the talkies appeared on the American horizon four or five years ago, Flaherty had enormous hopes that they might prove the salvation of the actualist cinema. If I remember, he sketched out forthwith an epic story of South Africa, with generation after generation of settlers pushing beyond the northern horizon, and breaking new ground in the wilderness. Much of its effect was to depend on the sound effects: on the roar of the Zambezi, the cries of wild animals in the bush at night, and — in one scene — the vast crackle of a bush fire. But we did not reckon at that time on the mechanics of the business. The talkie instrument is so crude as yet that it can only function decently in the controlled surroundings of a sound-proof studio. Indeed, so far as the talkies are concerned, the cinema has not only gone indoors: it has hermetically sealed the doors, the windows, and every conceivable passage to the open air. In *In Old Arizona*, the sweep of the foothills, and all the other wonders which have clung so desperately to the Western, had disappeared almost entirely. This first talkie of the wild west was a story of interiors — necessarily so. There is every reason to believe that Hollywood's outdoor tradition will perish still further while the microphone is perfecting itself.

After that, what? Returning to my sheep-station, they are at this time of the year gathering in the hirsels for the clipping, and the lambs are being separated from their mothers with much crying of old and young backwards and forwards. A dozen dogs are yelping excitedly as they turn the droves into the fank, and shepherds are whistling their orders and shouting in Gaelic. From the hill comes the low music of the burn over the rocks, which rises and falls with the wind and the rain, but never stops from one year's end to another. Tonight the sheep will go into the hill again, mothers will be re-united with lambs magically among thousands, and they will go up together unerringly to their own spot many miles away. The crying will not stop for hours, and distance and the quietness of the night will make it weirder than before. It has always been so, and the hill has no reality without it.

When the talkies give us an instrument which will record these things, and add, say, the cry of a whaup or a seagull, and give us the subtle distance of a boy singing on the other side of the loch, then, and then only, will it mean something for cinema proper. For the present one must prefer music.

(The Clarion, August 1929)

It is winter in the cinema world, one of these good old melodramatic winters in which furtive figures clutch unwanted offspring to desolate breasts, and snow falls and falls and falls. I know not how many silents are on the shelf. Others are being furbished up with spots and spotlings of noise — before, after, or indeed in any connection whatsoever — and so they yell lustily enough, but may yet be received into the bosom of the family.

For most of the said silents I have all the hardness of heart of a Warner brother. They were silents perforce, stories of personal relationships, best told in the conversational give-and-take which establishes the relationships of individuals. And for God's sake let the talkies take up their tale and be done with it. It may not, to be sure, be worth telling, but the talkies are certain to tell it better.

There is no use being all-embracing and indiscriminate in one's affection for silence. It is true that silence threw a pleasing mist over the inanities of story and the utter feebleness of character-drawing, and because of occasional lovelinesses we allowed our visual delight to cancel out what our intelligence revolted at. But now that the beautiful dumbbells have begun to talk, we have a less ambiguous measure of their quality.

Cinema — box-office cinema — has not, and never had, any innate love of visuals. It is an organization like the popular magazines — a story-telling, amusement-peddling organization of the popular sort, built on Ford principles. And asking it for the subtleties and difficulties of the visual is as futile as asking the *Saturday Evening Post* for a dissertation on the Critique of Judgement.

Take the following films: *In Old Arizona*: something about two guys, a girl and a murder. *The Wolf of Wall Street*: something about two guys, a girl and a near-murder. *Madam X*: something about a girl, many guys and a murder. *Broadway*: something about two guys, two girls and a murder. *The Doctor's Secret*: something about two guys, a girl and a taxi fatality. And so on and so on. Guys, girls, loves, jealousies and sudden deaths, varied by studio-murder-mysteries, behind-the-curtain mysteries, silent-house mysteries and musical comedies *ad infinitum*. Some of them, note you, perfectly sound as entertainment, with good acting, good singing, good spectacle, and honest craftsmanship in their technical entrails. But as exercises in the solidities, none of them start.

None of them, indeed, thought of starting. They are shows in the humble sense, side-shows, here today and gone tomorrow, and you will be wise to discipline yourself in the categories and limit your expectations of them. Do you sensibly expect Zukor and Lasky and John Maxwell to initiate you in the arts? Bless your sweet innocence!

The best of the present tendencies is to capitalize the attraction of the great music-hall artists and popular song-writers. Al Jolson in *The Singing Fool*, Maurice Chevalier in *Innocents of Paris* and at least two of the Four Marx Brothers in *The Coconuts* are brilliant figures, and the screen only adds to the gaiety of nations in giving them to the world at large. Music-hall is by all odds the greatest of popular media, and if the screen adds one cubit to its stature, you should thank the gods for it. It permits the popular entertainer to specialize in himself and achieve a measure of individual genius which escapes the more complicated efforts of the theatre. Harry Lauder, Will Fyffe, Billy Bennett, Ann Suter, Gracie Fields, Grock, the Fratellini Brothers: we will have them all properly distributed presently. Please heaven a half-witted cinema censor will not dim or dull the physical righteousness of Ann Suter or blot out a line of Billy Bennett's balladry. In an age of snifflings, pipings, pulitry and pornography, we need all the physical gusto and broadery we can get.

I shall say less for musical comedies, musical dramas and the like, for there indeed I am lost. Cochran wakes no fever in my breast, and the only time I ever saw a Shubert leg-show I walked out at the first interval with a twenty-dollar ticket in my fist. I went to see *Show Boat*, but the spectacle of that superb artist, Paul Robeson, 'Ole-Man-Rivering' between the face-to-face love-howls of hero and heroine was too much for me. I am therefore no guide. I am constitutionally against love-howls whether in Covent Garden or Piccadilly. They may have their place, but it is in the exclusively women's theatres which men may know to avoid. These, I regret to say, do not as yet exist.

The talkies, you may believe, will carry the love-howl to its most piercing perfection. *The Broadway Melody* stages singie tête-à-têtes with full orchestra in the privacy of a fifteenth-floor apartment. *Mother's Boy* is content with the back-room piano, but slops it identically. Al Jolson does it anyhow. They all howl and howl, and for the present the orthodox ambition in the hero heart is to make good as a songster. Who, outside the pastures of boobery, you ask, wants to be a singer anyhow? You do not understand. The talkie, in its naïve effort to tie up the old romance of success with the new opportunities, must wither the world to a musical-comedy stage. And there's an end on't.

Poor Maurice Chevalier! They have to turn his back to the audience in the love-scenes to prevent the supreme sophistication of the man breaking through their imbecility. Even as it is, every twitch of his shoulders is an invitation to the raspberry beds.

But these are only the first crude solutions of the talkie problem and may be borne with. The talkie is like a child of Prohibition introduced suddenly to the opportunities of a full-dress bar. It is mixing its drinks woefully and making an unconscionable mess of its innards. Theatre, music-hall, spectacle, silents — it mixes dollops of all four and misses in the mixture the virtue of each original constituent. *Broadway* is an excellent case in point. Presently, however, it will learn how to shake fairer cocktails.

More than cocktails I cannot promise you.

(*The Clarion*, September 1929)

Robert Herring recently made a short and swift judgement on the talkie situation which will bear some repetition. In the days of the silents, he says, there were already many who were trying to formulate some aesthetic of cinema, trying to show what it was the film's province to do, and what could be done by other means. Thus far we had actually got, and the dawn of dramatic importance was at long last touching (with roseate hue) the monumental slag-heaps of movie commercialism. It is this very seriousness of aim that the talkies have swept away. The old problems of what was or was not cinema went under as the new problems of sound and colour presented themselves. In the welter of back-stage dramas — all-talking, all-singing, all-dancing and all nonsense — nothing yet emerges of the same constructive consequence.

You must not hold Herring responsible for my phrasing, but the argument is sound enough. It bears repetition for the good reason that, if anything is to be done with the talkie business, we must start to think talkie in the self-same way as we once started to think silence; critics, producers, editors, all of us. We thought the silent cinema away from theatre; we thought it, with certain spasms of thinking, into its own world of mask and mime and movement. We articulated the world visually perceived, orchestrated its detail and played its effects. We rediscovered the principle of imagery which was lost with the poets. The same thing now has to be done for the world aurally perceived — for the world of sound.

There is no question at all of being against the new principle of synchronization, and anyone who defends the old system does not know (in sorrow and ashes) what he is talking about. One short experience of my own will illustrate why. When I had finished *Drifters*, there came the problem of music and, being no musician, I sat around for the experts to *fit it*. Several experts have at one time or another *fitted it*. There have been slices of Stravinsky, of Wagner, of Mussorgsky, of Mendelssohn and a dozen others. There have been snatches of 'Home Sweet Home' and 'Caller Herring', and any number of swishes and tinkles from the starboard side of the orchestra pit.

I shall not say how good or bad the different scores were, but this I can properly say, that not one of them gave me the film I cut. Here and there a score gets under a sequence and makes it six times bigger, but just as often its pulse-beat is not the pulse-beat of the film. It tortures the rhythm and strangles the march of the film to the point of agony. Here, indeed, I record an observation which blotted out my last lingering affection for the so-called silents. I have seen a sequence come alive with one score which was killed dead by another. I have seen sequences wriggling like worms cut in half because the music changed at the wrong time. I have seen a continuity lengthen and drag and flop because the music reached its natural peak some seconds before the cutting was ready for it. The music was releasing the audience from attention just when the film was calling for it.

It is not the fault of the musician. He does wonders if you consider the short time he is given for the preparation of the score. It may take months to cut a film, but he is given hours to cut the music. And, moreover, his library of selections is against him from the start. He is asked to build his house, not with bricks, but with rocks, each piece of music having its own obstinate individual existence. How, except by the crudest chance, then, will a piece of music match the equally individual existence of a stretch of film?

Such haphazardries are impossible in any serious work and I, for one, am glad to see the last of the score-as-you-please tradition. If sound is part of the life of a film — and it was from the beginning — let it be organized like the rest, and *synchronized*, so that no one-horse orchestra can murder it. In cinema accompaniment the timing is everything; the complementary effect is everything; let the quality of noise be what it likes.

At this point let me go a step further. It is not plain that there is much hope for the musical score even when it is made most especially for the film. Many of us thought so two or three years ago, for it promised something very much better than we were getting. We hailed the Meisel accompaniments for *Potemkin* and *Berlin* accordingly.

But I put it to you. Can we enslave the film to the mannered abstractions of music any more than we could to the theatre? We had to at one time, because music was the only organized world of sound we could use. It is, of course, a highly organized world, and perhaps the most subtly organized of all the worlds of art, but with its very arbitrary instruments, it is as stylized as the theatre. Necessarily so as the theatre was necessarily so, if we consider the conditions which produced both of them. One constructed according to one's tools, within the limits set by one's tools, and there could be no question of directly organizing either aural perception or visual.

It is different now. We can photograph sound and, photographing it, we can organize it. The wide-open world of sound is there for the taking, to be built to the purposes of art, not by strings and brasses and winds (though heaven knows they do it well), but in the simply registry of all the whispering nuances of life itself.

Cinema cannot refuse the help of music nor of choral singing, nor of any of the other mannered massings of sound, but I do think that the especial progress of cinema will lie in the pursuit of its own gifts. The theatre can orate and the orchestra can make music, but neither of them can go out under the winds and organize the actual. We shall tend on the whole to depart from both music and dialogue.

There must be a poetry of sound which none of us knows, a country whose satisfactions have been till now the monopoly of the blind. Meanings in footsteps, voices in trees, and words of the day and night everywhere. There must be massed choruses of sound in the factory and the street and among all men alive, ready to the hand of the builder, ebbing and flowing with life, rising and falling in a commentary and explanation of life. I know not the first thing about them, though I have, like everybody else, shut my eyes on hillsides and by the sea, and sat for hours trying to make something of the door-bangings and footfalls and crazy oddments of conversation that broke the plush darkness of a London night. We are tyros, all of us, with a new world opening up on the horizon. I see no reason why anyone at the moment should envy Columbus.

(The Clarion, January 1930)

4 · What I Look For

The editor asks me to stand forward on this festive occasion and speak a more general piece than is my humble custom. He thinks that the vast new audience of weekly readers may conceivably want to know what sort of things in cinema I believe in. The implication is that having seen the lion rampant of my flag you will come tearing after me every time I do battle on the fields of Wardour Street. I only wish I could follow the example of Wyndham Lewis (before Lewis had yet turned from the rip-roaring world) and publish my Blast of the Cinema. What things I should blast and what size of type I should blast them in! All the printing resources of the *New Clarion* could not find ink black enough for the soppies and the slobbies I would throw to the moon or the many, many monkey madnesses of showmanship I would gird and grind at. But let me be specific.

I am not a Garban. I see the Garbo, as a critic must, and I even like her well enough, but each time a new epic emerges from the presence, the worshippers among you will find me frigid. Once when Stiller directed her they let her be the crazy thing from another world she was meant to be. Now it is all cold commercial siren stuff, or a near-satanic tumbling from heaven to hell. Near-Satanic only, an imitation tumbling only, without conviction of space and time, and the fateful worlds one can fall to.

Nor am I a Dietrichite. I like her, again well enough, because Joe Sternberg, the director, likes her, and I like Joe Sternberg; but I see no other world in her either, nor aspect or illumining of the original Mother Earth. As I might explain, I am not for the fans at all, but all for this other world business. I do not ask to be taken to Jupiter, or the ends of the earth, or even beyond my own accustomed backyard, but of every film and every film talent I do ask a modicum of revelation. It may be a novelty of fact, or an angle of beauty, or an efficiency of technical demonstration. These will serve in the absence of better things, and I praise accordingly *Ideal Cinemagazine* for the novelty of fact, and Tissé, the Russian cameraman, for the beauty of angle, and think Cecil B. DeMille the greatest director in the world for sheer showmanship. Every film DeMille does I sit round the programme to see twice.

But there are greatnesses beyond these things: the sort of revelation that comes with Chaplin and Pudovkin, and every now and again from people like Hitchcock and Asquith and Lachman and Vidor and Sternberg and Flaherty and Roland Brown. It is my old-fashioned opinion that nothing less will serve us finally in our attention on cinema. It would be foolish to expect a lot of it, for revelation will remain, as ever, a difficult and rare experience; but consciously or not, we do ask a little of it every so often. Even a medium of professedly popular entertainment cannot quite escape that demand.

As I understand it, the first job of a critic is to stand as sensory instrument to the world of creation, and register this revelation as it comes along, and point people to it and, it may even be, do something to underline or elucidate it. In more recent films, for example, I should tell you that there was an infectious happiness about *Sunshine Susie* that was rare in its quality, and an unusual strength of description in *Beast of the City*, and a quality of stark staring vitality in Huston's acting of *A House Divided*. I should point to the especial decency of theme in *Arrowsmith*, and to the high intelligent import of Laurel and Hardy's clowning in *Laughing Gravy*, and to the great and moving beauty of really great films like *Kameradschaft*, *Mädchen in Uniform* and *Mutter Krausen*.

I look to register what actually moves: what hits the spectator at the midriff: what yanks him up by the hair of the head or the plain boot-straps to the plane of decent seeing. I see no reason why, because a film is made for the populace and made for money, we should exempt it from the ordinary duties of art.

But it is never a question, this criticism, of our seeing all things alike. If I am a Scotsman with an origin in the Black Sabbaths of the North, my judgement is bound to be more hard-bitten and even ruder on certain issues than that of an Englander. But the Englander, on the other hand, will be a far better guide to the metropolitan graces. This sort of thing you must expect with any critic. The asses' ears of particular, and sometimes indefensible, predilection, haunt even the philosopher.

On the other hand, there are certain serious issues of criticism which must concern a paper like the *Clarion* and readers of the *Clarion*, and on these you may very reasonably ask me to swing a bladder for you. Cinema is, by permission of our queer lop-sided and undisciplined system of society, a very haphazard affair, the effects and achievements of which are almost always dictated by the mind of the profit-monger. To any body of men interested in the better shaping of the world its influence is a serious matter. By romanticizing and dramatizing the issues of life, even by choosing the issues it will dramatize, it creates or crystallizes the loyalties on which people make their decisions. This, in its turn, has a great deal to do with public opinions.

I do not mean that the critic must examine in every film its Socialist implication or lack of it. It is enough if a critic is conscious of the general question and does his utmost to have the honours of life decently distributed. He has, of course, every opportunity of developing his distinctions. Along come the Russian films with their emphasis not on the personal life but on the mass life, their continuous attempt to dramatize the relation of a man to his community.

The documentary films at their best may push up similar issues of man and his environment, and often honour the common things of life which are beneath the silly notice of the studios. And as for the ordinary commercial film, it so often hides mere cheap showman's intention behind its excitement and its spectacle, that the critic must stand ready at all times to pass a scalpel (or a dollop of carbolic) over it. I am not sure how much we effect by so doing, but there is one consolation. The decent intention is the only one that can be publicized, and even the commercial showmen may yet hear of it.

(The *New Clarion*, 11 June 1932)

5 · The Logic of Comedy

The question of comedy has been much in my mind recently. As the magic mould of silence is broken, I find I regret the passing of the comedians more than any. We have a new talkie comedy, and much of it is excellent. A Roach slapstick I saw last week at the London Rialto was well in the Sennett tradition, and a mouse cartoon at the Capitol the week before was a thing of genius. But no Lloyds, no Keatons, and — mentioning the three I have held highest — no Chaplins or Langdons or Raymond Griffiths! I am thinking of the Harry Langdon whom Sennett billed to succeed Chaplin, the Christian innocent who made *Saturday Afternoon*, *Tramp, Tramp, Tramp*, and *The Strong Man*. Griffith broke forth in *Open All Night*, then took to satire in *Hands Up* and *He's a Prince*. His Shavian intelligence was the most unique exhibit in Hollywood three years ago. Like Langdon he was a master in the making when the talkies broke, and they meant more for him than for any other comic talent in the world. He can speak only in a whisper.

The silent screen climbed to comic heights which in the final estimate must be considered enormous, and this is fairly easy to understand. There, for one thing it had traditions behind it: the tradition of knockabout farce, which developed in the circus and the pantomime; the tradition of tragi-comic miming, which came out of the Comedy of Art; and the music-hall tradition which broke up the clown business into subtle and significant types like Chaplin and Langdon themselves. Silence, too, was an aid to the higher comedy rather than a hindrance. The clown at his best is a figure silhouetted against the horizon of human foible and fallibility. Silence, by adding one abstraction, the more confirms him in his philosophic significance.

(*The Clarion*, November 1929)

Chaplin has always been a wayward clown to follow in criticism. One might prove a logic of comedy for Grock, the oldest Fratellini, the Marx Brothers, Laurel and Hardy, and very particularly for Raymond Griffith and Harry Langdon. One has only to begin the task in the case of Chaplin to find his Charlot pirouetting on a left foot round the corner of the Law.

I have heard Griffith and Langdon and Chaplin all discuss the figures they attempted to be and, in the Hollywood I knew, Griffith and Langdon were far from being the lesser figures which the accidents of voice and capital have since made them. They were the real threats to Chaplin's supremacy, for their ideas in comedy were clear. Griffith was fed on Shaw, but had added a certain toughness of his own. The fun he created was the fun of satire, shading between the inconsequential of pure slapstick and the inconsequential which was a fine considered impertinence. It was satire, with a courage of comment which extended strangely to the princes and revolutionaries of Britain, the national and domestic gods of America, the economic considerations behind the Civil War, and laid longing eyes on such sacramental subject matter as the Arctic flights of Byrd and the Big Parade. There was a superb scenario going the rounds by which *Arms and the Man* was transferred to the battlefields of France, and another in which *Androcles and the Lion* was transferred in crazy fashion to the campus of an American University, with cheer leaders for the lions and cheer leaders for the Christians. Neither was made.

Langdon was another mind in comedy altogether. He called his clown the Christian Innocent and was certain in his own head of the texts that fitted it. He wandered pleasantly from picture to picture, braving in perpetual fairy tale, as a child might, the fearful romances of penny banks and Saturday afternoons and colds in the head and women who spoke to him in the street. He survived precipices, tornadoes, and wives, in a fashion which was not so much astonishing as expected, and even by Holy Writ promised to his kind. His very finest was a film called *The Strong Man*, in which, with a faith that was almost historical for Hollywood, Langdon somehow contrived to become the agent of the Lord in shattering the Walls of Jericho and confounding utterly the Wicked within it. He finished up, deservedly, as the village cop.

Chaplin also referred himself to religion. In one discussion with Donald Ogden Stewart, which gives effectively the measure of his comic conception, he upheld the Christian clown very brightly against the clown of the Anti-Christ. The comedy which was rooted in failure was set against the comedy rooted in superiority. Stewart mentioned the moment in *Hands Up*, when Griffith in the course of being hanged by the neck loosed an unforgettable grin on his executioners. Chaplin stood by the Testament, partly in consideration of the fun to be got by inflicting Christian innocents on the world, but more particularly for the tragedy latent in the idea. He was not quite so sure as Langdon that innocence proved its own reward. It could also be inadequacy, and failure, and futility.

But Chaplin has never in his films been quite so simple or straight-forward as this. His Charlot is respectability in straits, suburbia in tatters, a *petit-bourgeois* Ulysses against the horizon. He is also at odd moments the complete romantic, the dreamer, the tramp, whose strange Additions are stricken out by the most plain laws of Arith-metic. Or again, he is the corner boy of more proletarian persuasion, with the blackbird cleverness of the gutter in him, a streak of cruelty, and not a little common envy and hatred. These elements, if ill-assorted, can yet in some measure be held together in the imagina-tion. If the way of the wandering is something of an Odyssey, and the construction is picaresque rather than dramatic, Charlot may at least be as complex in his make-up and as various in his reactions as Poldy Bloom.

Unfortunately, the spirochaete of drama has been operating in Charlot ever since the litterateurs discovered him, and indecently flattered him by their discovery. Chaplin has been searching for rounded stories for his clown; and rounding his stories he has re-duced somewhat the high abstraction of his Charlot. For engaging Charlot too intimately in the pursuit of women and wealth, Chaplin is in a fair way to debasing him. The real disappointment about *City Lights* is that the noble tramp we knew has equated our common frustration to the meaner frustrations of sex; and our down-and-out of *Sunnyside* and *The Pilgrim* has sufficiently lost his independence to slobber over a matter of cash.

The central story of *City Lights*, which ought to be the whole story, is on an intimacy between Charlie and a millionaire which persists only when the millionaire is drunk. There is noble fun in the situa-tions it provokes. The kaleidoscopic changes between impossible luxury and the disillusionment of mornings-after are helped out by a musical commentary which is as intelligent as anything in the struc-ture of the film. There is even a *leit-motif* for the laws of arithmetic.

The good life of Charlie and his millionaire is wearily complicated, however, by another story about a blind girl which, in effect, spoils all their fun. Chaplin takes it seriously, and Charlot, under com-pulsion, takes it so very seriously that he is persuaded to send the blind girl to Vienna and cure her. So in a sad and sorry finale she gazes through her bright new eyes on the man of her dreams: tattered and torn for her, convicted and imprisoned and even shot-at-by-the-peashooters-of-small-boys for her. It is doubtful if at this peak of concentrated and manufactured tragedy Charlot survives. For you may reasonably observe that it is one thing to found comedy on the Christian myth and another thing altogether to compete with it.

It is possible, on a second viewing, to forget the implications of the tale and enjoy the incidental gags for what they are. They are always skilful, and the fine calculation of Chaplin's unmatchable craftsmanship has been written into them. It takes Chaplin to measure the nude detail of a piece of sculpture. But even the lesser moments of liquor swallowings, whistle swallowings and spaghetti swallowings have their little brilliancies of observation. The correction of a wine-glass angle when the whole bottle is pouring to perdition, the passing of the public attack of hiccups through the stages of apology, misery, desperation and anger: there are a thousand gems of the sort tucked away in corners. Chaplin's hands, too, are still unique in pantomime. The mask may have lost some of its quality, but the hands with their little tensions and uncertainties slip through a syllogism as easily as ever. If only Chaplin's story-telling, with its cliché figures and cliché symbolisms, were as delicate!

One sequence of *City Lights* deserves to be recorded separately because it is likely to become as classical a movement in comedy as the starvation sequence in *The Gold Rush*. Boxing scenes have been done a thousand times in slapstick, and Chaplin has appeared in at least two before now. This version is brilliant. It becomes, by an uncanny piling of gag on gag, colossally funny. But it has also the complete rhythm of ballet. Chaplin has always been at his greatest when he approached ballet, and *City Lights*, with its many disappointments, does have its roots in this original power.

(Artwork, Summer 1931)

Chaplin carries in his name so much of the history, tradition and past brilliance of cinema that it is difficult to criticize *Modern Times*. Personal affection is the death of good judgement. Many criticisms of the film have reflected the difficulty.

The theme—in so far as there is a theme—is that our rationalized world is crushing the individual—and that there is no place for a free and lively spirit in the world of machinery, big business and police. Chaplin is as much of a misfit with the workers as he is with the bosses. He fears the workers only a little less than their masters. Positively, there are many superb gags and enough of Chaplin's brilliant dance and mime to make any film distinguished. Negatively, it is disconnected and, in its overtones, sad, sentimental and defeatist.

Chaplin has taken life seriously enough to make an indictment against its present slaveries, and must be judged as seriously as the issue he raises. His sympathies are fiercely against exploitation, but he proves himself the loosest of thinkers. His position is that of the romantic anarchist. His hatred of capitalist machinery and organization gets mixed up with the anarchist's hatred of all machinery and organization together.

It is recognized that the only solution Chaplin could offer is a call to personal bravery. Taking to the high road is as near to suicide of the will as makes no matter.

Funny situations succeed each other and demonstrate great comic invention and execution. They become curiously more depressing as this romantic and trifling issue begins to emerge. Critics have said that Chaplin made the mistake of putting his best laughs in the first part. This is a wrong estimate. The truth is that you cannot laugh very heartily with a corpse in the house. This is not a reflection on the comedy but on the atmosphere. Chaplin himself chose it.

Chaplin's usual collection of stock characters and sentimentalities — the waif held for vagrancy, the dying father, the children begging for bread, the stealing of a loaf — look somewhat mannered. We may endorse his sympathies but not his clichés. His maintenance of pure mime with background music seems equally old-fashioned and uninspired.

Avoiding the possibilities of sound — and there are other possibilities than dialogue — he merely demonstrates that he has lost interest in the technique of his art. He has, under the new régime, discovered nothing and created nothing out of its vitalizing powers. In this, Chaplin proves yet again how near the anarchist may be to the die-hard Tory.

So, in spite of Chaplin's unique claim to our respect, and the basic genius of his comic figure, *Modern Times* proves to be doubly depressing. In his social statement and in his technical statement he has no progressive sense of belief to offer either his public or himself. He is funny but not gay. When his brilliance should inspire, he only dispirits. Chaplin has failed to bring forward his creative power into these Modern Times. He is out-of-date. Paradoxically, *Charlie at the Rink* and *Charlie the Champion* are as fresh as ever.

(*World Film News*, April 1936)

I was not in Hollywood when *The Woman of Paris* was made, but I sat around when its successor *The Woman of the Sea* was under way. *The Woman of the Sea* (aliases: *The Sea Gull*, etc., etc.) has become a mysterious item in film history because, immediately after its production, it passed into limbo. By a minor accident I must be one of the few outsiders who ever saw it or can tell the sad, sad story of its demise.

Chaplin wrote the successor to *The Woman of Paris* for Edna

Purviance and, as Von Sternberg had just then fallen foul of Metro in the production of *The Exquisite Sinner*, Chaplin gave him the job of directing it. I heard Von Sternberg's idea about the film and I heard Chaplin's, and it was fairly clear that the two minds were as separate as could be.

The story was a real Chaplin story, throwing a contrast between the woman who went from the fishing village to the big city and the woman who stayed at home. Sternberg was not yet the Sternberg of *The Docks of New York*. He was still a bit afraid of actors and actresses, and a trifle young and sentimental about art values. He played the story, not for its humanities, but for all the decorative values he could pull out of nets in the sunshine, waves on the shore, and so forth. It was, in an accurate sense, a rather lovely film.

Then on a pink carpet, I heard Chaplin describe the story as he had intended it to be. Chaplin, who understands decorative values not quite so well as my private jackdaw, laid all the emphasis on those elements which Sternberg had quite strictly missed: the home-liness of a fishing village, the sweat and the smell of a fishing village, the intimacy of one man with another, the accumulation of little intimate things which would make village life seem genuine and human against the abstract relationships of the city. Under the power of his description the carpet went insanely pinker.

Appreciating the Sternberg view, I could still understand fairly well why Chaplin did not allow the film to appear. However beautiful, it was not a film that had anything to do with the story he felt, or indeed with any story he could ever feel. Chaplin is above all a humanist. He is not a great film architect, and by no means an exponent of the purely visual values (of design, tempo, etc.) to be obtained in cinema. But he has a power over the significant detail of character and of situation which has to be experienced to be believed. *The Woman of Paris* itself was no great shakes as a story, but it all shakes together as a story well and intimately told. Film characters were at last characters: breathing and distinct: individual to their last braces' button.

René Clair's *Sous les Toits de Paris* does perform a similar sort of miracle. The story is slight and one that would look rather dull if you set it down in print. But you have to see Clair take a mono-syllabic *Non* out of a Paris midinette to know what film direction should look like. He likes people, he likes Paris, he likes flirtations on stairs, and whispered requests that receive monosyllabic *Nons* from midinettes. He likes people who sell popular songs and use assembled crowds to stage a bit of honest pocket-picking. He likes the peoples of the cafés, and the garrets, and one-roomed, two-roomed joints in which they live. He likes the glimpses one can get of fat women and thin men and somewhat un-baptist young ladies through skylights and street windows. He likes them all with a gusto which is French, but which is so admirably good-natured and so wisely informed, that what would be given an air of tom-peepery by the average director, has only the genius in observation of a de Maupassant or a Chaplin. 'By a single word, give me to understand wherein one cab horse differs from fifty others before and behind it', was the test-piece in art set by Flaubert. René Clair can do it.

Sous les Toits does not snap to a finish as a good box-office film should do. Its structure will not bear a lot of analysis. Its roofs — beautifully shot as they are — are not roofs which have anything to do with the sky. Its *apache* fight — for a climax — is a poor amateur job which Clair, by much sound trickery, tries to avoid. But the people of *Sous les Toits*, though you only meet them for the brevity of a single gesture, will stay in your head. There is a colour about the greater American film stars (about Beery, Gilbert, Bancroft, Garbo, Cooper) which ensures your remembering them for what they, in themselves, are; and so they are from picture to picture. Here, in *Sous les Toits*, is a talent which ensures your remembering a hundred people for what the director has made them be.

(*The Clarion*, January 1931)

I am not sure where to place Laurel and Hardy. Indeed I am not sure if they should be placed at all. The case of Chaplin is a warning. The pundits have had their will of him, and his comedy has distressed itself with the responsibilities they have laid upon it. It would be a pity if critical analysis spoiled yet another gift of honest slapstick.

But the higher comedy is important stuff and is worth distinguishing. When comedy is merely a matter of artificial situation and expert gags, as in the case of Harold Lloyd and, to some extent, in the case of Buster Keaton, you laugh and are done with it. They are clever fellows to work their way through such amusing scrapes, but they mean no more. Keaton shows admirably the distinction between the higher and the lower comedy. His mask is a very significant thing with its dumb registration of things felt. It might pass through life registering a heap of things most deeply felt. But it does not. In every Keaton story the action whoops in reel five to allow Buster Keaton the clown to become Mr Keaton the romantic achiever of all things, and the fun of his face sums up nothing but a temporary pretence.

Clowns are the world's incompetents. They are bound to the wheel of incompetence or they cease to be clowns.

Chaplin once, in *The Gold Rush*, broke the underlying significance of his rôle and spoiled a great film. He forgot Charlot the outcast to become a millionaire and marry the girl, like any John Gilbert or Ronald Colman. Clowns cannot possibly stoop to such romance. They are, in essence, super realists: that is to say, they are tragedians in disguise. Their endings are happy for everybody but themselves.

Chaplin's ancient endings were true clown endings, when he walked down an endless road in *Sunnyside*, and planted impossibly endless fields in *A Dog's Life*, and straddled the hopeless boundary of slavery and death in *Pay Day*. My point is that clowning, when it passes beyond the naïvetés of the fun of the fair, becomes an infernal responsibility to its practitioners. It becomes an art, subject to discipline, subject I am afraid to idea. Anyone can be foolish. The test of your great clown is whether, with all his fooling, he means something.

Laurel, as you know, is a quiet man and Hardy a robust and fat one. They are famous for the world they tumble about them. They have but to touch the garden gate and it collapses in ruins before their eyes. Do what they will, the bricks of their houses dislodge on their inoffensive and embarrassed heads, the water-butt leaps up to meet them, the window slams on their fingers. It is no wonder if sometimes in desperation they give up the impossible task of staving off chaos and, in an orgy of destruction, welcome it.

They are perhaps the Civil Servants of comedy. Nothing on earth would please them better than a quiet permanence in all things. The garden gate, the water-butt, and the window smooth on its roller, are their symbols of ease.

Laughing Gravy starts with a hiccup in the middle of the night. They are disturbed by it, disturbed by the hiccup itself, disturbed by the fact that it will wake the landlord. They represent the vast multitude in this world who worry about hiccups and about landlords.

The hiccup goes on its way. It wakes the dog and the dog most certainly wakes the landlord. The landlord, who has forbidden dogs, throws the dog into the snow. Laurel and Hardy, boobs that they are, pity it. Hardy goes in his nightshirt to bring it back, and the door, of course, slams behind him. He tries to get back in a knotted sheet and it drops him in yet another water-butt. He splashes the icy water in futile fury. He is definitely not one of the innocents whom angels guard. Few are.

So from step to step, in the simple continuity of an ordinary suburban night, one destruction follows another. They wash the dog furtively to wake no one, and spill the water and drop the bath to wake everyone. The landlord, maddening under the strain, breaks down his own precious door and smashes his own precious window. By the end, suburbia is in tatters.

Yet through it all there remains the curious continuity of two figures, one thin and one fat, which deplore the disturbance they are creating. They hate it, and would avoid it if they could. They are men of peace. But in this case the meek are not blessed. They do not inherit the earth. They inherit chaos. Chaos most active and violent and diabolical takes advantage of their inhibitions.

I find Hardy an improving clown. His gestures grow large. He begins to appeal hopelessly to his audience in the classical fashion of clowns. He begins to demonstrate a large and splendid selection of angers and petulances. He was once the minor partner, but now looks like becoming the major one.

Laurel improves into blankness. He can do nothing right and never will. Hardy, with a fine optimism, will try and fail. Laurel, poor devil, knows he has failed before he tries.

There is no wonder the life they lead goes to the heart of the multitude. A few million commuters in London alone will find good reason to laugh at them. There is not a gag of suburban fear and suburban futility in Laurel and Hardy they will not appreciate.

(*Everyman*, 29 October 1931)

Of all the new films I find it easiest to recommend *Fra Diavolo*. Laurel and Hardy, though the Film Society does not agree, are superb clowns at their best and first-rate tumblers at their worst. Here they have been added to a full-length version of the Auber opera, to tumble as comic bandits in the train of Fra Diavolo himself. The upshot of the piece is accordingly not theirs, but what are Laurel and Hardy without command of the upshot? Theirs is their own right to pull the world to pieces: by logic of destruction to demolish utterly one or another select section of suburbia! The finale is necessary to them. It gives fundamental point to their clowning that the hopeful idiot and tragic yokel in all of us should so combine to make a complete mess of things. Here they touch noses and wiggle fingers and fall down wells and get uproariously drunk and make preposterous efforts to hang each other, but too incidentally to achieve their own special effect. As clowns of a now considerable reputation they should know better than to get lost in somebody else's seven-reeler. If they are still funny, it is because they could not be less.

(*New Britain*, 24 May 1933)

The best of the week is Buster Keaton's *Passionate Plumber*. Jimmy Durante, the Schnozzle of ferocious sighs and four-syllabled excitements, is with him. The film adds little to the Keaton myth, but it is a good hour's fooling. The virtue of Keaton is that while he does not reach for the more cosmic honours of clowning, he is never feeble. I hear the world about me complain for the days when the frozen-faced comedian was silent. They speak of the mask which was essentially of silence, of the greater courage and more desperate self-discipline which that mask implied. I am afraid you will see little of this in *The Passionate Plumber*. It is another loss you must put down to the talkies.

In the silent days every comedy had to be a comedy of situation. The visual emphasis of the medium made action and event necessary for any considerable effect. Verbal play, however snappy, is no equivalent. It may get the laughs as they say, but this arithmetical computation of laughter is a poor guide to fun. It is one of the fallacies of the commercial philosophy, that 'they count 'em'. The tragedy in this case is that Keaton had once a reputation for greatness. Now, when situation has been buried alive in wisecracks, he is merely another good comedian.

Here I should record a question asked me recently by Alfred Hitchcock. 'Is cinema, then, so much a matter of violence?' For the argument in which it was put, I answered 'Yes'. Hitchcock went on to say that once he believed there was nothing in the novel which cinema could not do: the continuity of story, the description of character, the atmosphere behind, and the leisurely commentary on all three. He had come to doubt it. Those of you who have followed Hitchcock's work will appreciate the significance of both the question and the explanation. They explain a great deal, if not all, of that skilful but sometimes ineffective meandering which has unspeeded so many of his films.

Hitchcock asked his question rhetorically, with the air of one who for a year or two had been making a slow and bitter discovery. Action, of course, is the ultimate material in cinema. The first movies were introduced to the pavement crowds with the stentorian cry of 'They move, they move.' We forget that original truth periodically and always come back to the rediscovery of it. We have rediscovered it with the Westerns, with the epics, with the *Vaudevilles* and the *Potemkins*; and we are rediscovering it now with the Disneys. Always it is the same old story of visible event: in a new guise and in response to a new deadening influence. Of which, as you can imagine, the talkies with their everlasting verbal flipflap, are the most deadening of all. The great pity is that comedy, which was once in slapstick so much a matter of movement, has been tempted more than any other genre. It was more than any other vulnerable to the specious attraction of the wisecrack: and the wisecrack is smothering it.

I hope I do not muddle the issue by talking in the same breath of violence, movement and situation. I only mean that cinema with its capacity for event should keep things happening: pulling its tension in drama from the violence (and in complement, from the suspense) of happening. The recommendation of Aristotle was that action comes first and the characters after. 'The end aimed at in drama is the representation not of qualities of character, but of some action.' The distinction will serve even better for cinema. If we try, either in Hitchcock incident or in Hollywood verbalism, to emphasize the mere detail, the unity and the drive of event which make a film important are being destroyed. And masks, the greatest of all the gifts of the silent comedy, are become mere faces again.

(*Everyman*, 28 April 1932)

The quintessential virtue of buffoonery is discovered in the hangover. The merely funny causes its eruption of belly-laugh and is soon done: the larger idiocy engages the conscience. It is a head laugh and invokes a certain subconscious pondering. In it—the pundit Kant would say—the Imagination is related to the Faculty of Ideas, under a subjective presupposition of the Moral Feeling in Man. This arduously but more authoritatively means the same thing. There is a hangover. Of associations and appreciations which are a trifle profound.

I believe the philosophical explanation of it is that your born buffoon plays old Harry with the categories of reciprocity. They are the local daemons who preside over all habitation of the flesh: the laws of sense, the laws of consequence, the laws of fol-di-rol and fol-di-ree and other formulae of Philistia. You cannot bust them, but so blessed is the mind of man, that you can conceive of busting them. Your buffoon urges your fancy to an impossible emancipation, and this is your only clue in life for a really good laugh. You are kidding yourself to death.

In fact, you are quite literally kidding yourself to death, for obviously if such emancipation were realized you would perish: if, like Langdon, you jumped over a precipice and trusted the gods; if, like Chaplin, you set forth into the Arctic with an N.S.E.W. scribbled on a hunk of paper; if, like the oldest of the Fratellinis, you did not appreciate the difference between your shadow and your enemy. If, to put it very plainly, you hated your physical company so far as to will its destruction. The eldest Fratellini fights with his shadow fiercely, and screams, with possibly a note of agony. It is very funny as you see it, but something more.

I introduce this dissertation as a species of advance applause for the Three Marx Brothers, late of *The Coconuts* and now of *Animal Crackers*. They are great clowns, and may yet, like Grock, Chaplin and the Fratellini, become historical ones. If, that is to say, the commercial cinema permits them to polish their rôles, and refine the Idea that is in them. It is, I admit, a good deal to ask of an institution which has destroyed Langdon and cast away Raymond Griffith. What rare and noble clowns these two might have been!

As it is, the Marx Brothers are a howling success. Their rôles and methods are similar to the ones they took in *The Coconuts*, but I fancy somewhat developed. Groucho, the talker, plays fast and loose with every conversational convention there is: puns outrageously, but makes speeches which get brilliantly nowhere; destroys every continuity of expression or thought presented to him; and insults his polite listeners to the rollicking satisfaction of every suppressed desire in the bosom of man.

Chico, the Wop, is the villain as before, a dark scheming villain bubbling over with joy for the infinite desire of villainy within him. 'I don't want you to steal it,' says the girl. 'Then I can't take it,' says Chico. And certainly he can't. It must be villainy or nothing. He is an Iago, a bare-faced Iago, with the ambition in villainy of Macbeth — blessedly disproportioned to all possible existence.

But Harpo, the dumb member, is the greatest emancipator of all. His capacity for pocket-picking is prodigious in its skill; his capacity at cheating at cards is prodigious in its nakedness; and to this he attaches the bright-eyed devilry of a mischievous child. The first two, by the extravagance of their emancipation, are absurd. Harpo, however, achieves the complete syllogism of emancipation. He is also insane. Capable, as it turns out, of most cheerfully murdering the entire cast, friend and foe alike, and himself to the bargain.

That, I submit, in all psychology, is a clown equipment which is more fascinating in its fact than in its possibility than any we have seen since Chaplin. If I understand Chaplin aright he takes comedy to the point of tragedy by reminding one that the little man, the *homme moyen*, who so brilliantly succeeds against odds, can only impossibly do so. Harpo comes near to proving, as Prince Myshkin did before him, that the place for all fun (as for all innocence), when it grows really prodigious, is a booby-hatch.

Animal Crackers is of course not an exercise in the logic of comedy. There are a few perfect examples like Langdon's *Saturday Afternoon* and *The Strong Man*, Grock's act, and Chaplin's *Pay Day* and *The Pilgrim*, but, as a rule, the logic gets lost in other matters and the presentation of the idea is incomplete. So there are some dud leads in

Animal Crackers. Harpo, for instance, should not interpolate a serious harp solo, even if it happens to be a good one; and Chico should carry his villainy quite completely into his piano work. In *Animal Crackers* there is a beginning to that, but no doubt it will go further. Groucho, too, should be tireless in his talking, to the last bell. He is not.

The one supreme moment to record is the last one. There is a nymph whom Harpo has been pursuing like any satyr throughout the film. In the last bright murderous scene he hunts among his victims till he finds her, arranges himself appropriately and with the final and complete satisfaction of absolute lunacy gives himself the necessary knock-out. It is the prettiest happy ending since Langdon, the Cop and Hero, stumbled and was led forth on patrol by the blind girl.

(The Clarion, December 1930)

The Marx Brothers have a sense of continuity in their comedy. From *Coconuts* and *Animal Crackers*, the Brothers graduate into *Monkey Business*. They insist on the jungle. This, of course, is very right of them. They are wild men, who, if they did not find a jungle ready to hand, would certainly invent one.

It is, I take it, the particular function of comedy to destroy the more trifling dignities of this earth: quality varies with the shape and size of the dignities it destroys. Pantomime goes with a whack to the seat of the pants; slapstick goes with peel or pie to any section of the anatomy which presents itself; Shaw, a Mack Sennett of the Parlour, trips up the prejudices. The quality deepens till, in Swift, you tumble up the human race itself. In this event, the laughter of mankind at its own sorry self is liable to echo down a couple of centuries.

The Marx Brothers are moderately solid clowns. They have the single weakness of taking their music seriously. Chico the Wop is liable to pursue his piano keys as if he really meant them. Harpo the Lunatic slips back miserably into sanity when he addresses the harp. But, taking the Brothers all in all, they do get through a large amount of necessary destruction. They are guerrilla warriors and lack the more solid sense of artists like Chaplin, but they are smart around the rocks.

In *The Coconuts* they turned the respectable Rotarian state of Florida into the sports ground of a booby-hatch, and very little was left of its vaunted climate and real estate when they had passed through it. In *Animal Crackers* they proceeded to the palatial interiors of Long Island. In *Monkey Business* they arrive as stowaways to devastate an Atlantic liner. There is a story somewhere of a gangster feud and an ocean romance, but since it is the job of a Marx Brother to destroy all such evidence of social equilibrium, you will catch only passing glimpses of either. The rest is anarchy.

Groucho attends, as usual, to the verbal continuities of life. He eliminates them, and, of course, talks incessantly. He sees to it that no idea gets anywhere, or, if somewhere, that its final destination will be of the maximum unimportance to the human race. In this, Groucho brings to cinema America's strange genius for nonsense. He belongs to the tradition which has produced Bugs Baer and Ted Cook among the columnists, Robert Benchley and Donald Ogden Stewart among the writers. But there are a thousand exponents of varying talent in and around the newspapers, magazines and music-halls. They represent together a brilliance of idiocy which is quite easily America's most civilized contribution to this section of the century. The only weakness of it is that it is frothy stuff. This may be due to a national mind which has not yet got down to the job of social criticism. It is in its first fine youthful stage of making fun of anything and everything, quite indiscriminately. Stewart once confessed to me that his *Crazy Fool* was as good as *Candide*, and he spoke in good faith. The difference, of course, is in the skittles they skittle. Voltaire went for Leibnitz. *The Crazy Fool* just failed in the bubbling of its enthusiasm to go for Big Business.

Poor old Groucho's chief distinction is that he is the world's best murderer of party manners.

Chico the Wop is, unfortunately, not quite so much in evidence in *Monkey Business*. There was a certain desperate villainy in him in *Animal Crackers* of which one hoped all things. He had all the makings of a comic Ishmael. One could conceive of him harbouring deep and dire stratagems for seizing this Atlantic liner, or firing it, or scuttling it. No such deep stratagems are given to him.

The largest part of the Marxian effort comes, of course, from the Brother Harpo. He is Mad Hatter altogether, with fairy tale in him. The others, for all their craziness, belong to this world. Harpo, in some fashion best understood by children and their fellow-innocents, belongs to another. It is difficult to separate him from the gang, but I find him individually the most considerable clown, apart from Chaplin, in the whole of cinema. There are patches of him in *Monkey Business* of a brilliance which not even Chaplin has touched since *The Gold Rush*. He is, like Chaplin, silent. Like Chaplin he has a capacity for sudden mad bursts of comedy. The classical example is the pillow scene in *The Gold Rush*, but Harpo's whoopee with the passports is not a bit inferior.

Such moments belong exclusively to the great clowns. I can think only of Chaplin and Grock and the Fratellini and Herb Williams as having the power of them. I commend you in this regard to an examination of Harpo's invasion of the Punch and Judy Show in *Monkey Business*. Like the best of Chaplin, it climbs in comedy, till, in a last crazy shot, it goes out of sight altogether. The last crazy shot in question is of Harpo disappearing on a scooter like some fairy figure from Grimms'.

It is best to be doubtful always of where the screen's comedians will take us. There is something in the mechanics of the business—Box Office Control and Committee Production—which destroys the good things cinema creates. In cinema the geese that lay the golden eggs are quite invariably done to death in the name of scientific and mass production. Other clowns have shown similar powers and have gone in a year or two in oblivion. The history of cinema is full of ideas and rôles well started, which have been lost in the day-to-day whimmery of cheap showmen. Chaplin is unique. He has had the capital power, as well as the ability, to develop his rôle.

The Marx Brothers, to judge from a music-hall appearance, are powerless by themselves. They need not only the capital for production but also a director who will stay with them and bring the idea that is in them to greater power and point. But whether any commercial company is capable of seeing to this, I doubt. Comedy when it begins to be really good, is, like tragedy, too large an affair altogether for the commercial conditions which determine the film business.

(*Everyman*, 15 October 1931)

There is, on West End screens, a very pretty sense of how the public peace or complacency can be best disturbed. At a time when the country is asking what is wrong with the Labour Party, Messrs Atlee, Bevin and Greenwood might learn from it. In easy foot-work, length of reach and unexpectedness of crosses, they are by all odds inferior in equipment to the Marx Brothers. I recommend *A Day at the Races* as a classical exercise in Opposition. Messrs A, B and G may catch from it, if they care, that secret of high anarchy without which no body of criticism (His Majesty's or any other) was ever worth the bother of maintaining. It may help them if they regard Groucho's home for rich neurasthenics as a pleasant commentary on our Defence Departments and the plight of the unfortunate race horse Nelly—so pestered by duns that it has to be accommodated on the fifteenth floor and fed on the bedroom mattresses—as not dissimilar to that of the League of Nations. But, as people who are too serious by half and not enough, they will mostly learn from the Tactic of Inconsequence.

When faced with the Sublime (Niagara, Baldwin or Mussolini), Kant from Koenigsberg recommends, like any trade union leader, a snivelling glance to the starry heavens above, though it is difficult to see why when he so accurately defines the sublime as 'the mere ability to think which shows a faculty of mind *far surpassing any standard of sense*'. Being less provincial philosophers, the Marx Brothers take the definition at its word. With a whoop they are round the corner of Nonsense and what happens to the Kantian devotee is nobody's business. At the very least it is what Groucho does to Margaret Dumont in the operating theatre of his neurasthenic sanatorium. In what Basil Wright describes as a 'nightmare tangle of voodoo, dentistry and hairdressing', the one thing which is finally disentangled is the divine symposium of the dignities and snobberies which Miss Dumont so happily represents in every Marx Brothers comedy. Sociological students will appreciate that nothing is so likely to perform this feat, as a 'tangle of voodoo, dentistry and hairdressing'.

It may be that others, more gently, have applied the same critical tactic, and all good satirists do. The special secret of the Marx Brothers is in the physical quality they have been able to add. We have had nothing like their sense of direct action since Gulliver invited the insults of the arboreal Yahoos. The mechanistic persistence of Chico's crookedness, the enthusiastic sacrifice of sense and sanity to speed and certainty on the part of Groucho, the mad dashes of Harpo after any and every indiscriminate suggestion, have a passion about them which no statement in a slower medium could hope to match. It is in this that the Marxes make their chief contribution to the cinema. They have made its physical speed an essential part of their art. Anyone who has seen the relatively crude efforts on the music-hall stage to achieve a similar frenzy — whether in the antics of the Crazy Gang at the Palladium or in the vaudeville version of the Marx Brothers themselves — must recognize the importance of this cinematic asset.

In one matter *A Day at the Races* represents a dangerous deviation from the true Marxist doctrine. It has been described by good critics as 'striking a perfect balance between fantasy and reality', meaning that the background of young musical-comedy love, with tearful heroine and hero bellowing to the moon (reality), fits with perfect balance into the extravagance of the Marxian antics (fantasy). The other view is that having gone so far to debunk the niceties of human intercourse it would have been simple decency on the part of the Brothers to debunk love's young dream as well. In previous films they have done it and I am sure only considerations of the box office have dictated respect in this instance. Their previous treatment of love's young dream has lost them half a million dollars a picture.

Be that as it may, there is enough in this epic of social sabotage to make *A Day at the Races* a very distinguished performance. Our students, Attlee, Bevin and Greenwood, have only to find political equivalents for mixing a Negro sing-song with the Pied Piper, middle-aged romance with paper hanging, Ascot with a traffic jam and a ceremonial reception with a night in Harlem; and the quality of His Majesty's Opposition will be up to standard in no time.

(*World Film News*, September 1937)

Joe Sternberg is one of the few directors whose every work one sees as a matter of course. He stepped rather suddenly into the film world in 1925 with a film called *The Salvation Hunters*, which he had financed with his last five thousand dollars. He has been interesting ever since. *The Salvation Hunters* was a young man's gamble. His stars were taken from the ranks of Poverty Row extras; his story was right outside the Hollywood tradition. It was a sad romantic affair of how a young man tried to escape from the dreary existence of a dredger. The dredger with its slime was, of course, symbolic. The ending, with its two young lovers moving off into the rising sun, was equally symbolic. Sternberg began with a great hankering for good things.

You should remember the simple, rather naïve and sentimental idealism of that first effort when you see *Shanghai Express*. Dietrich stars. Like that exotic and meaningless lady herself, the film is a masterpiece of the toilette. That only. Its photography is astonishing; its sets are expensive and detailed to an ingenious and extravagant degree; its technique in dissolve and continuity is unique. You might see the film for its good looks alone. But it is coldbloodedly lacking in every virtue which made Sternberg a lad of promise.

A great deal must have happened over the years to turn the simple romanticist into this sophisticated purveyor of the meretricious Dietrich. I wish I knew what it was. I knew Sternberg just after his *Salvation Hunters* and liked him immensely. He had made a fine picture for Metro called *The Exquisite Sinner*, and had been heaved off the pay-roll for adding some genuine local colour to a Breton scene.

It struck me that sensibility of his peculiarly intensive and introspective sort was not a very healthy equipment for a hard world and, in face of his strange progress, I am sure I was right. There is, as you can imagine, no place for the introspectionist in a commercial film world which is as objective in its conceptions as in its accounts. A director of this instinct is bound to have a solitary and (as commerce goes) an unsuccessful life of it. Sternberg, I think, was weak. Hating the notion of this commercial unsuccess, he has thrown his sensibility to the winds and accepted the hokum of his masters. His aesthetic conscience is now devoted to making the hokum as good-looking as possible. As you might believe, it is almost pathologically good-looking, as by one whose conscience is stricken.

I give you this Sternberg saga because it tells more clearly than any personal story I know how even great spirits may fail in film. The temptation of commercial success is a rather damnable one. There are dollars past dreaming and power and publicity to satisfy every vanity, for anyone who will mesmerize the hicks of the world.

I watched Sternberg make still another picture, *The Woman of the Sea*, for Chaplin. The story was Chaplin's, and humanist to a degree: with fishermen that toiled, and sweated, and lived and loved as proletarians do. Introspective as before, Sternberg could not see it like Chaplin. Instead, he played with the symbolism of the sea till the fishermen and the fish were forgotten. It would have meant something just as fine in its different way as Chaplin's version, but he went on to doubt himself. He wanted to be a success, and here plainly and pessimistically was the one way to be unsuccessful. The film as a result was neither Chaplin's version nor Sternberg's. It was a strangely beautiful and empty affair — possibly the most beautiful I have ever seen — of net patterns, sea patterns and hair in the wind. When a director dies, he becomes a photographer!

Well, here is *Shanghai Express*. Joe Sternberg is now the great Josef von Sternberg, having given up the struggle for good: a director so successful that even Adolf Zukor is pleased to hold his hand for a brief condescended moment. He has made films with Jannings and Bancroft: *Paying the Penalty*, *Docks of New York*, others of equally exquisite hokum; and Paramount has blessed his name for the money they made. Once from the top of the tree he made a last desperate gesture to his past in *The Case of Lena Smith*, a fine film, which failed; but that is now forgotten and there will never be a repetition. He has found Dietrich and is safe for more dollars, more power, more success than ever. What weak-willed director would not launch a thousand cameras for Dietrich, giving up hope of salvation hereafter? Sternberg has. He has the 'von' and the little warm thankful hand of Adolf Zukor for his pains.

Shanghai Express follows the progress of a train from Pekin to Shanghai, finding its story among the passengers as *The Blue Express* did only recently. Dietrich is Shanghai Lily, a lady of no reputation. Clive Brook is an old lover meeting her again; hating her past, but still very much in love with her. They fall into the hands of Chinese revolutionaries and Dietrich saves Clive, and Clive saves Dietrich; and in that last mutual service the dust is shaken out of Lily's petals and the doubter damns himself for having doubted. This high argument is staged with stupendous care, stupendous skill, and with the air of most stupendous importance.

I remember one shot of the Shanghai express pulling into a wayside station in the early evening. It is one of the half-dozen greatest shots ever taken, and I would see the film for that alone. It is, however, the only noble moment in the film. The scenes of Chinese street life are massive, Napoleonic in their sense of detail and presented very pleasantly in dissolve; the minor acting is fine; but the rest is Dietrich. She is shown in seven thousand and one poses, each one of them photographed magnificently. For me, seven thousand poses of Dietrich (or seventy) are Dietrich *ad nauseam*. Her pose of mystery I find too studied, her make-up too artificial, her every gesture and word too deliberate for any issue in drama save the very gravest. Sternberg perhaps is still after that ancient intensity. When themes are thin it is a hankering that can bring one very close to the ridiculous.

(*Everyman*, 14 April 1932)

Shanghai Express is an extraordinary work from a photographic point of view, and all my advisers tell me that the Dietrich nose, eye and underlip are 'lovely'. I confess I was watching von Sternberg more closely. He is a director of parts, whose every film has had great qualities to recommend it. Something of strength is missing, however, in his creative make-up. If one cannot by taking thought add a cubit to one's stature, one can no more by great gifts of photography add power to a feeble story.

All Sternberg's stories seem to fade off into almost pathetic unimportance. There is, I think, no doubt that he makes his own choice, for almost always the central character is a figure who, like Jannings in *The Blue Angel* and Esther Ralston in *The Case of Lena Smith*, has been specially wronged by the world. This affection for the outcast is the trade mark of the Sternberg cinema. But, except in the *Lena Smith* case, the personal tragedy is always somehow too adventitious for the greatest effect. It is felt sympathetically, but not built into that world of accepted fact which alone can make tragedy real. Jannings, in *The Blue Angel*, was an old fool of a professor whose physical inhibitions overcame him when honest men are in dignity digging their graves. Dietrich, in *Shanghai Express*, is a lady of the very slimmest social justification.

I always regard Sternberg as the most Jewish of directors, and far more typical of the racial inspiration than the luxurious DeMille. 'The Jew is either at your throat or at your feet.' It is a distinction those who know Jews in the world of art can readily appreciate.

More objective than most, they can be more subjective than most. Sternberg is a curious combination of the extremes. I have known him, I think, personally, and a man of finer sensibility I never met. But this side of him mingles strangely with a colossal respect for the more ordinary grandeur of the world. The combination explains *Shanghai Express*. Vast settings are there most splendidly produced, and Dietrich is at the centre of them, an outcast after the Sternberg heart, seeking your sympathy. It is doubtful, however, if you feel her case very directly. When cases are serious, an advocate should be simple. When the beautiful and expensive flurry of *Shanghai Express* is over you may well ask yourself what all the shooting was about. Very little one can remember after a fortnight! If it were not Sternberg one would not worry about that, but his ability is rare enough (he is still a young man of thirty-five) to command our concern.

(The Clarion, May 1932)

Eric von Stroheim is the crazy man of the film world. He cut *Greed* to sixty reels and defied Hollywood to make it less, at which they sacked him and hired an infidel to bring it down to a humble ten. They are always sacking von Stroheim. The infidel cut and cut and gave up at twenty-five, and, when he too was fired, explained that Stroheim's sixty was a masterpiece, anyway.

Of course, Hollywood respected von Stroheim for his stand at sixty. Anyone who will threaten to entertain you for twelve hours on end is plainly in the grand manner. They gave him yet another and yet another film to do. Each time the story has been the same. Stroheim has gone whoopee and shot to the moon, and found himself unemployed before the picture hit the headlines.

He paid himself into the première of his own *Merry Widow*, though *The Merry Widow* went on to make a fortune. *The Wedding March* which followed became one of those traditional productions, which company after company fail on. It soared into the millions. I saw great slices of it shot and great hunks of financiers' hair torn from the roots in the process. But not a frame of what I saw appeared in the final version. When Paramount bought and finished the film, Stroheim was on the outside as before.

Yet for most of us von Stroheim is the director of all directors, and I think largely because of this superlative disregard for the financiers who back him. If he feels like shooting, he shoots, and damns the pennies. If he wants one last detail on a set, he will hold up the world at a thousand dollars per tick to get it. If the gesture of a single tenth-rate extra is to be perfected, he will rehearse it for a couple of hours and hold every star in the cast waiting till it is done. The public issue of the film means nothing to him in comparison with its issue of craftsmanship.

The principals in the desert scene of *Greed* he put into hospital by actually shooting the scene in Death Valley and sweating them under the Californian sun till they achieved the realism he wanted. That sort of thing does not, I know, prove him a great artist, but it does demonstrate a virtue which is necessary in some measure to every director. Surrounded by a thousand technicians and a thousand interests which conflict with this job of pure creation, a director has to have something of Lenin in him to come through. Strangely enough, there is not an artist who ever appeared under him who will hear a word against von Stroheim. In a world of commercial flip-flap he does stand so surely for the larger intensities of art.

The Lost Squadron uses him as an actor only, in yet another of those sinister Teutonic rôles he made famous. The interesting point is that he is cast as the crazy film director he is supposed to be: with such a passion for realism that he pours acid on control wires and sacrifices the lives of his stunt airmen for a movie effect.

This sort of thing, of course, is not quite the measure of von Stroheim the director; for if he did smash things to pieces to get his stuff, be sure he took the biggest wallop himself.

Just for a minute, however, you do get something like a genuine picture of the man: when, standing dreadfully erect before the set, he screams 'Cameras!' I have seen him do that with very similar passion and I have seen him go off the hoop as he does subsequently, and be very much the blood-curdling creature of temperament he demonstrates. It is worth seeing. He is the villain of the piece in this case, but you may believe with me that a single gesture of such villainy is worth a great deal of more flat-footed orthodoxy. 'What are a few deaths to the art of Benvenuto?'

(*Everyman*, 26 May 1932)

The case of William Wyler is a rather curious one. He is an odd member of the Laemmle tribe: origin Swiss; and, like every other member of the tribe across the world, he has answered the tocsin of Uncle Carl and joined the family at Universal City. But there must be something in the Laemmle blood, because Wyler has taken a line of his own. He is very nearly the most serious of Hollywood's directors, and almost certainly the best poet. I have a notion he will become the director we once expected Vidor to be. Like Vidor he wanders in strange country but, unlike Vidor, he has the courage of it.

Hell's Heroes, a film of the early thirties, told the queer story of three bad hombres who sacrificed their lives to deliver a child to a frontier town, and Wyler directed it magnificently. With its perverse parallel to the tale of the Three Wise Men, the delivery of the child on Christmas Day, and the last man falling dead as the local choir broke into the carol of 'Holy Night', the story itself missed hokum by a hairbreadth. Only a director of unusual ability could have steered it past into genuine emotion.

In *A House Divided*, Wyler lives dangerously again. Here, the story concerns the father and son theme which Eugene O'Neill made great in *Desire under the Elms* and Douglas in *The House with the Green Shutters*. In this case the son is weak and the father is strong, the father takes a new wife, and wife and son fall in love with each other. The story is set against a background of sea. Walter Huston plays the father.

I saw Huston play the father rôle in the New York Theatre Guild's production of *Desire under the Elms*. He played it for the great and intense thing it is, and caught the Calvinist passion of the rôle with a certainty that seemed a trifle bewildering in the atmosphere of Metropolitan America. When Calvinism has disappeared from its own country, dare one expect to find it honoured among the Philistines? But if that was strange, it is stranger still to find the outlook and the issue reappearing in a Hollywood film.

I am all for this William Wyler; he has a taste for the greater gestures and is still steering them past the hokum they so easily invoke. It is difficult to stage a tough old warrior of the Calvinist school, and achieve sympathy for him. If there is kindness in him, he would not show it; and 90 per cent of the slovenly little humanities which people expect will wither under his discipline. But Wyler and Huston put him over. It is not often that the ancient virtue of pity and terror creeps into a film. Here it does.

(*Everyman*, 24 March 1932)

Cecil B. DeMille is the sort of prophet who has honour in his own country. He has been an enormous success ever since that first bright moment in his cinema career when, pressed for an alibi for some unusual photography, he invented the term 'Rembrandt lighting'. He got away with that one and, for that matter, has got away with most things since. After Rembrandt it was Moses and *The Ten Commandments*; after Moses it was a certain carpenter of Nazareth in *The King of Kings*.

DeMille is a showman in the grand manner. He shrinks at nothing — at no importance, at no dramatic issue either side of the Styx — in his passionate ambition to tell the world about something or other. He loves size, and the bigger his subject the greater the gusto in putting it over. The birth of Israel, the birth of Christianity, the birth of Soviet Russia (in *Volga Volga*): come as large as they like, DeMille will spit on his hands and make a rollicking showman's job of them. He is the Jack the Giant Killer of the cinema world and, like his original, he works by guile. He reduces everything he handles to the same good old melodramatic formula — Pleasures, Passions, and the Price to Pay. And no matter what it is — the story of Moses, the story of Mary Magdalene or the story of the Revolution — having once lured them on to that beanstalk, he slays them easily.

The latest in Pleasures, Passions and the Price to Pay is *Dynamite*. I enjoyed this film but I would not happily see it twice. DeMille is so good a craftsman that he is always worth watching, and his slightly Hebraic sense of splendour is always inclined to be vivid. There is no bathroom like a Cecil DeMille bathroom. His plumbing, as a New York newspaperman once reported of the new seventeen-million-dollar Paramount Theatre, is palatial. All technicians of the ball and plug trade will please note.

This *Dynamite* film covers a heap of territory. It has (1) a prison with prisoner awaiting execution, (2) a high society lady in her high society world with (*a*) a swimming-pool and bathing belles, (*b*) a battalion of female archers, (*c*) a regiment of Aero Wheel racers, (*d*) a bemillioned interior with cocktail bar, cocktail party, petting party, bathroom and other offices complete. The society lady married the murderer to get the cash on grandpapa's will. Last-minute confession scene. Murderer (incidentally miner) gets off. Story spreads via super-chromo'd ten-cylinder to mining town. Three shots to do justice to the proletarian world of coal, all three of them bad; but for makeweight a speech by hero about coal turning to diamonds in so many million years. Cecil B. DeMille records the fact proudly. It brings him closer to his subject so to speak, and the tale proceeds, as you guessed, to a grand old explosion among the future diamonds. The third party to be eliminated (Conrad Nagel as the Price to Pay) is thereby eliminated, the high society lady loves her labourer, and capital and the proletariat go into a personal fade-out.

The crazy thing about all this is that it takes you everywhere and gets you nowhere. You have a great deal of life under observation but see nothing graciously and nothing well. DeMille is careful to make his miner despise the social luxury, but the terms are not real. Nothing is real, not even the miners. They have explosions, they disappear on impressive rescuing expeditions, but not a brass scuttleful of coal is heaved during the entire proceedings. Nothing ordinary is worth a foot of film for DeMille — only the murders and the confessions and the cocktail parties and the dying children and the explosions among future diamonds. And let him do these things ever so well, as he often does, unreality is in their bones from the beginning.

(The Clarion, May 1930)

It is a long time since I had so brave and powerful a film as *Kameradschaft* to write about. We scribblers on cinema wander about for the most part making the best of second-class jobs. Some are slick, some are able, some are good fun. We whoop them up in criticism rather desperately. We know that the only thing that matters is evidence of a fine purpose and a great imagination; it is the single and only measuring stick of painting and sculpture and the other arts. But what can we do? Cinema is a popular medium and one of the incomprehensible heresies of our social order is that the old *vox populi* is the voice of a second-rate god. The big ones come seldom.

I hate to do it, but I must lean out from the pulpit in this way to get *Kaméradschaft* into its proper category. I do not think it is a world shaker; it is not as big in size as *Storm over Asia*, or as important among the classics as *Turksib*, or as fine in its quality as *Earth*, but it does belong to the greater company.

First, for its theme. It tells how disaster comes to the miners on the French side of the Franco-German frontier and how, in the shadow of that disaster, national distinctions are wiped out, and frontiers are broken down, in the common effort to save the men entombed. The theme has size. It reaches out from the usual smaller issues to a larger one in which the lives of men and women and families and villages and nations are given dramatic substance. Drama ripples out from the exploding pit in sea circles. That is what the dropping of a great theme into a slice of life must inevitably do.

Pabst, who made the film, is a very able director. He can manage crowds with grandeur and hold the difficult details of half a dozen stories and sub-stories in the pester and movement of his crowds; and he can keep his thematic emphasis through the lot. But I have one objection to his work. He is sentimental, as every Teuton (except possibly Bach and Heine and Frederick the Great) has been before him. He cannot leave his theme be. Here you will find the point about brotherhood emphasized far too much. The frontiers are broken down too much; the contrast of the war is played too much; the symbolic hand-clasp is held for exactly four seconds too long. You will hear that the brotherhood of workers is greater than the brotherhood of nationals. You will hear a lot about that and so far so good.

You may ask yourself logically at that point what they are being brothers about. If they are uniting, what are they uniting for, and what against? Pabst will not tell you. The film finishes (as significantly for director Pabst as for Franco-German relations) in the re-establishing of the frontier barrier that was broken down so magnificently four reels before.

Looked at in this way, he has merely told us splendidly that when men are dying there is no nationality. But we know that already: even, curiously enough, in the war. One of my strongest recollections is of a ship shot to pieces by a submarine and a wounded crew bound up by the submarine commander himself. Perhaps you want international sentiment to develop a little further. Perhaps, in Marxian fashion, you would prefer an economic basis for the development, and good solid machinery to establish it. Pabst, I am afraid, takes us no further than the submarine commander.

You must see *Kameradschaft*. It is the grandest story of international bandaging ever made. It will bring tears to your eyes and honour to your bosom. You will like the men and women (fine people all of them) who mill and mass and struggle through breaking props and piling gases to give body and bravery to the film. You will salute a thousand well-turned episodes and a thousand really noble photographies. And you will realize at the end that this Pabst is a great director and *Kameradschaft* a great film. I merely emphasize the other aspect in case Socialists of more sentimental persuasion find their internationalist conscience satisfied by it. They are, often, so easily served!

If you answer me and say that this international bandaging is all one can expect from a film, I shall probably agree with you. Even as it stands *Kameradschaft* is superb propaganda for international understanding. No one can see it without realizing the futility of frontiers and the common aspirations of common people the world over. Perhaps, after all, the further move is not with the film-makers but with the politicians. Let Pabst and the film directors do the sentiment and the politicians the organizing. . . . If only the politicians would do the organizing!

(*The Clarion*, March 1932)

On a swift generalization, it is remarkable how Fritz Lang's instinct runs to bigger ideas than any other director; but it is just as remarkable how little he ever makes of them. *M* is in the grandiose manner Lang established in such films as *Metropolis*. Its theme is taken from the Dusseldorf murders. Its hero is a sex pervert who murders little girls.

By its subject-matter the film is unusual in all conscience, but I doubt if, on examination, it proves to be anything more than a plain thriller. Lang's photography is always excellent, of course, and his description of a mood or situation can often be brilliantly brief. In this example the murder of one child is followed in the adventures of a toy balloon; and the approaching, growing and finally commanding mania of the murder is translated in the simple whistling of a motif from Grieg. But, if we look behind to the theme itself, we find that Lang's inspiration is only second-rate.

Metropolis, for all its pretension of setting and high flying issue between capital and labour, concluded sillily and sentimentally that 'it was love that made the world go round'. As H. G. Wells pointed out at the time, it was an infant conception without knowledge of society or science. Lang, I think, only ever peeps into the great problems. Looking into the hinterlands of space and time and the mind itself—in *The Girl in the Moon*, in *Metropolis*, in *Mabuse*, and in *M* he is satisfied in the end with the honours of melodrama.

The concluding scene of *M* is in the basement of an old battered distillery. The murderer has been run down, not by the police but by the thieves of the town, who find that the now desperate activities of the law are spoiling their business. To effect his running down, the thieves have organized the city beggars to watch every quarter, every street and every section of a street. But with the murderer crushed and cringing before the underworld, the whole drama is climaxed in a trial scene in which thief and pervert argue the relative merits of their case. It is a fantastic way of bringing so derelict a spirit as the Dusseldorf murderer into the realms of sympathy, but obviously not a tragic way.

It may possibly be asked if the whole idea of the film is not a little perverse: if anything is to be gained by creating sympathy for such a character. The test is always in the telling. Whatever the derelict—a creature of jealousy like Othello, or ambition like Macbeth, or of madness like this man from Dusseldorf—it makes no odds in theory to the writer of tragedy. As a human figure, both possible in fact and relatable in fact to the warring issues of existence, he can be brought to sympathy and made an instrument of great appreciation and great art. The sociological argument is beside the point. If he must be kicked from the social midst—hung, imprisoned, or shut in a padded cell—the sociologist may be done with him. The artist is not. By that very fate he becomes for the tragedian the broken, incomplete figure of man who gives him his occasion and his opportunity.

When Peter Lorre, who plays the murderer, screams out 'I couldn't help it!' you will probably be moved. That is the centre of the piece, the theme itself; terrifying and, in the usual curious way, uplifting. But in that poignant moment one appreciates all the more the opportunity that has been lost. If this was the story, if this possession by devils and most foul destruction by devils was the story, the film's theatrical excursions into underworld organization, housebreaking and the like are irrelevant. Lang has, as usual, peeped into his big subject and been satisfied with a glimpse. The best that can be said for the film is that no other director one knows would have thought of the Dusseldorf murderer for his hero. In this Lang shares honours with Dostoievsky and the best of them. But Lang has only thought of his subject; he has not felt it. *M*, like *Frankenstein*, is a full-blown tragedy that has been diminished in the creation to a mere 'sensational'.

(Everyman, 16 June 1932)

Ernst Lubitsch is one of the master craftsmen of the cinema. Consider, for example, *The Man I Killed*, the tragic anti-war story of the French youth who, conscience-stricken for his killing of a German youth, goes to make peace with the German's people. You may consider the story sentimental in its substance—for, war or no war, we do a lot of killing in our day—but you will have no doubt at all about Lubitsch. I cannot remember a film so beautifully made, so completely fine in its execution.

Perhaps I can indicate its quality better by describing a simpler illustration. Before Flaherty went off to the Aran Islands to make his *Man of Aran*, I had him up in the Black Country doing work for the E.M.B. He passed from pottery to glass, and from glass to steel, making short studies of English workmen. I saw the material a hundred times, and by all the laws of repetition should have been bored with it. But there is this same quality of great craftsmanship in it which makes one see it always with a certain new surprise. A man is making a pot, say. Your ordinary director will describe it; your good director will describe it well. He may even, if good enough, pick out those details of expression and of hands which bring character to the man and beauty to the work. But what will you say if the director beats the potter to his own movements, anticipating each puckering of the brows, each extended gesture of the hands in contemplation, and moves his camera about as though it were the mind and spirit of the man himself? I cannot tell you how it is done, nor could Flaherty. As always in art, to feeling which is fine enough and craft which is practised enough, these strange other world abilities are added.

Lubitsch does not often depart from comedy to make serious films. His last one was *The Patriot* in the late days of the Silents: with Emil Jannings as the mad Czar Paul. It was a huge performance with great acting, intense action, and some amazing camera movements in the corridors of the Palace.

The Man I Killed is a simpler film, lower in key, with none of the mad happening of *The Patriot* to build on. The youth, praised by the Priest, goes on his journey. The German family, living on the memory of their dead son, receive him as a friend of the son, and he finds it impossible to make the confession he intended. There are scenes of the old citizens of the German town at their beer; there are some homely interiors; and the only happenings are that the old father comes to like this foreign youth and turn from his hatred of the French, and the German youth's girl falls in love with the man he was killed by. Little enough, if you like, to make movement of, or make climactic intensities of. But Lubitsch's camera glides magically in and out of these ordinary scenes, taking the details of expression and character and essential story on its way. Watch it particularly in the last scene, as it goes from the youth playing his violin to the girl, to the old couple, and watch how there is expectation, and expectation surprised, in every foot of the gyro's passage. The actors are Lionel Barrymore, Phillips Holmes, and Nancy Carroll. As always happens under Lubitsch direction, they were never so modulated or so good.

Lubitsch sketches his character with a single pose, or a single gesture, taken in the camera's stride. He does his work so easily that you hardly know it is being done.

(*Everyman*, 23 June 1932)

Quick Millions is a very remarkable film. It is so much tougher than its gangster predecessors that *Scandal Sheet* and *The Front Page* seem bedtime stories in comparison. Indeed it gets so close to the hoodlums it deals with that it has all the flavour of a personal experience. It is, strangely enough for Hollywood, realist to the bone. It does not romanticize its racketeering; it describes it. It even explains it. It is on the way to being, apart from its drama, a sociological document.

Behind the racketeering story, of course, is the story of private enterprise gone riot. *Quick Millions* reaches through to it bitingly. The toughest article present is not the chief gangster, nor even the henchman who finally puts him on the spot; it is the writer and director of the film, Roland Brown. He presents each factor of the racketeer game, the buying and selling and grafting in high places which make it possible, without batting an eyelash. He makes big business in its American version a big joke.

In the tale a truck driver undertakes to get rich at the expense of society, and he does so with a facility which only to Englanders will seem bewildering. He works a garage racket, which means that under pain and penalty of one destruction or another he levies a weekly protection fee from garage proprietors. Being an intelligent organizer he smashes a few cars in the street and sees to it that co-operating garages are supplied with custom. He works the building racket, which means that for a weekly tribute he refrains from (*a*) bombing, (*b*) killing and (*c*) otherwise sabotaging on the premises in question. His henchman, when he breaks from the decency of his principal's control, edges in on the milk racket and the cloak and suit racket. A machine-gun play on a few milk-cans, a mud spray on a few dresses, pave the way for both.

The police are impotent, for their chiefs are either bought outright or scared of some private revelation. Their personal scandals are on file in the racketeer's palatial office. Superior organization, as he explains lucidly, is everything. In a world in which social purpose is strictly lacking in society's managers, and everyone is impeachable, it is definitely everything.

This is not a fantastic picture of American life, but the nearest thing to bald-headed revelation the movies have ever given us. In one American city recently I sat in on a detective sergeant's description of the city management, which had every one of these elements detailed. Public authority is going to pieces everywhere. Prohibition is a cause. It has done everything to make law-breaking an honoured and established pursuit. It has brought honest citizens into a direct dependence on hoodlums. They would be inefficient hoodlums if they did not improve their grip. But Prohibition is not the whole cause. The silly scramble for wealth, the utter lack of ambition outside the scramble for wealth, the fact that leadership has become divorced from a primary loyalty to the State, the fact that the State has lost the power to create a loyalty to itself, make order impossible. You cannot educate a people in grabbing while the grabbing is good — and no Prosperity speech by an American President has meant anything more since Roosevelt — and expected the grabbers to confine themselves to the ranks of High Finance.

Quick Millions will tell you much of this and it will tell you in a manner which is altogether unique. This is Roland Brown's first film and he has begun his technique where Hollywood and the Germans and the Russians left off. This is a faster film than a Russian, and without recourse to the click-clack and eyestrain of the *montage* business. It is so fast, and moreover so smooth in its quick continuity, that it makes the *montage* business look crude and old-fashioned.

And if anyone still remembers *Berlin* with an unwarranted affection he had better see *Quick Millions* demonstrate how *Berlin*, without loss of complexity, might have been made articulate. Poor Milestone, who with his *Front Page* was supposed to create something of a revolution in the tempo of tale-telling, is a dullard alongside this new and very amateur director. Brown does not know what to do with an actor when he sees one. So long as he makes the gesture that gives Brown his continuity, he can be as good or as bad as he likes. But what continuity!

You will find blemishes in the film: notably a couple of impotent speeches by reformers and a more impotent resolution by big businessmen to do this, that and the other thing. Forget them and concentrate on this director's demonstration of how to start a story in forty-five seconds and end it in twenty. The subtlety of attendant detail I leave you to examine for yourselves. More often than not it makes the very acting unnecessary.

(*The Clarion*, August 1931)

King Vidor's *Hallelujah* is an all Negro film. This is to the good, for the Negroes, like any other spontaneous species of the human race, have a great deal in them that is cinematic; in both the visual novelty of their bodies and the wrapt emotionalism of their ways of expression. Moreover, Vidor is a serious director. I saw something of him in Hollywood and liked him for that seriousness, and I would not miss anything he did. He is an intimate and unofficial disciple of Chaplin: no man can be that and be tawdry.

The principal virtue in *Hallelujah* is in the intention, for glorifying the Negro is not the easiest of tasks in paleface America. For the rest I was disappointed. I was so anxious to see the film that I went to its very first appearance, and disappointment may take colour from too much expectancy; but there it is. It is difficult to knock a film like that for, heaven knows, it is better than most and required a labour in the making one should respect. I must, however, on your behalf insist on superlatives.

The trouble with *Hallelujah* is that setting out to glorify the Negro it does much less than it might. The film tells you about a Negro of honest and pleasant home-town associations who falls for a vamp, takes to religious revivalism, falls once more for the vamp, is cuckolded, murders, does time, and arrives back for a fade out on the plantation again. All of which is rather threadbare. In cinema the big opportunities are the cotton picking, the delivery of the cotton at the market, the Negro cabaret, the revival scenes, the lumber yard to which the Negro, as renegade preacher, descends. All of them admit of song and sound most rhythmic, and none of them achieves it. The film is badly cut, almost without knowledge of Russian achievement in that field, and almost any big mass scene in, say, the *Village of Sin* (Russian), *Storm over Asia* (Russian), or in the *New Babylon* (also Russian) would shame *Hallelujah*.

I apologize for this judgement and again you must see this film rather than others. I was perhaps too acutely conscious of the possibilities of the original material. I have not seen too much of the American Negro, but I have certainly seen better cabaret stuff, better revival scenes and heard better renderings of Negro songs than the film gave me. The point is that the intensity which is instinct in everything Negro did not come through. I question, too, if this rather sordid preoccupation with vamps and Aimée Macpherson evangelism, represents the dramatic truth of the Negro. I note, from a publicity puff, that Vidor freed the Negro from misunderstanding just as Abe Lincoln freed him from slavery. Both statements are exaggerated.

(*The Clarion*, February 1930)

Tabu is a South Seas film in the *Moana* tradition. It went into production with the very proudest and most classical story the world's drama has ever evolved. A boy and a girl love each other—the gods sanctify the girl and make her tabu—the boy breaks the tabu—the gods destroy him. In one version or another it is the story which made Socrates and the Greek Tragedies and Corneille and Racine. If you remember the futile academics of your youth, it was as each dramatist solved the problem: for the gods or against the gods: for society and against the personal or for the personal and against society: that he was allowed by the professors to carry the banner of classicism or romanticism.

I myself was schooled by Calvanism to the classical version and have been content to see the gods obliterate the little tabu-breakers: the Antigones and Hippolytuses and Horaces. And who would not be, who has heard an audience at the Comédie Française roar their welcome to the *qu'il mourut* of Horace itself? Unfortunately, the Murnau-Flaherty work is not to be ranked with Corneille. To defy the gods is a terrible thing, and they have failed to make it terrible. The standard is there for everyone to see.

One should, I suppose, be grateful for South Sea settings and Polynesian maidens and the sterling rhythms of the hula-hula. The photography, when it is not fussy and finicky and too dam' beautiful by half, is the wonderful photography which says what it wants to say. The Polynesian bodies when they are not overposed are the decent god-like bodies *Moana* taught us to expect. The hula-hula dance I found at first a trifle exhibitionist, lacking by a hairbreadth in spontaneity and, therefore, in purity. It was not the dance of Moana. But it stays in the head. There is a moment in it when the youths and maidens glide into the ring of villagers which must be as great a split second as there is in all cinema. And more than that. In the middle of the ceremonial the boy moves to the girl he is losing. Their faces light up as they infect the dance suddenly with their happiness. The danger infects it and the beat of the dance gathers and increases about them. This is true dance, for it is drama.

I must say less of the efforts of the director to pursue the lovers to their fate. The thunder and lightning, which the original dramatic proposition calls for, is seriously absent. The film fuddles. Murnau leaves a long and arduous sub-title to describe the escape to another island across 'a raging Pacific'. This is a mistake from which the film never recovers. You may not in cinema mention a raging Pacific in a footnote.

When retribution comes, it comes clumsily by way of dance halls and drink and some episodic pearl diving. I cannot myself swear to the sequence of events: I could not follow it through the heel-tapping of guitar and accordion numbers. I can only record that high tragedy in this case is not the steamroller affair it used to be. There is no little red flag marching ahead of it. It lacks the note of the inevitable.

There is, on the whole, relief when the messenger of the gods drops off a schooner (its name is *Moana*) and beats Tahiti and civilization to the job of destroying the protagonists. When heroes get muddled and forget to be heroes, destruction is obviously the best thing for them. The quicker the better.

You will gather that *Tabu* is not quite a masterpiece. The drowning of the boy in the last sequence is good: the old messenger of the gods is a grand tragic figure at all points, indeed the only protagonist worthy of buskins; there is, too, some considerable dramatic value in the notion of Fate striking and missing in the shark sequence. With the last part of the dance, they belong to that larger world of cinema which one hardly ever glimpses in the commercial movies. They are worth collecting. And you must see *Tabu*, if only to realize how very great and pure a film *Moana* was.

It is difficult, of course, to tease out from the final account the individual contributions of Flaherty and Murnau. My own opinion is, that all the good things come from Flaherty and all the bad ones from Murnau. They were the wrong people to work together. Flaherty is a naturalist director, with an eye only for the spontaneities and the decencies, and a mind only for stories that go to the heart of things. Murnau was a studio product, a manipulator of artificial effects, a manager of exaggeration, introspective, perverse: an artist who never smelt an honest wind in his life. Flaherty was an explorer in the South Seas; Murnau was at worst a tripper, at best an exploiter. *Tabu* must have been a dogfight!

(*The Clarion*, October 1931)

7 · Hollywood Looks at Life

Hollywood has always had the good sense to loose an occasional salute to the common life. Behind its luxuries there has always been a suggestion of origin in Kankakee or Kalamazoo. Behind the gowns and gauderies there has been a frank allowance that the lady inside them started under honest parents as a shop girl. Tales of the Frontier and the Railroads and the Gangs and the War have remained still more faithful to the notion that rank was but the guinea stamp and a man was a man for a' that.

The manhood may have been romanticized, but behind it, dimly, has been the presupposition that common things have virtues and that straight-up braveries are the essence of nobility. It is this presupposition which has made me prefer American films to English ones. I imagine most people are with me.

Say what you will of the Americans: they do not take their subjects and settings from one silly stratum of near-society. They use the stuff in front of their noses, even if they colour it with the baby pinks and baby blues of happy endings and luxury finales. Not one of us but knows their soda fountains better than our own cafés, their cops better than our police, their department stores better than our shops, their newspapers and business offices better than Fleet Street and the City.

There is a limit, of course: the limit reflected in the baby blues and baby pinks: the showman's fear of introducing the sordid. Hollywood has made a dream world even of its realities. I know there may be a case for filling the world's head with dreams, but one finds it a relief when a story of commoners stays rooted to the solid earth. We want it romanticized just the same, but we want our romance with the sweat and the smells thrown in. It is a better romance.

One great effort to break through to this braver world was King Vidor's *The Crowd*. It failed commercially, because people were too accustomed to the usual halcyon treatment of human life to stand it. It told the story of two young people, who married with all the hopes and intentions outlined in American magazines and movie philosophy and finished up as most folk do, cultivating their back garden on five pounds a week and a family. It cut across Hollywood's world audiences like a whip. It hurt them.

As well offer bread and meat to a dope-fiend as give movie audiences the plain honour of families and affections. So it seemed. But I am not sure that the dope is working quite so well as it used to do. *Bad Girl* came along some time ago and made a great success. *Taxi*, which pursues the same tradition of *petit bourgeois* trials and tribulations, is careful to mix its family drama with a gangster feud, and spice it with three solid killings. You will like the film, however, for James Cagney's very decent presentation of a hard-boiled young taxi-driver, and for the friendly detail of his house and home.

The Champ brings King Vidor back into the big lights, after the sad adventures of *The Crowd* and *Hallelujah*. Vidor is a good director who takes films seriously, his one fault being a tendency to equate seriousness with pessimism. This fallacy is very common in America: I leave the sociologists to guess why.

With *The Champ* he is on safe ground. He has Jackie Cooper and Wallace Beery, and a tale about a prize-fighter, ex-champion of the world, who tries to come back for his son's sake. Beery kills himself in the process. It is told with a great deal of skill, and the relations of the derelict father and worshipping son are sketched with a good deal of humour. You must be left, however, to endure the heart failure of the final episode as best you can. It means that Jackie can be taken at long last to a nice home, a good education and a fitting environment. The film tells you so, and presumably romance is thereby satisfied. There is one scene in *The Champ* where Beery arises after a dirty night and goes through the odd gestures of coming properly to life again. From the chorus of reminiscent chuckles around me, I was led to believe that Beery had made a masterpiece of it. The reminiscent chuckles are passed on for your consideration.

(*Everyman*, 14 January 1932)

Street Scene is from the play by Elmer Rice: a sad, pessimistic play describing the domestic tangles of a tenement building in downtown New York. That is the old town, where the aristocratic quarters of fifty years ago are the slums of today. There, racial elements are mixed as only metropolitan America knows how to mix them: in this case Russian Jews with Italians with Irish with Swedes with Germans. If you knew Halsted Street, Chicago, you would call that a simple mixture, but it is sufficient to make *Street Scene* the first in-seeing picture of American life we have had.

Here is the real America, where a thousand bewildered foreign peoples dig in their toes and fight desperately for a foothold in the promised land. There are economic footholds and spiritual ones. This is about the spiritual ones.

Elmer Rice, before he wrote *Street Scene*, wrote a superb skit on

Hollywood, calling it, in the Swiftian manner, *A Voyage to Puerilia*. He knows Hollywood, and he has taken no chance on the infantile adaptations served out to intellectual dramatists. He adapted the play himself. It is so faithful a reproduction that the film, like the play, is confined to the single tenement set in which the protagonists laugh and fight and dream and weep and murder each other. The only variants for film purposes are the cuttings from close-up to close-up, the long tracking shots to and from the doorway, and the odd surrounding details of elevated railroads, roofs, and passing traffic.

This may sound very dull to those of you who are keyed to the swooping and swinging of movement, which is regarded as the essence of film. But, after all, it is an account of people and of what may happen to them in a day or a night on their own doorstep. Both Rice and Vidor, the director, were wise not to be tempted beyond their thesis. Even as it stands it is a better job than the stage production. The variety of the movement within the limits set is a feat of great skill, and I think only Vidor of all directors could have brought it off. The music, too, with its Blues commentary on the story, and its fragments of jazz (the folk-songs of these very American tenements) adds a quality to the film which the play could not attempt.

I found myself stirred by *Street Scene*, simply because it was serious about something and stuck to its gesture. Yet in the ultimate I am as out of sympathy with it, as I am with Rice's earlier *Adding Machine*. In America, to be serious is to be pessimistic, and I cannot follow the process of thought. In this case misunderstandings happen and murders happen, and everyone is more or less derelict in a world he cannot master. The Russians call this 'defeatism' and class it as the sin against the Holy Spirit. In that, they are strangely true to the classical tradition of dramatic values, where—whatever happened—the potential or the promise of life was also indicated, and the true balance kept.

The Blues are bad medicine when they are of the Gershwin variety. I believe they are even shallow medicine. Better the Negro rendering, where the horn goes heroic. *Street Scene* is pure Rhapsody in Blue.

(*Everyman*, 21 January 1932)

Seldom does cinema provide so captivating and wholesome a film as *Three-Cornered Moon*, the story of an American family's fortunes during the depression. Some films are clever, some funny, and all too many bear the thin excellence of technical skill; but a fine observation is the rarest of qualities in this mass art of ours. It prefers to stumble through the wider hoops of romance and sensation: afraid of the minutiae of living things and living people: incapable, seemingly, of the themes which touch the common routine of our affections. Compare *Three-Cornered Moon* with the films which deal, in the Cabell phrase, with the 'regions beyond life': where the ordinary is not sublimated but side-stepped, and the ambition (not always, nor altogether commercial) is to take the plain citizen 'out of himself'.

What relief to come back from the pyrotechnics of super spies, super crooks, and super monsters to the even more sensational pyrotechnics of an ordinary household, where the plain citizen can be 'inside himself' again, and where the trials and triumphs, though they are small, are blessedly recognizable as his own. The Rimplegars, in Gertrude Tonkonogy's story, are a rich Brooklyn family reduced by the depression to a bank remainder of one dollar sixty-five. They are, like every family in the world, an incredible mixture. The mother, brilliantly played by Mary Boland, is incapable of anything except affection; but it is enough to make her a great lady indeed. The daughter, Claudette Colbert, is bright as a blackbird, but senselessly involved in an affair with an aesthete — who is a pretty foul specimen of an aesthete. One brother is muddling through a law apprenticeship, another through an athletic career at Yale, another through the mad preliminaries of theatrical hope. With wealth behind them, they might tumble along till doomsday: ridiculously concerned in their own inconsequent affairs: quarrelling and fighting to their hearts' content: the delighted mother dancing equally inconsequent and equally inefficient attendance on their squabbles and their stomach-aches. It is, in other words, that rarest of all good things, a family seen from the inside: and so accurate in its detail and affectionate in its drawing that it is, without a doubt, autobiographical.

When the crash comes, what a masterpiece of half comic, half desperate self-sacrifice the family becomes. There is no nonsense about the uprising affection the situation produces, and that is the film's principal attraction. But it is there, working them all to death, in shoe factories, public baths, public libraries, second-rate touring companies, as inefficient, as free in complaint and, with pretty judgement on the part of the author, just as ridiculous as before. You are not asked to sympathize with their fallen fortunes, for that would have been the weakest of gambits. You are merely asked to observe the strange and incomprehensible fact that blood is thicker than water: even when, as in this case, it is of plutocratic density.

You will like the Rimplegars. Their family fortitude will not, I hope, lull you into a false state of satisfaction regarding the depression for all the family fortitude in the world will neither excuse it nor solve it. Here, however, are people drawn from the life and drawn so ably that they have the presence and importance of personal acquaintance. That is so rare a feat in cinema that I give you *Three-Cornered Moon* as very much the film of the year. The honours of it go to the author. She has done her people proud.

(*New Britain*, 20 September 1933)

I went searching for Tom Mix the other week. I wanted to see how the ancient tougheries were standing up against the Cagneys, the Gleasons, and the Tracys. With Cagney in *The Picture Snatcher*, Gleason in *Orders is Orders*, Tracy in *Private Jones*, all parading their more fashionable braveries to the moon, academic research in this very important matter seemed an ordinary critical duty. If I also wanted to slide off the metropolitan pavement into a cool stretch of Wyoming foot-hills, I make no apology for a rustic's nostalgia.

Mix was riding the wind in *Rustlers Round Up* at Camberwell; in *The Fourth Horseman* at Herne Hill; in *Rough Riding Romeo* at Walworth Road; in *Death Valley* (or was it *Defiant*?) at Forest Hill. Indeed, I gathered that our West End emphasis is not altogether shared by a very large number of citizens beyond the Elephant and Castle. There is something to be said for their preference.

The Western saga is simple, but there are some curious and precious qualities in it. Behind the paraphernalia of good hombres and bad hombres, ranch conspiracies and banditries, rustlings and rides to the rescue, there is so plentiful a splashing of hills and horses and fresh air that one only realizes on seeing it again how cabined, confined, and claustrophilic our other films are. In a world so plain in its villainy and diffident in its heroism, the belly-aching spiritual (or only sexual), which is nine parts of the West End emphasis, seems more than remote. It is clear that Mix, at the first whimpering smell of it, would shift from one foot to the other, mutter illiterate apology, and take his leave. You may reckon indeed that the persisting diffidence is something of a persisting decency shying away from all such sickness in the blood. It represents the instinct of common men, to free themselves not only from complications but also from complexes. The world it rules may be a simple world, where the principles of law are understood even by cow-punchers, and I am not sure that the technique of lying and deceit in which all of us so proudly graduate is not better suited to the particular villainies we fight, but the other has dignity.

It is this quality more than any other that the Cagney heroes lack. They are bravos in their own way, though obviously the world has become too deep for them. The Western's straight to the mark solution for bandits and bad men has become a posturing protest in, say, *Private Jones*. Jones thinks the war is bunk and persists against odds in toughly saying so. Mix would have said very little. He would merely have shot a couple of politicians and woven some magical hemp round several profiteers. I notice that our metropolitan toughs roll into action only on the more orthodox occasions. They will push a moll in the face, smack her garter a yard high, tip a drink down her blouse, and square up on all possible personal occasions. So much for a general belief in direct action. But it is kindergarten stuff. You may regard it as commendable after a surfeit of Christian propriety and social complacency; you may even think it significant of a new and rising temper in the world by which ordinary men will again liquidate the smells they register; it is, on the other hand, too uncertain of itself, too ineffective, to give any considerable satisfaction. If dignity attaches to the Western hero, there is this deeper reason for it: that he does also carry protest to an active conclusion.

This larger argument apart, there is still nothing in cinema to compare with the movement which these Westerns so easily and consistently command. The horses are fine in themselves, but pressed in the crescendo of rides to the rescue, and cross-timed with the events they hasten to help, they give you the simple essence of good cinema. The Western moves; it delights the eye with progressive and developing movement; it stirs with most visible happening. It is superior to everything except event; and it plays its story against a landscape noble in itself. Its avoidance of the more complex, and possibly more reasonable, versions of personal romance need not bother you. It would be better, I know, if the little girl looked more like a rancher's daughter and less like a dolled-up stenographer, and you may even find that in this regard the cow-puncher's diffidence is overdone; but in *Rustlers Round Up* you will find a note of compensation. Where in any more sophisticated rendering (outside D. H. Lawrence) have you heard a proposal of marriage fortified by a speech in praise of stallions? The boys and girls of Camberwell were delighted.

(New Britain, 2 August 1933)

Cimarron takes a tough young newspaper editor through those generations that saw the building of Oklahoma, from the opening of the Indian Reservations and the first rush for the land, through the building of city and State, up to the last mad discovery of oil. That is recent history and a matter of two generations or three at most; but it gives you themes in space and time and creation.

Hollywood, which knows what to do with space and also—occasionally—with creation, has never been very strong on Time. You may remember the effort of Lillian Gish to rock a cradle through the ages in Griffith's *Intolerance*. The Massacre of the Huguenots was there, if I remember, matched in modern history with a trial for murder in twentieth-century New York. *The Vanishing American*, a later effort, began splendidly with the passing of tribe after tribe across the prairies and the wiping out of each by its successor, but fell down on a modern episode where Noah Beery (sheriff and villain) pinched a bit of land from Richard Dix (Indian and hero), and Dix, being an Indian and coloured, couldn't marry Lois Wilson, the local lipsticked schoolmistress. The Indian infants in a touching if rickety scene waved penny flags and repeated the Oath of Allegiance.

It used to be one of the copy-book headlines that you couldn't get the hang of the local event and give it its reference in history. This is particularly true of a tribe like the Americans. They have Mencken but no prophet: the *American Mercury*, but no criticism.

But *Cimarron* is a step ahead, even if it slips up a trifle on logic. Dix (again Dix), the symbolic hard-baked American of the Oklahoma land rush, the hard-baked editor who lays down the law and defends an editorial from both hips, remains the everlasting hunter of new-fangled enterprises. The war with Spain. The Great War. The opening of the Oklahoma oilfields. Just like that, uncritically and any-old-how, following the fashion in whatever is new and tough, and leaving the old lady at home to build up the *Oklahoma Gazette* and prosper on the want-ads.

I am not sure myself if the Oklahoma land rush, the building of Oklahoma, the Spanish-American War, the Great War and the Oklahoma oilfields, make a straight flush—and you may agree with me—but the film does get across that particular stretch of history and does make it feel like history. That is the accident I refer to. This film has the size of time, and that is the most wonderful and the most difficult thing on God's earth to get into any job. With even a hint of that you may forgive a film anything.

Chang, which ran a trifle to expert showmanship in sections, achieved it by the odd patience with which Burmese natives started hacking down trees at the end to rebuild the homes they built laboriously enough at the beginning. The quality of ease and patience made the show. Time is in character: mostly in ease, mostly in patience, seldom in dramatics: in a handful of corn thrown into the earth generation after generation through all the less pertinent sequences of disaster and death. The Greek sculptors avoided the peak of action.

Cimarron, if it has anything, has a hint of this continuity of essential character. It is good that men should ride off to war and things, and leave their ladies on the domestic watch tower. You and I may, in a sense, want to investigate the wars a little and discover what the gesture is all about; for you never know about wars and the gesture may be a fake one. Even the garden patch can be a long way from home. Apart from that, the principal truth stands and any sense of tribal criticism at all will pick you the real deaths from the dud ones. *Cimarron*'s director is Wesley Ruggles. He is, I understand, young and coming.

(*The Clarion*, March 1931)

A most remarkable film is *Beast of the City*, and one of the very few which, in justice, must be seen again and again. It is a long time since I felt that about a film, but when you observe the creative detail of its first two reels you will realize why a technician should be interested. American films as a rule swing into their story with a directness which excludes the more gracious details of life on the way. The story is given you; the characters, the action, the threat, the climax, the *dénouement*; on the best models everything moves swiftly to its appointed end without too much concern for those more incidental humanities which are the breath of life to the greater dramas and the greater novels. *Beast of the City* is a curious exception to the American rule. It strides into its action, but with a generosity of bystanders and bystanders' comments which rounds out the scene and gives one a deep and impressive sense of reality.

You may remember the technique used in that remarkable stage play by Rice, *The Adding Machine*. There the whole effect of life in the city was created by the cashier's monotonous repetition of the dollars and cents of her cheques. It went on and on in variations of 'two dollars' and 'forty cents' till it raised your hair with its insistence. So at the beginning of *Beast of the City*. The radio announcer at police headquarters calls the police waggons, strung out across the city, and gives them their several instructions. 'Calling car three-seven-one . . . three-seven-one . . . Calling car five-two-four . . . five-two-four. . .' The succeeding details of robbery and murder and rape pile up in monotone, and the camera roves round the city giving visible substance to the dramatic narration. The cars with their individuals of police officers move into action, and in its swing the camera picks up the details of this and that on the sidewalks. The effect is colossal.

The story of heroic cops and villainous bandits is less important than this incidental quality of method. I laughed with my neighbours when the police department took its oath to the Constitution, and laughed again when they vindicated it with fifty sudden deaths in the last act. There was indeed a great deal of naïvety in the film of the type which over-gestures the heroic and makes duty an exercise in exhibitionism. When the detectives move down in phalanx on the hoodlums in the last act they do so with a disregard for strategy which astonishes even the girls of the audience. They are open to the wide; so unnecessarily so, that the sacrifice of their forty lives passes from bravery to the ridiculous.

I don't know why American enthusiasm should be so unhumoured when the enthusiasms are moral ones. If the theme is one of national virtue as in *Cimarron*, or of civic virtue as in *Beast of the City*, you can lay almost any odds you like that America's stupid pulpiteering manner will spoil the effect. It is in this case particularly unfortunate, for otherwise the film is magnificent. The power of the initial scene is something to take really seriously. It indicated a method which makes previous documentary methods as developed in Russia seem crude and unsatisfactory. Now and again cinema has touched on the impressionist. It was impressionist in that 'knife, knife, knife' scene in *Blackmail*, and again in the trial scene in *Murder*, where the comments of the jury were piled up artificially to force the mind of a doubting member. *Quick Millions* took us a step further when it passed swiftly from one peak of action to another to build up the bravery of a character. But the *Beast of the City* technique is better still. If you can hang odd catches of conversation together, to illumine the life of the city, you are doing something rather revolutionary and rather grand. Carl Sandburg in *The Windy City* and T. S. Eliot in *The Waste Land* have done the same sort of thing in poetry, trying desperately with this gathering of significant trifles to articulate a complex modern world. Cinema has been slow to follow their lead, but with *Beast of the City* it begins to demonstrate a method by which it can do its realist powers justice and become imaginative. Brabin directed.

(*Everyman*, 19 May 1932)

Variety, best of all the cinema gossip papers, tells us we must expect more gangster pictures. After seeing *The Public Enemy* I am not so sure that this is the bad news it sounds. The Westerns created Epic by repeating themselves: by the very threat of monotony escaping into bigger things. Few of the movie subjects have suffered a similar transmutation because they were done with before they were well started.

One of the stranger curses of the game is that, like other female worlds, it follows the fashions. A hit in horror films or animal films is followed with a rush by others of the species: quickly conceived and as quickly executed to exploit the newly discovered taste. The public mind is thought of rather pathetically as some citadel fortified and defended against an enemy. One little breach in the walls and our entertainers are piling pell-mell after each other to seize the advantage.

This superficial outlook has been disastrous because the weakness of the repetitions is liable to kill a field of material for years. A batch of sea films flop (because they are bad films, of course, not because they are sea films), and the word goes round that sea films are 'out'. Or a plenitude of war films puts war films 'out'. So, innocently, is the plain fact of the matter lost sight of—that a good story with the original issues of life in it emerges from any material whatsoever.

This is a long but necessary introduction to *The Public Enemy*. We have had gangster films by the dozen over the past year, and this is yet another of them. But it is a good film—good in itself—and all question of fashion is immediately beside the point. I found myself liking it much better than my fellow-critics, and you will have to make your own careful judgement on its merits.

My impression was that there was something at the heart of it more solid than any gangster film before has shown. Not the shootings: there were better in *Beast of the City*. Not the continuity: *Quick Millions* makes it look ragged. The achievement of *The Public Enemy* is that it gets closer to the person of the gangster, to the mind that works behind the gangster, to the possibility of the gangster, than any previous film of the sort. It does make him credible, and that represents a very noteworthy exercise in the higher revelation.

For this, one must be grateful to a story which contains some of the pertinent social facts. Most of us are guided in our film theory by the notion that cinema has nothing to do with the novel and a very great deal to do with the short story. We look for an action begun, executed, and resolved, with a certain directness. We are enslaved to the Greek conception of Unity in Time, as the dramatists who follow Greek theory have never been.

The Public Enemy makes the big plunge and follows a life history spasmodically through its several ages. The boy becomes the pool-room youth, the pool-room youth the consequent tough, the tough the gunman, the gunman the bright and burnished 'big shot' himself. It all really happens. That is to say, we do in a fashion grow up with the youth, and, as familiars must, we find him as possible an acquaintance at the end as he was at the beginning.

This is something different from our detached acceptance of the 'big shots' in the average gangster film. They are melodramatic set-ups. This, because we have seen it grow, is more nearly a living gangster. A living character, of course, is the first necessity of a living drama. What happens to him is immediately important. What fate befalls him has not only life and death in it, but is as liable to have the elementary laws of philosophy in it.

I shall not put the matter too high, but *The Public Enemy* noses sufficiently into the larger world of appreciation to command your attention. Cagney lives and perishes as the gangster, and such sterling dames as Joan Blondell and Jean Harlow walk casually in and out of the picture. It is whispered down Wardour Street that the censor has had his way with them. This may account for the strange poppings of their exits and entrances.

(The New Clarion, 2 July 1932)

The Mayor of Hell follows the sociological line and describes an experiment in self-government in an American reformatory. The reformatory is a studio set-up, and the boys are ordinary little Hollywood actors, registering mass emotion to the crack of a directorial whip. Fortunately the theme is better than the film, and I, for one, shall say nothing to discourage Hollywood in the pursuit of other social problems of the sort. Play them as they may, it is better to have them romanticizing reform than romanticizing rackets.

Far too little justice has been done to the side of American life which this reformatory theme represents. No country, in its universities, has studied the liberal aspects of social service so carefully and so laboriously; and it is good to remember that Chicago produced Clarence Darrow, the finest of all humanitarians in our day, at much the same time as Al Capone. The principles of reform laid down by American liberals may appear somewhat sentimental and tender-minded. You may even believe that Darrow's belief that crime is illness is not deep enough, and that Judge Lindsey's psychological clinic for children in Denver does not sufficiently comprehend the economic sources of crime, but the justice they represent is wiser and, to some extent, it works.

So with the film. Its conclusions are easy, but, in its plea for children's courts from which the penitentiary atmosphere is eliminated, and for reform schools that really reform, it does a magnificent piece of propaganda for the more sensible treatment of wayward children.

What happens is something like this. Cagney, a young war heeler, is given a job as deputy commissioner to a reform school. In the

American municipal racket it means that for services rendered—
gangster services at polling booths—he is given the right to take a
rake-off on contracts. No more is expected of him. But he falls in
love, and listens to his lady's ideas of reform, and puts them into
practice. The boys are let loose to do the things they want to do: to
do woodwork if they are natural carpenters, to draw if they are
made that way, to run their own stores, organize their own affairs,
and administer their own laws. All this, as one might expect in a
Hollywood film, they immediately do, with only minor casualties.
They become, indeed, decent law-abiding little citizens, and potential
pillars of the *status quo*.

It may be that *Mayor of Hell* was inspired by *The Road to Life*,
which dealt similarly with a bunch of ragamuffins. If so, it raises a
pretty distinction in sociological argument. I found the uplift note
pretty strong in *Mayor of Hell*; and, if anything, the toughery of
Cagney makes him a more plausible reformer of boys than the scout-
master approach of his counterpart in the other film. But *The Road
to Life* had a stronger argument. Its notion of boys learning to be
useful, learning to make things, learning to take a creative part in
society is no different in principle, no higher in aim, than the theme
of this American film. The superiority lies in the fact that the boys
are offered a rôle and a regime they can genuinely believe in and
enjoy. I doubt, for example, if you can really exorcise the smash and
grab spirit in youth when smash and grab—in only slightly different
forms— is the most honoured practice of society. And I doubt if
you can, with any final success, teach youngsters to be useful when
every snob value in the land is associated with uselessness. *The
Mayor of Hell* gracefully skips any such considerations.

(New Britain, 29 November 1933)

With *Gabriel Over The White House* Hollywood makes a first
hurried and hectic dash into the field of politics. I hear that there is
great concern in America lest by adding its weight in this way to
direct propaganda cinema may upset the balance of politics; but you
will be wise to reserve your judgement on the principle till you have
viewed the product. As you might imagine, Hollywood is liable to
pursue the sensations and romances of political issue and is hardly
likely to face the ordinary realities of political construction. In this
example, Hollywood's political conclusions are, to say the least,
simple.

You will appreciate how very simple if I give you the line of the
story. A new American President has just been elected, and it is plain
that his high-winded election promises will pass into limbo in the

usual way. He is a good party man, a roysterer, a 'good-fellow', in
the old-time American sense: more than likely to use the spoils of
office for the personal benefit of himself and his friends. He is
involved in a motor-car accident, suffers concussion, and emerges
as a New Man. At frequent intervals, he casts up his eyes in a nor-
therly direction (inspiration from God) and listens queerly to
ghostly choruses (heavenly choirs by Cosmopolitan Productions
Inc.). On special occasions, a trumpet solo off stage witnesses the
presence of Gabriel himself.

All this is dandy. As the mistress of his roystering days very gravely
puts it, 'There is the old Judd . . . there is this great gaunt ghost who
is the new Judd . . . and there is the THIRD BEING . . .' With this
holy trinity in charge at the White House, the political fireworks are
all set for a Hollywood fiesta. Are you surprised that the cleaning
up of (*a*) America and (*b*) the World, is carried out forthwith! I was
not; for, in student days, I walked the wards of an asylum and, once
a week, saw the self-same miracle performed under the self-same
conditions. Eyes were turned upwards, ghostly voices spoke, Gabriel
played a two-fingered exercise on his cornet; and dictatorships were
achieved, and the ills of the world were solved, by the Perfect Faith of
raving lunacy.

I found the sequence of events exciting to a degree. The new
President has Quixote lashed to the mast in the matter of easy solutions. The Secretary of State baulks him, so he fires the Secretary of
State; and, for good measure, he sacks the rest of the Cabinet as well.
Congress criticizes; he adjourns Congress. The unemployed march
on Washington; he forms a labour army in which the unemployed
(forgetful of labour doctrine) happily accept a soldier's pay. When
the gangsters challenge the White House itself, they are wiped out
by a dozen armoured cars and a firing squad. Last miracle of all, the
statesmen of the world are brought together in holy harmony, and
the Peace of the World is achieved. And how, my pretty politicians,
how? By assembling the might of America's navy and America's
air force, and telling said statesmen they will be blown to hell if they
don't do as America tells them. In the English version a diplomatic
alteration has been made. It is an Anglo-American combine of
navies and aircraft which bullies the world into peaceful submission.
Wheesht, Stalin!

You will not wonder that on achieving so swift and satisfactory a
millennium, our Mr President Judd collapses under the strain. And
you will be delighted, as I was, to hear him, with returning consciousness, speak in the roystering accents of the good old days. He calls,
as anyone would, for his Pendy; the concussion has passed away.

But do you think the film allows us to utter the gargantuan peal of laughter which is trembling at our gizzards? Not on your life! The film, not weary with well-doing, murders the President off, lest, by the odd chance of returning sanity, this strange millennium be embarrassed. Depressing the necessary button with his heavenly forefinger, Gabriel fades out on a high C.

It would be scurvy of me to set against this fairy tale of politics the thought of the ordinary realities which politics involve, of the day-to-day building of organizations, of the persistent wars between constructive and destructive forces, wise and stupid and plain ordinary forces, which prevent easy conclusions and slick results. Perhaps the business is altogether too dull and painful for the easy manipulations of cinema romance; and original sin (or original incapacity) is too sorry a deterrent to the halcyon endings which cinema demands. I do not, therefore, object overmuch to the fairy-tale form. It is dangerous, like other drugs, but not half so dangerous as the underlying suggestion, in this case, that a benevolent dictator-ship can curb rapacity, and that peace can be commanded by a jingo display of war power.

(*New Britain*, 14 June 1933)

Propaganda is an excellent mistress, but a blustering fool of a matron. In more incidental function, she gives spice, purpose and most necessary prejudice to life. With right to command, she outbawls one's every instinct of proportion. If, perchance, she wears the draperies of Pure Patriotism, heaven help the producer who is tied to her! Her great skirts whirl in a pompous flurry of reds, whites and blues, stars, stripes and whatnots; and she outbellows the bull of Bashan with her blather.

You will gather from this that I have no stomach for the American navy parade in *Hell Divers*. Its patriotism is of a brand that would be indecent coming from anywhere. Coming from a country of *émigrés*, where patriotism is even less mature and critical than the European species, it demonstrates a complete disregard for the international decencies. The air squadrons of the American navy fly past. They parade in magnificent patterns across five reels of film. They swerve, swoop, hurtle and nose-dive sensationally for the world to see. And to what end? That the world will observe the killing power of their bombs, the fearful, diabolical engine of des-truction they represent! That is the thrilling issue of this singularly blatant and unpleasant film.

The parade, I will confess, is good to look at: as it could not fail to be. There is something in flight itself—even to see—that catches you in your landlocked midriff, and gives an almost physical sense of release. That command of space which is the artist's chief end, whether in sculpture, in writing, or in film, is here achieved with a single take-off or a single spiral. Add clouds and the world above the clouds, and you add poetry with each sunlit vista. It is all such sure-fire, inspiring spectacle that the bombs beneath and the gas tanks under seem a vulgar impertinence.

Wallace Beery is the hero of *Hell Divers* — or, rather, he co-heroes with Clark Gable. They are rivals, doing each other dirt at every turn; but, with any experience of films of the American services, you know that this is only their little bluff. Back of their rivalry, they are buddies under the skin, true blue sons of the squadron . . . and the devil take the hindmost Chinee or Nicaraguan! They love their officers, love their work, jump to it with or without occasion, and carry on the very best tradition of recruiting posters the world over.

The sequence which will amaze you most is the description of an aircraft carrier landing aeroplanes at sea. The ship is turned into a beehive for a hundred buzzing aeroplanes; taking off and landing with military precision, turning the deck into a most impressive parade ground. The aeroplanes are, in fact, old-fashioned: slower and clumsier and 'blinder' than our own. That may give the warriors among you some consolation.

All this is fine. Where you may find life less plausible is in the finale, when the Gable outfit crashes and Beery is sent to the rescue. Gable is washing about in breakers that would smash the skull of an elephant and break the bones of a Brontosaurus, but Beery saves him none the less. And not content with this, Beery proceeds to the Great Sacrifice itself: forfeiting his great husky hulk of a life for the 'dark-eyed gabble-gabble of the femmes'. It gives the film the concluding spectacle of a burial at sea. The ship's company is marshalled on deck, the bugles blow and the flag flutters as per patriotic recipe.

You will — as usual — pardon the details. They are not important, but certainly demonstrate what a job it is to make a decent personal story for a piece of blatant propaganda. Every situation is manufactured, every dramatic crisis forced, every heroism sentimental. Only the flying spectacle comes through. That, if you can forget its implications, will take your breath away.

Arrowsmith is about publicity — which is the little rather snuffy-nosed brother of Propaganda. It tells, as you probably know from the Sinclair Lewis novel, the sad story of an American who once upon a time hated publicity. He was a research worker and discovered a serum and went to the Caribbean to demonstrate it in a plague of bubonic. The serum came through, and the medical came back to

New York to shun publicity as a plague even worse than bubonic. With any great instinct in research he might have discovered a serum for publicity, too. But he did not think of that. He merely humped into melodramatic gestures of personal integrity, and shunned it. Here I am not so sure what the issue is, but I liked the film very well for the fine acting of Colman as the medical, for the superb direction of John Ford (a great director at all times) and for the unusually fine art direction. It is a good film: slick to a degree in its sequence and beautifully shot.

I see there are objections to the Caribbean sequence, which is supposed to be — in heavy contrast to the rest of the film — too 'studio'. I thought it all 'studio' and the Negro spiritual effects, which accompanied the bubonic in the jungle, no more unreal in drama than the fantastic laboratory settings, and the strange laboratory habits of the research worker, Colman, and the miraculous muddlings among the beakers and test-tubes. Happily one does not expect realities in such a film. One accepts the studio props and the studio presentation and hopes that within these artificial limits something real and live will issue.

In this case I think it does. It is unusual to see an honest worker made a hero of: and it is almost revolutionary in a Hollywood film to see him heroicized in terms of his work. This is so much a matter for praise that one can forget the little snail tracks of box-office intention which emerge from time to time.

As for that ultimate issue between the honest worker and the publicity merchant, I wonder if it is the desperate affair the film would have us suppose. It is bad to have scientific results prostituted for a headline. But how otherwise can scientific results be spread to the populace except by simplifying them and dramatizing them? And how otherwise can public institutions establish their necessary public relations, except by translating their plans and results into the vernacular of luncheons and news stories?

That is my single objection to a good film. Sinclair Lewis is always bludgeoning some fake villain, and you must expect it from him.

(*Everyman*, 7 April 1932)

The Last Gangster, I heard, was just another gangster film and my informant was Sydney Carroll. 'Personally I have no use for it', he writes. 'It seems to me to pander to a morbid interest in murderers and city thugs and the scenes in which the gangster and his son are put through a sort of third degree are too horrifying for description.' Fortunately, I had another and different tipster in O'Brien, scenario chief at M.G.M., and the world's greatest expert on short stories.

I was interested to see what he, in high contrast, thought the best M.G.M. film for ages.

Well, this business of being 'too horrifying for description' you will have to cut out as no argument at all. So for that matter is the description of the dead in *Salammbo* and, for a 'morbid interest in murders', your recollection may refer you to *Hamlet*. The test is surely whether pity goes with the terror and the high resolution of tragedy comes out of the mixture. Gangster film or no, you had better have a close look at this Edward G. Robinson picture for, if my eyes do not deceive me, it is pretty close to the real thing. I shall always count the ennoblement of the maniac in *M* as one of the weirdest and bravest things the cinema has done and the ennoblement of this selfish, arrogant killer in *The Last Gangster* is not different in kind. The basic elements of true tragedy are there. Without letting up on the selfishness, arrogance and evil, here also is courage to make up the human balance. When the film has swung fiercely through the terrors of the gaol of Alcatraz and has tortured the gangster step by step and brought him finally, ashen grey, to his knees, there has been enough of human dignity in the process to make the balance swing not unbeautifully in the sunlight.

I could wish perhaps that Krauss or Lorre or Muni or Laughton had played the part, for Robinson, first-rate actor as he is, does not quite make the level of the idea. The film makes a hero of his figure of evil and a not unworthy child of Paradise Lost, but he lacks the subtlety to hold the two elements together. I wish too that the sub-plot in which the gangster's innocent wife flies to the arms of James Stewart and brings up the gangster's son in respectability, were less smarmy. Poor son of a gangster if James Stewart be the alternative and poor Hollywood if this be really the last of the gangsters. It had better dig up a new slice of evil for, heaven knows, it is no good at good.

(*World Film News*, January 1938)

8 · The Cinema of Ideas

Great writers have had bad luck with cinema. Herman Melville's *Moby Dick*, greatest of all sea stories, became a sentimental vehicle for John Barrymore's profile, and the malice of the Great White Whale was suppressed at last in a hide of indiarubber. The only importance of *Peter Pan* and *A Kiss for Cinderella* in the history of the cinema was that they lost a great deal of money and abolished whimsy for ever from Hollywood's repertoire. *The Admirable Crichton* prospered, but in the disguise of *Woman to Woman*. Mr Shaw, with *How He Lied to Her Husband*, turned out to be a poor scenario writer in a medium which demanded action. The size of Anna Karenina escaped the Garbo, and the devil of Dostoievsky was not in *The Brothers Karamazov*. The single blessing of *Don Quixote* was that the butchery of its manufacture produced *La Douce France*, one of the best satires ever written on the movies. Only Shakespeare has done well. There was life in the Fairbanks account of *The Taming of the Shrew*, and something of the ancient flash came through the Hebraic spectacle of *A Midsummer Night's Dream*. Not even in alien accent does poetry completely perish.

There is a difference about Mr Wells's entry into cinema. Hearing perhaps of these other strange transformations, he has had the courage to attend on the movie world in person. He has himself turned his book into the terms of movie. And lest anyone, seeing the film, doubt what he intended it to be, he has published his treatment. It is *Things to Come*. Arriving so far, he has at least beaten the example of Mr Maeterlinck, who, after a luxurious passage to Hollywood and an equally luxurious welcome, was told that they hoped, with patience, to make him as great as Rex Beach. Maeterlinck did not finish. Hollywood found to its horror that his leading lady was a bee.

I hope I am not prejudiced by the professional reading of scripts, but I find the published version of *Things to Come* fascinating and easy and vivid to read. For anyone with eyes to see and a mind's eye to conjure up the images he is meant to see, a film description has many advantages over plain narrative. Events, characterizations, and the argument of the drama are whipped into a running shape more precisely and with less meandering than the narrative form permits. Something certainly is lost. Those sandwiched encyclopaedic slices of fact which give size to *Moby Dick*, and the rolling introductions which 'establish' the stories of Scott, must unfortunately go by the board. The deviations of description and commentary and plot within plot are impossible. But a mounting action and a tempo'd climax of argument and event give the film description its own virtue. For this alone *Things to Come* must be a revelation to most people. Here they will see the stuff of which films are made, and, by its origin, it is big stuff which has not often come the way of a film director.

One thing about Wells is that he lives and learns to the minute. I have seen Shaw sink dully, and, for once, dumbly, before a description of the possibilities of cinema. Against this is the vision of Wells sitting watching, month after month, the wildest experiments the London Film Society could conjure up for him. In so far as he has confessed in my own theatre at the G.P.O. that he was in course of 'learning' from us, I may, I hope, claim the right to examine him on his first result.

Let me set down the story in brief and be done with it. In his introductory word, Wells calls it a 'spectacle'. It is not, like the book *The Shape of Things to Come*, 'a discussion of social and political forces', but a 'display' of them; for 'a film is no place for argument.' The subsequent arguments of its readers and spectators were not the less violent for that. The spectacle is certainly a strange one.

It is 1940 or perhaps a little before, and the good families of Everytown are preparing for Christmas. War breaks out and disrupts the families, dragging out from 1940 to 1970. Civilization disappears and Everytown reverts to medieval conditions. The technique of our era of science is lost. The Black Death comes. In the stage of final desolation the reversion to the primitive is complete. Mechanical knowledge is vaguely remembered, and buying and selling is a matter of old clo' bazaars where the effects of the ancient gentry are the prize of bandits' mistresses. The great patriots' war goes on under the leadership of petty chiefs and savage gangsters.

At this point the old Wellsian finger wags, and out of Basra comes a new dominating force which restores civilization and the world. It is, of course, as every Wellsian knows, the power of the technicians and scientists, mobilized and regimented to reorganize what the politicians and the soldiers, with their imbecile nationalism, have destroyed. As a saving qualification, however, even with the dictatorship of the technicians, perfection does not altogether come. The question of the haves and the have-nots they solve. The deeper question of the do's and the do-nots remains. There is revolution in the Utopia of 2055: on the question of whether two young people should be sacrificed by science in a journey to the moon. That revolution is not resolved, and the film ends, as Wells promised, 'in a note of interrogation among the stars'.

The story goes with a clip, making light of marching armies, landscapes of tanks and poison gas, and scenes of death and desolation as vast as London Town. The chronicle rips over the years of Everytown with the destructive gusto of a tornado making for Miami. 'The Tower Bridge of London in ruins. No signs of human life. Seagulls and crows. The Thames, partly blocked with debris, has overflowed its damaged banks.' This, one effect in thousands, gives every assurance of spectacle. But one problem drums in my head. Can patriotism be mobilized to its own evident destruction over thirty years? Is the human spirit so craven as to endure the destruction of civilization in the name of whatsoever patriotism? On a more practical and political level, would an armed proletariat stand for it? Wells was not in the war of 1914–18, or he would have sensed how near the breaking-point men can be not in thirty years but in three. The facts are there to guide political philosophy. The Russians broke in three, the Germans in four, and there were, shall we say, certain difficulties appearing among British, French, and Italians alike.

It is an important issue for the film, for I doubt if any thesis can sell so vast a dereliction of the human spirit as these thirty years of death and desolation represent. Few at heart will believe in it, and where there is no belief there is only melodrama. On a first impression of the treatment I would say that too much of one's common experience is left out of account. I remember a certain Peter Kerrigan magnificently challenging a crowded St Andrew's Hall in Glasgow to 'pit him oot' and receiving no answer. There are no Peter Kerrigans in *Things to Come* — not at least for thirty years — nor flywheels of Russian example to hold the desolation in check.

On a lower level there are other doubts, particularly about these technicians who take the place of the proletariat of Marxist theory and create the first liquidating dictatorship. This is to put faith in a class of society which in the past has shown no inclination to serve any but the highest bidder, and as a class has demonstrated no political consciousness at all. The experts walked out of Russia with their masters. It is an axiom of Marxism that only the proletariat know the burden of Fascism and war, and may be trusted to destroy the system responsible. This one may at least comprehend. That a privileged and honoured class like the experts should find fire and determination enough to give new laws to society is a trifle more difficult to appreciate.

These are the essential issues of *Things to Come* and more important than any mere question of film treatment. Being important issues they, of course, affect the treatment considerably. As a result of this lack of faith in the common people there are, for example, no common people in the film, save as soldiers and victims, and no braveries or humanities of common people. A photographic art is, in the last resort, an art of the ordinary. It may by its many fantastic devices create vision and spectacle, but a shot of a child or a spontaneous gesture will bring you slap bang into cinema's own essential virtue. These scenes of war and pestilence, of a craven or non-existent people, these star-finding technicians, have not the life's blood of such common observation. They are rather the projection of an argument which one feels is itself out of touch with common observation.

The film reflects this difference. There are marchings and counter-marchings of time — abstract, spectacular, melodramatic, fantastic — but they are no more humanly true than the effects of *Metropolis*. It is a great story and a great tract, but, if I may say the worst, it is no more intimate in its human reference than a spectacle by DeMille.

There is, of course, the argument that it is high time the spectacles of DeMille found the quality of a great writer and time that we had a great tract in cinema. That miracle has certainly come to pass. There will be more thinking over *Things to Come* than over any film since *Deserter*. There is a greater sense of social warning and a better instruction in citizenship than in any previous film whatsoever. It is perhaps the measure of *Things to Come* that it sets out in most popular fashion to make the millions think. The important thing is that the first of our great writers has taken this medium of millions and studied it and used it to address the world.

I will not say that Wells is as good in the cinema medium as he is in his own. It would be foolish to expect this, for the idiom of the cinema is a young man's idiom asking even newer complexities of mould than Joyce himself. Wells gives the show away in pretty fashion when he tells us that the music specially written by Arthur Bliss for the film may be had on gramophone discs. Any real film man will laugh at the possibility of such a divorce, and suggest mildly that where there is so much of pure music there must be less of pure film. In yet another direction I do not find any of these heartbreaking qualities of time and suspense with which a more poetic Pudovkin introduces his great scenes and sets them against the far horizons of drama.

But these are academic points. What I greatly admire is that this brave old master has out-faced us all with the size and scope of his vision, and that this clever old master has seen a way, within the vicious limitations of commercial cinema, to advance a great social argument. Before these two major facts I do not care how unsubtle his sound band is. The mental band is all right, and when, pray, did cinema ever give consideration to *that*?

(*Glasgow Herald*, 29 October 1935)

Don Quixote is still the greatest of the enchanted wanderers and, whatever film is made of him, something of the idea must inevitably be left to excite the imagination. In Pabst's film something does remain and, sorry rag that it is, it is enough to give the film an almost revolutionary distinction. We do not often take our films into the higher and wider adventures and never, except possibly in Chaplin, into the irrational regions of philosophy. Surfeited with the too, too local anecdotes of Shepherd's Bush and Hollywood, it is pleasant to remind ourselves that cinema may also deal with ideas.

The film is a triumph of photography, with a peak in the windmill scene which must delight everyone who respects the powers of the camera. The acting presence of Chaliapin, too, is something so unique in itself that it commands respect. But the film and the idea within the film: that is another story altogether.

Chaliapin needed a mountain top to give film proportion to his gestures; and the idea of Quixote needed wind and space and horizon to give it size in cinema. But no, the poor devil staggers through five hundred close-ups of face and posture, with a rabble of grotesquely inferior studio actors jostling him for each. Never, except in the final windmill scene, does the film begin to open out. Even the battle with the sheep and the freeing of the thieves are cabined and confined: with an over-filtered photography depriving them of their last vestige of air. A dropsical curse this super-photography sometimes is!

From a directorial point of view this lack of space has a disastrous effect on the whole film. How, except against images of isolation, is Quixote conceivable? The romantic lunatic as a hero might be a great subject, but his dream needs the detached substance of poetry to make him a figure of drama and not of a lunatic asylum. If sympathy is to be got for him, or heroism or tragedy added to the tatterdemalion grandeur of his hopes, it is only against other-world horizons that he can properly be figured. And that, in cinema, is definitely not to be done by close-ups.

Don Quixote does not come over. We note the gestures of his knight errantry and, impossibly connotated as Cervantes makes them, they mean, or should mean, something real. The injustice which sleeps neither night nor day, the chastity which is the first rule of knighthood, the chains which must be broken, the giants, the magicians, even the lances and the helmets and the Rosinantes have reference in the common philosophy. But here, there is no deep familiarity in our contact with them, though every Tom, Dick and Harry of us has waved his similar plumes. How, in jostling studio streets or scrappy close-set encounter of sheep, prisoners, wine bags and comic tournament, could there be!

One directorial occasion will suffice to indicate how *Don Quixote* goes dead. Quixote has emerged from the tourney and, raising his helmet, recognizes Carrasco as the fake adversary. It is a moderately important moment when he says pathetically: 'I have been tricked, they have made a fool of me': and a more important moment still when, with a last muster of essential dignity, he rides off through the jeering populace. That dignity meant everything to the representation of the idea. It should have been staged mountain high: the audience with Quixote, the laughter breaking in waves of the sea over him. But no: one far shot of Quixote riding off, and the crowd of monkey extras yelling their heads off into the camera! I never saw a great occasion so shoddily done, and that it came from a man of ordinarily fine understanding like Pabst I cannot understand.

Quixote, of course, is not necessarily this figure of tragedy. It is only one of the many possible ways of playing him. You may affirm that his pursuit of Romance in a world of two-times-two makes him more naturally a figure of comedy. You may follow the pundits and say that he is the pilloried representative of chivalry and a figure of satire. Or you may note the cumulative quietness and affection of the Cervantes narrative and say he is just as possibly a figure of picaresque or of fairy-tale. On any one of these counts this Pabst-Chaliapin interpretation has equally failed.

Chaliapin has played the figure too high for either comedy or satire. He presents Quixote from the first as distraught and a madman, and holds this note of overwrought insanity to the end. Quixote is as heavily outlined as Boris Goudonov. So detached from ordinary recognition is he, so much a figure for certification, that you neither laugh at him nor make fun of him.

As for fairy-tale, the touch is not light enough, the vision too pedestrian. The wine bags are just ordinary wine bags, the sheep just ordinary sheep, the tourney just a plain bad tourney. You see them as such, and for all the director and the camera tell you there is nothing more. You might have seen them as Quixote saw them, for giants and magicians and fearful affrays, and captured that double vision of phenomena which is the essence of fairy-tale, but Pabst (Teuton though he is) has forgotten the possibility. Quixote is just a poor stick.

In spite of complaint the film stays curiously in the head. It may seem that Pabst has done a scurvy job by this English version and allowed a tenth assistant cameraman to cut it; but it is difficult not to sympathize with a poor benighted Pabst doomed to direct the notoriously undirectable Chaliapin and mix him with the somewhat unmixable Robey. The job may have been impossible from the beginning. In the problem of a German directing Chaliapin and Robey in a language which he (probably) and Chaliapin (almost certainly) did not understand may be found a sufficient excuse for the curiously undramatic and unmeasured wordage which accompanies the film. But whatever the final judgement on the film, it is certain to turn the molecules of criticism. And that is a unique distinction.

(New Britain, 7 June 1933)

The Reverend Galsworthy's famous sermon on gentility, *The Skin Game*, has been turned into a film. Hitchcock is the new preacher, but the sermon remains very much as before. It is still the funny, rollicking yarn it always was.

If you remember, the Hillcrists, who are the landed gentry, are at outs with the Hornblowers, who are the industrial gentry. You never saw such a fight of hooligans. They storm and threaten and kick each other's shins; they accumulate every species of muck from rotten eggs to cods' entrails and slosh it over each other's heads; they turn to blackmail and reputation-dirtying with an ease which would astonish and even stagger the most hard-baked criminal. At the end of it, the Reverend Galsworthy asks his famous question: 'What's the use of gentility if it can't stand fire?' The operative word is 'gentility'.

I first heard that tag line years ago and have never ceased to find diversion in inventing answers for it. That, however, was in the days before the Raspberries (American and Hungarian) short-circuited criticism.

There is, of course, an issue between these landed and industrial gentries. The landed gentry, it seems, do not want the nasty chimney smoke drifting over their demesne. The industrial gentry, it seems, think the landed gentry a bunch of snobs. There is (for the moment) some question of whether a certain peasant's cottage will be held by the landed landlord or blotted out by the industrial landlord. There is also the very grave question of whether a proletarian damsel of doubtful origin can be the sort of person a landlord (landed or industrial) would care to have around. On this last matter, as you can imagine, both landlords are agreed.

If you like your fights faked, this one may stir you. Otherwise, I am afraid, you will find it a very unfunny farce indeed. For, of course, Mr Hillcrist and Mr Hornblower never fought at all. They fell into each other's arms seventy and eighty years ago. Mr Hillcrist put his money in Mr Hornblower's business and Mr Hornblower bought some of Mr Hillcrist's land and they have been as thick as thieves ever since. And well they might be. What birds of a feather they were, and are.

Can you really imagine Mr Hillcrist worrying about the industrial smoke over his demesne? Why, it was the merriest thing in the world when he found coal under it, and no trouble of conscience at all to have it ripped up and slaughtered and uglied by workers' slums if the royalties were forthcoming. Can you really imagine Mr Hillcrist worrying about the poor peasant in the corner field? Did he not put his fields to sheep and easy profits, and drive him into Mr Hornblower's factories? Did he not otherwise burn him out of that very cottage and drive him to a wilderness overseas, Hillcrist himself not caring a hoot in hell where he went?

I can assure you of a fine time at *The Skin Game* if you have a neighbourly neighbour you can poke in the ribs and chuckle with: it is full of such jokes. It will give you all sorts of opportunities for casting your mind back on the other fruits of that English gentility which Mr Hillcrist so splendidly represents. You will hear of the honest land-love the Reverend G. claims for him, and think of his criminal neglect of his drainage system. You will hear the Reverend G. blubbering about his sportsmanship, and think of the tenants he has rowed across the ferry. This was the Highland Hillcrist's equivalent for bumping off. The rest was hat-touching, forelock-pulling, fifteen shillings a week and a bag of meal.

As for Mr Hornblower, he was so shocked when Chloe turned out to be a proletarian damsel of doubtful origin, that he left that part of the country for ever: retaining only a controlling share in the local company. It was strange for Mr Hornblower to be so shocked, because at that very moment he was pimp to a thousand Chloes in his very own factories. It was hardly so strange that he should worry mostly about the shock to his system and very little about poor Chloe herself. But you may depend on it he got over what shock there was. In another parish over the hill he set up his mansion with the rest of them, and has been Lord Hornblower to this day.

No, you could not expect the Reverend Galsworthy to know these more intimate details of the Hornblower family history. Like the other literary toadies of his generation, he sobs on a short front.

The film itself I must proclaim for the fine job it is. It is a smooth account, with all the ingenuity in character. But when, oh, when, will Hitchcock get a theme that will match with his powers of production? This has all the air of being more important than the previous ones, but when you come to think of it, what a shallow and contemptible theme it is!

(*The Clarion*, November 1931)

All Quiet on the Western Front is Universal City's version of Remarque's picaresque war novel. The film is built on a larger scale than the book, and considering the crudity and naivety, and the still unmastered complexities of the sound-film medium in which it is presented, it is a braver and bigger piece of work than the original.

Not better. Writing a novel is a moderately simple business, and simpler to do well. One man sees it through from start to finish, without any more interference from an outside world than he cares to stand for. At the worst he can, like Joyce or Lawrence, publish in France: but always he has the will of his medium. His materials are cheap.

With cinema it is very different. For every foot of film you shoot, you may put down 6d for the material film alone. Your actors, sets, and equipment, your regimental staff of cameramen, art directors, electricians, carpenters, and the rest, come over and above. Your most humble effort in cinema carried you therefore into a maelstrom of high finance—a maelstrom in which the promoters, backers, bankers, and other riff-raff of private enterprise tumble and curvet like so many dogfish, snapping for dividends. They require safe-guards for your every move, and reduce the essential gamble of art to such vulgar certainty as their own minds command. They will not trust their funds into a world of art or inspiration, for that indeed would be trusting them out of their sight. By that fact is the film director limited. He is in strait-jacket to the devil. There are few occasions when he breaks through.

All Quiet is the exceptional occasion. The tracks of the companion-ing pig are to be found only at the theatre entrance. A lady with one leg naked to the hip stands over the doorway at the Alhambra bidding the vulgar suppose that the film concentrates on the higher nudities. The film, however, is consistently earnest and for quite considerable passages intelligent. I have heard that the director's ending was scrapped for an ending suggested by the favourite son of one of the bosses, but by that time you will be too grateful for a deal of honest directing to worry about the soft-headed symbolism of a single last shot.

The film handles war material a thousand times better than any previous Hollywood film has known how to. It gathers them up relentlessly, more detail and more, till the mass of detail registers the size and significance of war itself. Any private story there may be is cast strictly in proportion to the size and significance of that larger reality. This, you may well believe, is almost revolutionary in Hollywood film technique.

There is, however, something more in *All Quiet* than the bravery of the war scenes. There are passages of intimate feeling — intimate war feeling — which show quite unusual power of insight for a film production. These passages, I admit, are balanced at least equally by passages of mother love and youthful whimpering in which the insight is more nearly Hollywoodesque, but the greater moments are none the less real. In the best of these you might be sitting with Gorki, and I found some satisfaction in the thought that this best was provided by the long-lost Raymond Griffith. He is the French soldier whom the youth stabs to death in the panic of the retreat and, dying, he becomes a cynical mask of death that delivers in a flash all that any anti-war film could wish to say. The youth might well scream through the night watches in such a presence.

Oh yes, it is a good film, but, that justice be balanced, I shall put down certain qualifications. I did not like the whining mamma of the 'leave' episode; and I did not like the boy's prayers over the hospital death-bed of his friend. In moments of the greatest personal emotion there must be a decent limit to fluency, and no suspicion of exhibitionism. The stuttering Shakespearian model stands: 'Pray do not mock me. . . . I am a very foolish blind old man. . . .' This film, like others, tends to take the high spots easily, and the sentimental and the slick are blood brethren in the field of art. The boy, for example, talks much too much when the mask of death is driving him mad. The essence of madness is surely silence, as any trip to a madhouse will testify. The silence may be broken suddenly and perhaps terribly, but the beastly thing about the business is that it sinks intolerably back into silence again.

Once or twice, however, the film does reach that final stabbing restraint: once when the boy kisses the hand of the little French girl (she of the higher nudity), once when he finds the last of his comrades dead on his shoulders, and once again when on a morning in spring, the boy himself is killed. On these occasions the Western Front is indeed most poignantly quiet.

This unevenness in *All Quiet* may or may not be due to a weakness or confusion in the idea controlling it. It is concerned, as the book was, with the futility of war and, to be sure, some wars are futile enough. But, complaining too much about the futility of a particular war, it carries over into a pacifist complaint against war in general. And that is dangerous ground for drama. The embittered protest of outraged youth becomes too closely associated with the quite different protest against all life-doctrine, and apt to set up a deal of whining. It may be dirty — as the film maintains — to die for one's country, but there must always, of course, be some country — define that country how you please — for which it is in the original sense good to die and to discipline for; the two processes being in principle identical.

In this case there is no ironsided assurance of one country or another, one positive life or another, behind the film; and the conclusion of futility is on the whole too easily bought. Youth dies without having lived or died for anything in particular. This is not true tragedy. The essence of that highest of all philosophic forms is that the size and articulation of death is only complementary to the size and articulation of the life that is set against it. Here death is terrible enough, but all that is lost is a rather sentimental undefined demonstration of youthfulness. The film deduces no considered or deepening reason why one should weep for it.

(The Clarion, July 1930)

Frankenstein is the sensation of the day. It is not as I write the best film in London; but it will make more money than any of them. I watch the local intelligentsia go through the usual agonies of despite when a popular crasher comes along, but away they toddle to see what it is all about. So, I imagine, will most people.

In *Frankenstein* we advance majestically from the sevenpenny novelette to the penny blood. It sets out to scare you to death and it succeeds. This may or may not be an important thing to do, but the yokel in you will snoop up to the Chamber of Horrors and plunk down the necessary penny. There is no use me saying that its direction is comical, its general level of acting atrocious, its romantic relief a last word in infantile imagining: when Frankenstein's monster is upon you, tearing and rending, and growling and whining, the yokel in you will rise and acclaim and tell me to take my criticism to the devil.

This only proves what one of my comrades-in-arms is forever telling me. Skill doesn't matter; cleverness certainly doesn't matter: only the idea matters. In *Frankenstein* the idea is altogether novel in cinema. What does it matter if it is presented idiotically, if the imagination that went to its making is the imagination of a rabbit: it is sensational enough in itself to emerge from any directorial murdering.

The film tells you of the strange manufacture of a human being and of what befell between this manufactured man and the world he stumbled into. He had a raw beginning. A crazy young doctor gathers corpses from graves and charnel houses and anatomists' slabs and moulds their dead pieces together. As men have done before him, he calls down fire from Heaven and pours life into this creature of his making. He is a strangely pathetic figure at first, raising stiff arms in wonder to the light, and taking orders like some great lumbering baby. But, gathering strength, he gets gradually out of hand. He murders his keeper, breaks from the watch-tower of Frankenstein, and terrifies an entire countryside with savage attacks on everything he encounters.

You may trust the film to tell you how awesome in sound and sight such an unnatural customer may be. When the bats fly low and night's in the sky, Universal Studios are at their best.

The finale is of a brute savagery in the pursuing mob which easily beats in subnormality the efforts of any single monster born or created. They drive him into a windmill and burn him, screaming and screeching, to death. As George Atkinson demonstrates, the film rises in glee to the foul sadistic excitement of an Alabama manhunt.

There are two moments in this film altogether magnificent: the gesture of the monster as he raises his eyes to the light for the first time, and his reaction to the first sight of a child. How anything of this beauty got into a film so crudely inspired, I cannot conceive. I can only think that the episodes were in Mrs Shelley's book, and that Boris Karloff, who played the monster, was bigger by a mile than Carl Laemmle junior and his scenario department.

Indeed I am sure of Karloff's part in the business, for he brings a curious beauty to the rôle which the script does not intend. The story is stacked against any sympathy with the monster; his brain is supposed to be a criminal brain; he is supposed to be a savage, congenitally wrong. But, seeing the film, I thought there was a greater human dignity in him than in all the miserable little Anglo-American fools who yapped round his great heels. I even found a certain perverse pleasure in his disembowelling of the idiots.

Of course, the whole trouble is that Hollywood has cheapened a great theme. This monster might be anything. It might be a symbol of every creation whatsoever, for each must inevitably take life to itself and pass beyond the power of its maker. It might be a symbol of machinery which, invented in good faith, becomes by the stupidity of its manipulators the degrading monster it is. It might, like any figure of Greek tragedy, represent the power from which some last gift of grace is lacking; or, in still another rendering, represent the

Rogozhin to Prince Myshkin, the Hyde to every human Jekyll. Shakespeare made Caliban of such a figure, giving it the brutish reference of ancient eras and first strugglings from slime.

There is no end to the possible significances, except in the limits of your imagination. All Hollywood saw, however, was a bogey man and a chance to whoop up the boys with straw in their ears. I admit they have done it well. The scene where life is born (by aid of a 'ray beyond the violet ray', a ten-foot spark-gap, and a melodramatic thunderstorm) is good value for money; and the art director who created the sets deserves a special hand. The stumbling entrances, the off-stage whinings, the fantastic agonies of Karloff in the final flames, are quite physical in their effect. But here's to the straw in yours ears! May you quake!

(Everyman, 4 February 1932)

Like most people who work at cinema, I see too many films: respecting most of them for the labour and the ingenuity I know they contain and, in one way or another, learning from all; but it is seldom enough that a film bowls you over. *The Life of Emile Zola* is one of the fine ones which begin as a film and end as an experience: like *Potemkin*, *Earth*, *Deserter*, *Man of Aran*, *Pasteur*, and, with all its faults, *The Good Earth*.

On the sweeping canvas of late nineteenth-century France, Hollywood has staged in this life of Zola as dramatic a battle for truth as ever the cinema managed in fact or fiction. Most people will wonder how they came to be interested, but, considered as a form of expiation, there is good reason for its fire. No one would be more likely to appreciate the disintegration that goes on in the successful artist and the pains of the artist in the face of vested interests than the writers and directors of Hollywood.

The quality of the film derives from this feeling of secret autobiography and, of course, from Paul Muni. As a piece of acting his account of the character of Zola is enormously skilled: jumping from age to age of the man; changing his gait, his speech, his idiosyncrasies, his mind: developing his literary character with such an uncanny sense of detail that, before we know it, we are facing a picture that so pleasantly reminds one of H. G. Wells that it cannot be far from the great Zola himself.

One sequence when Zola is a poor young man receiving his first fat cheque for *Nana* is a most moving little patch of film acting, and heavens knows what with. Another, when Zola makes his defence of truth at the Dreyfus libel trial, has the temerity to run eight hundred feet or so, or four times longer than the newsreels would allow our best political orators. Muni gets away with it. This I find queer enough. He has, at times, more annoying mannerisms than any actor I know, yet this power of settling into the clothes of his character amounts almost to transubstantiation.

The principal theme of the story is not, as we have heard, the Dreyfus trial. Hollywood and its directors have taken deeper account of the writer himself: the progressive writer, successful, finally complacent, shocked into the old fire by the political scandal which the Dreyfus case represented. Whatever the literary accuracy may be, it is a story which feels good all the way and in the great trial scene when judges act like curs and generals like jackals, it becomes, for a moment, majestic. A curious point is that Cézanne has been made the driving force of Zola's life. He appears as a much lighter figure than the bearded tough of the portraits and a more romantic figure than the fierce old psalmist Cézanne actually was; but let it be registered as the most bewildering thing of the year. Hollywood has paid this tribute to the man who, more than anyone in the last half-century, despised everything that Hollywood stands for.

(*World Film News*, November 1937)

Dead End was a serious and successful play on Broadway. It is equally serious and successful as a film. It is beautifully directed by William Wyler, who is not only one of the great directors, but one of the rare two or three whose sense of drama is as adult as his skill. It is profuse in human sympathy as it dives down into the tenements of East Side New York and discovers the teeming tragedy of the poor. What more can we ask? We have challenged the cinema to grow up and take stock of society, and here it does both. We have cursed its dream life and sugar-stick endings. Here is real life and — as one gangster generation dies of its own evil and a new generation is marched off to the reformatory — here is the spondaic ending of honest observation.

Yet, and in spite of watching the film with eagerness and respect, I dislike it intensely and it won't do at all. It is aquarium stuff. It looks at people distantly, like fish, and its sympathy is cold with distance. The poor, poor beggars, are poor; they are uncomfortable; they breed thieves and gangsters and a curse on the conditions that breed them; they struggle against overwhelming odds and what break are they given in achieving the good life? That is the theme and the thesis. It sounds all right; but who was it said that there was more reality in a louse on a dirty bagman than in all this sorrow for the working class? Granted the poverty, the discomfort, the struggle against odds, no slice of humanity is so dim and sad as *Dead End* observes. They laugh and fight and love one another and, except to the sympathizers from without, their dreams of escape are not more important than the rich grip on life they already signify. It is this that *Dead End* misses. It lacks gusto.

Perhaps I am no great shakes as a reformer, but I feel a trifle bewildered when I see anaemia made the price of reform. In *Dead End* the heroine, poor dear, wants a cottage in the country away from 'all this' and the architect hero, poor dear, feels so savage he could pull down 'all this' with his bare hands. Well, I say, let the L.C.C. boys and all such look to that; and they will. But who, except the dramatist and the poet, will see to it that the deeper virtues are not lost in the process? Here, emphatically, there is no contact with these deeper virtues. The poor fish swim round and round with sad eyes and no escape: as though escape were outside, along Riverside Avenue and into the Bronx, and not inside, laughing and loving one another and kicking up hell at injustice and being themselves.

I urge the point because there is one thing the cinema preciously possesses. It began in the gutter and still trails the clouds of glory with which its vulgar origin was invested. But as we ask it to go deep, be sure we are not just asking it to go middle class. And be sure that the next phase of cinema may not be to eliminate the Cagneys in favour of the Colmans, and indeed to Colmanize Cagney himself. Behind all the arguments about the future of British films there has been an alignment which reflects this fear, and it is far more important for the future than all the divisions over national *v.* international, small films *v.* large. Some of us say the future is where vitality is, and never mind the art of cinema for the present. It would be a pity if we achieved everything and lost our sense of smell.

(*World Film News*, January 1938)

Captains Courageous, I am told, is the film of the month among the general releases, and I believe it, though I can never find my way in the idiotic labyrinth of premières, first runs, second runs, and the kind I see at the Crystal in the Borough. These, of course, are the best ones, for by the time a film gets to the Crystal the spit and polish have gone, the confidence trick of presentation and ballyhoo is an old damp squib of months ago, and *Lost Horizon*, *Mr Deeds*, and the Hoot Gibsons, they all come even at last on the bill boards. They have to talk across the hard floors and the waste spaces of the peanuts to be good, with nothing to warm them except what is inside themselves, and that is as it should be. The Crystal is the place to pick the classics all right. Only the elemental survives under its last ironic timeless eye.

But *Captains Courageous*, I know, will pass down the line in triumph and, except for its miserable and indeed bloody last reel, it will be for the boys of the old Dover Road what the cinema was thirty-five years ago in the then abandoned skating-rinks. I cannot be a critic at all about this film. It has everything I asked for thirty-five years ago — the sea and the fishing-schooners and fog on the Grand Banks and fishing cod from a dory with hand lines one after the other — and then a race between the schooners in a high wind, with noses ploughing under and throwing water high over the fo'c'sle, and the hull heeling over till it seems impossible it will ever come back, and the mast straining under the bravery of brave men, till it cracks.

I confess I have been fortunate since. I have gone to sea as I vowed and fished cod one after the other with hand lines one after the other, and there isn't a whip of wind or water, or a hull heeling over so it didn't seem it would come back, that I couldn't match; and the reality was as good as the dream, as all realities are when you look into them. The only difference, perhaps, that it wasn't mostly on the Grand Banks and the only fish I ever loaded into a Grand Banks schooner was some raw bootleg liquor in the days of Prohibition. But here, with *Captains Courageous*, I fall for it as hard as ever and all over again, and will quite certainly join a schooner at Gloucester, Mass., as soon as I can get there, and in spite of the Swiss advertisements and the Travel and Industrial Association of Great Britain and Ireland, saving their presence.

Maybe when I get to Gloucester, Mass., I shall not hold so strongly for racing till the foremast goes; and there is a point in navigational ethics in crossing a bank in a high sea, just to beat the other fellow, which I shall discuss at length, if not soberly, with the skipper. I have no doubt either, that we shall get by without losing the brave and noble Spencer Tracy when the mast goes and indulging in a long heart-to-heart talk with him before he finally disappears below the waves. I feel certain that at the end of our trip, when we unload our cod and sell them smart, that we shall not have a grand slam burial service for the hundreds of drowned sailormen we have left behind us, with weeping women and other nonsense stacked to the skyline, and a daft statue of an emaciated man-at-the-wheel towering over us, his eyes staring nowhere a good mariner's should. But all that is best in the film I shall have and easily; and that is how the sea is the one thing that never disappoints a man — and how good a sea film *Captains Courageous* is. A bit of exaggeration perhaps at the high spots, but basically all that a fishing film should be — with everybody in their right places round the table in the saloon, and the mixture of dirt, and discipline and ribaldry just right, and none of that sissy swagger that is coming these days into every ship afloat, what with education and the cruises and the pyjama parties on the Atlantic, so there is no sea tradition left, except in the stokeholds.

I should say that for this breath-taking reality of the sea — or, shall we say, the breath-taking reality of the romance of the sea made real — the film is better than Kipling, except that Kipling couldn't conceivably have made such an over-nauseating mess of that last reel. The Americans have handled the essential story well. The little prig of a boy who is due for salvation at the hands of fishermen is a very son of a bitch of a boy as played by Freddie Bartholomew, and his saving at the hands and heart of a Portuguese fisherman named Spencer Tracy is as nice and delicate a job of work as Spencer Tracy ever did. He even sold me a rather sappy address to the night sky and the angels and sang something about 'Don't cry little fish' in a harsh and horrible voice which, I confess, is my idea of singing on the Grand Banks of Newfoundland. Only the long and dithering death of the man withdrew my loyalties. I can explain it only by saying that I don't mind old Captain Ahab dying as a hero should, when, as any fool can see, it is the time for Destiny and the Great White Whale to come for him. But watery graves, which happen by accident and only to be sad about them, are not good fishing, nor good film, but only bad Louis B. Mayer and melodramatic slobbering of the worst. When I get to Gloucester, Mass., Louis B. Mayer will quite positively not be present. He would drown anybody, including me, for his box office.

Victor Fleming directed and I would like to hear his explanation of how so good a film — though, you will have gathered, simple-minded — managed to foul its lines so stupidly coming into harbour. For the death of our hero is but the signal for a general collapse in which Lionel Barrymore's seamanship, good film direction, and the tight little story of the making of a man, suddenly go off the earth together with Spencer Tracy. It is notorious that Americans, not content with the lugubrious sentimentality of Mothers' Day, have also created a Fathers' Day, and that is the trouble. What a people, what a people! The boy's father is brought in and there are dreadful goings on about fathers getting close to their sons, laying alongside their little hearts, close hauling their what-nots, and being pals to them, and other horrifying sickness of the sort, with the little hand finally closed in the fat sloppy hand of American paternity. Here, I regret to say, I leave the ship. Who does not know that fathers, like skippers, exist to slam hell out of their sons — and sons, fathers?

(*World Film News*, December 1937)

9 · Hitchcock, Asquith and the English Cinema

Hitchcock is the best director, the slickest craftsman, the sharpest observer and finest master of detail in all England. There is no doubt about this. He has these qualities so abundantly that in their sum they give him a style which is his and no one else's. A Hitchcock film is a Hitchcock film — and never a bad one — and this, if you will believe me, is an achievement of character where so many hands, grubby and otherwise, contribute to the final result of a film.

Yet for all these virtues Hitchcock is no more than the world's best director of unimportant pictures. Not one he has made has outlasted a couple of twelvemonths, or will — unless something radical happens to change his standard of satisfaction and give his talents something solid to be bright about.

As the credit and future of British cinema rests very much in Hitchcock's hands it would be best to make a job of the analysis. Here is *Murder*, a story of a young lady falsely accused. She is a poor benighted creature (Norah Baring) who works her hands around in a Baring way and cannot remember anything. She cannot remember anything and the usual potent courtroom atmospherics emphasize the blank. She is sentenced to death and so far so good. At this crucial point in the lady's career, however, it is plain that we must proceed to set her free again. We do so. With ins and outs, sometimes interesting, not often urgent, but with due Hitchcock regard for the absolute in-and-outness of this world, we do so.

We find a hero in the person of an actor-manager who is also a knight. Your attention is thereby directed to the magnificence of the apartments of the actor-manager-knight class. It is also directed to the sentiments of one who would, on his own confession, use the technique of his Art to unravel the tangles of Life. (*Sic.*) We find an aide for our hero in the person of a poorish stage-manager. Your attention is thereby directed to the comic table manners of poorish stage-managers when eating with resplendent actor-manager-knights. We proceed on our quest. Our hero shaves. This directs your attention to the possibility (unique to the talkie) of uttering the thoughts of a face. In fact we make a high spot of it by uttering the thoughts of two faces, to wit the face shaving and the face reflected.

Moreover we make the radio the excuse for an undercurrent of commentary music.

The heart of our hero is, by this novel use of talkie technique, cheered in his murder researches. He proceeds to the place where the body lay and spends his night in a lodging house. There is no reason why he should, but your attention is thereby directed to the plague that a landlady's children can be to an awaking plutocrat. And so sensitive has Hitchcock become to the comic horrors of poverty, your attention is directed most ably. A child squalls and squawks through-out the scene. This too is novel, for where is the theatre that can guarantee the like? We proceed to find our true murderer as trapeze-act in a circus. This is especially lucky, for it not only directs your attention to the cinematic possibilities of a trapeze-act (originally exploited in *Vaudeville*) but it presents you incidentally, if there be such a mental distinction in the Hitchcock philosophy, with ele-phants, clowns, dwarfs and dressing-rooms. The murderer hangs himself with his own trapeze-rope and outwits the censor. The benighted lady is set free. Our proposition is complete.

I believe I am putting the matter fairly and with due regard for the film's excellences. My criticism is that the excellences are incidental excellences. They dress out the banal issue so that the separate scenes hold you as they would not, under a lesser director, come near to doing. But the issue pokes its empty face at you, at every turn.

I am not saying that the life of a lady means nothing as an issue: I am suggesting that in this case it never ceases to be anything but a trumped-up occasion for Hitchcock's cleverness. It may be because Hitchcock is too intelligent to take an affair like that seriously. It may also be that Hitchcock thought it was a serious affair and engaged himself at the midriff to do his deepest by it. In that case *Murder* is a flop all ends up for Hitchcock as a large-size director.

Now catalogue the talkie novelties, for you will hear much of them in the parlours of the highbrow.

(1) The scene in the jury-room. Sir John is the last juror to hold out against the verdict of Guilty. The mental pressure from his fellow jurors is built up in mass and tempo by cutting-in the faces and phrases with growing close-up and loudening voice; the faces have their characteristic phrases, they are repeated, quicker and quicker; a chorus of 'What do you think of that, Sir John?' mounts up through the sing-song babel. This sort of technique has been used by the advanced play-writers (Rice, Connelly, Dos Passos, etc.), and has been developed by the B.B.C. The principle of construction is sound, but the value of each demonstration depends of course on the variety and suggestion value of the sound images which go to the making of

it, that is to say on the imagination which goes to the choice of the sound images. In this case they are obvious and ordinary.

(2) The shaving scene already mentioned. The mind speaks off stage. In this case the voice is straight. It was a husky whisper and dramatically opposed to the straight voice in one of the high spots of *Hell's Heroes*. The *Hell's Heroes* job was stronger.

(3) The death sentence. This is not seen. It is plain that we have had enough of the courtroom — and other movie courtrooms — already, and have exhausted the visual interest. The silent film would have had to repeat. The talkie need not. The death sentence is heard. The visual accompaniment is the meandering of a caretaker through the deserted jury-room, picking up an odd cigar, wiping a desk, etc., etc. This is fine and the best thing in the film. By its weight of understatement — that is to say, apart from its technical novelty — it almost makes the gimcrack death sentence solid.

There remains to add that Hitchcock is the only English director who can put the English poor on the screen with any verisimilitude. Perhaps as time goes on and success comes over him, Hitchcock tends to love them less and exploit them more, to see them strictly from the outside and be snobbish. He finds it more a matter of regret that they have no dinner jackets than that they have no dinners. But apart from that he is the one director who is familiar with them to the point of genuine observation.

I write so much about Hitchcock for the good reason that he is the only English director worth writing so much about. One large disturbance in the slats of his ambition, such as I am attempting to give him, and he would be a great director indeed. At the moment he resembles too much the luxury forward line at Stamford Bridge: he is pretty to watch in front of the uprights but somewhat apathetic about the issue thereof. Will Hitchcock, for a change, take counsel of Arnold Bennett, and give us a film of the Potteries or of Manchester or of Middlesbrough — with the personals in their proper places and the life of a community instead of a benighted lady at stake? That is something not only worth doing but, for the sake of the commonweal, something urgent to be done. It is already within his scope; it stands, however, as a challenge to his depth.

(*The Clarion*, October 1930)

A new Hitchcock film is something of an event in the English year, Hitchcock has a personal style of his own direction, which can be recognized. He has a long record of good work, with large slices here and there of supremely intelligent work. He is known to have a freer hand than most in direction and to have odd thoughts of greatness.

It is no wonder, therefore, if in criticism we exalt him a trifle. With a national cinema growing up under our eyes, we need strong and individual directors more than anything else. Financiers and impresarios you can buy two a penny. Directors who have something to say and the power to say it, you can only close your fingers and wish for.

Rich and Strange is the story of a young couple who cross the earthball on a holiday, and drift, in shipboard fashion, to new loyalties. An adventuress so-called disrupts the male and a colonial planter disrupts the female. In the main it is a meandering tale built up on the slim behaviourism of two or three characters and the minutiae of their relationships. The end of the story is that the couple are shipwrecked and saved by a Chinese junk. In that oddest of all spots in the world they discover the great mercy of having a baby.

The most important thing about the film is not so much the story. It is the sudden emphasis it lays on weaknesses in Hitchcock's make-up. I have guessed before that these existed, but have never seen so clearly what new opportunities of direction must be given him if he is to build up his talent to the very grand affair we expect it to be.

In trying new material Hitchcock has found himself outside both his experience and his imagination. He has already proved himself as a director of London types and Londonesque melodrama. This new and greater canvas of seven seas and half a world has caught him short.

Think of the theme for a moment. You have in the background the journey across the earthball, and Marseilles and Suez, and Colombo and Singapore to play with. That must surely mean something to the story. You may think of it more deeply as a demonstration of the fact that even the world and its wonders can only teach people to be themselves. Whatever you think, you cannot avoid the background. It is the material of your drama and your cinema both.

The success of the film as a study of people and as a slice of cinema depended, therefore, on Hitchcock's ability to make that journey live. He fails, and entirely because his mind does not quite appreciate the wonders of the world he is trying to use. He is in this sense the supreme provincial your true-born Londoner tends to be. He knows people but not things, situations and episodes but not events. His sense of space, time, and the other elements of barbarian religion, is almost nil.

The shipwreck is like the ship itself, a fake and a frost, composed of half a dozen studio effects. The scenes abroad have nothing that influence the story even by a trifle. They cannot be rich and strange because not one of them is newly observed. It would have been good to have added to the film some sense of strange trafficking and curious merchandise, but if anything, the greater weakness is the weakness of the ship. By its very nature a ship is a living thing, worth the grace of cinema, and in missing it, Hitchcock has very literally missed the boat. It is not as Hitchcock makes it just a collection of rails to look over, and evening skies to go mooney about. It moves; it passes with not a little triumph through an entire ocean, with all sorts of things stowed away in its mysterious belly.

But let me indicate the charm of Hitchcock's direction of his separate episodes. You will have heard before now of 'the Hitchcock touch'. This consists in his great ability to give a novel twist to his sketch of an episode. The man and woman are quarrelling desperately in some Oriental room: Hitchcock punctuates that episode with the apologetic entry of a Chinaman who wants to sweep the floor. The man, again, has just clinched his appointment for a first essay in infidelity: he walks idiotically into a ventilator. The film is full of details of the kind, sometimes amusing, always clever, sometimes merely clever.

I would suggest that Hitchcock's concentration on such details is at least a part of his worry in the world. Reaching for the smart touch, as often as not he irresponsibly destroys the characters he has been building up and throws away his sequence. In Chaplin you do not mind the beaded story of moments and episodes. In a dramatic director like Hitchcock you must. A film is not like the celebrated Rosary, an affair of moments to be counted over, every one apart. It is a procession of people and events that march along: preferably, of course, going somewhere.

I believe the highbrows, in their praise of him, have sent Hitchcock off in the wrong direction, as they have sent many another: Chaplin, for example. They have picked out his clever little pieces, stressed them and analysed them till they are almost everything in his directorial make-up. We have waited patiently for the swing of event (preferably of great event) to come into his films, something that would associate him more profoundly with the dramatic wants of common people. Something serious, I am afraid, will have to happen to Hitchcock before we get it.

(*Everyman*, 24 December 1931)

Tell England is the work of Anthony Asquith and Geoffrey Barkas. From internal evidence it would seem that Asquith is responsible for the interpretation of the story; Barkas for the organization of the scenes of mass warfare. Asquith, again, within the limits usually attached to directors in commercial production, is probably responsible for the cutting. Who was responsible for the final scenario, and who for the final condition of the film, I cannot guess. The film, I calculate, has been shot round a thousand and one winders in the making. It carries the customary evidence of studio uncertainties.

You will gather from this the suggestion that Asquith has had a certain burden to bear in acting knee-wife to Raymond's rather sissified story of English heroism on the shores of Gallipoli.

Yet *Tell England* is undoubtedly the biggest job so far performed in the history of English cinema. There have been better jobs and more finished jobs, but not bigger ones. Looking back over a long sequence of minor efforts, the last attempt to add an element of importance to an English film was, curiously enough, in the film which gave Barkas his reputation : *Q Ships*. You will remember how in that picture one of the German officers acted as a sort of recording angel for the dead submarine commanders. He assumed a size in tragedy which, in fact, made *Q Ships*, not the epic of the British Navy it was meant to be, but the epic of the German U boats.

Since then we have inclined so much to Blackmails and Murders that one had almost come to forget that importance had any possible relation to English cinema. *Tell England* is a brave effort to stop the rot. It is a young man's effort. It is the effort of a man whose ideas of human importance are not mine. But if you have any sense of proportion in films you are bound to take it seriously. It is in a higher category altogether than other English films, however you place it in that higher category.

I make these nice distinctions because I have had a great deal of trouble in coming to a critical conclusion about *Tell England*. I have had to see it twice, and should properly, no doubt, see it twice again. The difficulty has been to separate the intelligence of Asquith as a technician and his great ambition as an artist from the thoroughly false importances which either the Raymond story or Asquith's own mind has imposed on the fabric of the film.

Of skill there is no doubt whatever. Some of the connectives between scene and scene are classical in brevity and point. The variations in the treatment of the three separate advances on the peninsula indicate an intelligence in visuals which is for anyone to study. The handling of rhythms is not so strong, but the percussive cutting of one shot-and-shell sequence is better than anything of the sort from Russia.

But it is when you have granted these things, when you come to the cause it celebrates, the sentiments that inform it, the stuffing with which it is stuffed so to speak, that the trouble starts. For to be plain, admiring the film, I do not like it : I would as quickly put it on the tumbril as any film I ever saw. For what is the upshot of this Gallipoli of Asquith's? It is in part a filthy massacre, and that part of the story is well told. But in its other part it attempts, as Tragedy must, a justification of that massacre. Tragedy, however, is no Tragedy unless the justification is just. It is no Tragedy unless the human dignity that arises above the death and destruction is a deep-laid dignity, and the human vision which throws death back into its true propor- tion to life is a vision of something fairly ultimate. *Tell England*'s ultimate will not bear a great deal of examination.

To be blunt about it, Asquith's rather trifling hero dies specifically for — (i) Fay Compton, (ii) a couple of swans, and (iii) afternoon tea on the domestic lawn. He dies for an England which may indeed be Asquith's England, but which is hardly an England worth dying for. For on its own evidence, it is a leisure-class England which has lost contact with fundamentals, with the toiling earth and the men who go with it. It is a complacent and effete England, which — if it exists — one would rather die to wipe from the map in a more local war.

Unfortunately, these false choices extend to Gallipoli. In the presence of death officers commanding and men commanded reach an uncommon equality, or Shirley would be no poet. And gunfire of the splendid fury illustrated by Asquith comes certainly within the category. But the old English film tradition prevails. Officers are heroes and men are comic relief. Officers die, with personal wonder- ings, worryings, and all evidence of being human about it. O.d.'s are content to fall anonymously in a welter of pseudo-proletarian jokes that a self-respecting village idiot would be ashamed of.

Undoubtedly the strongest thing about *Tell England* is something that emerges quite accidentally from it. It is not Asquith's young Rupert Brookes who wonder and worry and die for the immaculate lawns of England, but the battalions of poor devils who, without wondering or worrying, do a great deal of dying to provide a back- ground for them.

I have thus far been blaming Asquith for the false emphases which ruin *Tell England*, but I am probably wrong. The false emphasis can all be traced back to the Raymond book, and it was folly, not in Asquith but in his principals to attempt to build a Gallipoli on its tawdry foundations. A film of Gallipoli to be genuine must be either a rollicking cynical farce like *Shoulder Arms* or a drab tragedy which finishes not in honour but in futility. For a brief second during the film Asquith himself thought so. The box-office wallahs, no doubt, prevailed. As it is, Asquith really has set his hand manfully to the most impossible job that was open to him.

(*The Clarion*, May 1931)

I have seldom seen an English film that gave me so much pleasure as *Dance Pretty Lady*. If you would see how movement should be put together and most ordinary exits and entrances turned into a poetry of movement, you will find a whole curriculum in this film. And more. One of Asquith's great talents is his power of giving conversational point to action and character. He slips in details of observation which are, on their own account, a running commentary on both. Plastered hair, a stiff collar, or a room's decorations become in his hands a character sketch; the window of a hansom cab underlines a period. There is no other director who can do it so well; there is no other director who can even do it.

Always, too, looking at Asquith's films, you realize how well he knows his painters. I suppose the little references to one or another, the consciousness in this case that Degas should not be shamed in his own subject, can mean little to some audiences. Asquith can at least defend himself on the Kantian maxim, that one may only appreciate as one would wish the whole world to appreciate. It is a maxim never, never in evidence in the film world, but heaven knows cinema could do with a little of it.

Dance Pretty Lady is a delight to the eye: be assured of that. I cannot, however, say so much for its appeal to the imagination. It represents filigree work, most delicate, on a story that could not possibly make a big film. A little ballet dancer (much too young to be allowed to fall in love with anybody) falls in love with a sculptor. She will not let him have her 'because she would feel a sneak'. The sculptor goes off in a tantrum, lets another man, 'a dirty rotter', have her instead. The sculptor comes back for a quick and sudden and quite banal happy ending.

That is the tiding of great joy which Asquith (of Balliol and I know not what other traditions of English leadership) has spent a year in fetching us. A more cynical and shameful waste of time I cannot imagine. I may tend to over-emphasize our need for leadership and the film's great capacity for giving it, but was there ever another film director trained so specifically and deliberately and cold-bloodedly for the job as Asquith? This is it, bless you. Claptrap about a virginity. Why, the entire sentiment that makes a plot like that possible went into discard with the good, prosperous, complacent old Victoria. It was, relatively, an important matter then. But it is mere infant fodder now when you consider the new problems we carry in our bellies, and think of the new emphases we must in mercy to ourselves create out of our different world.

Flaherty was sitting with me at *Dance Pretty Lady*, and he is a good judge. He was as fascinated as I was myself. But his summing up was this: 'If that boy ever gets a story you will see the film of your life.' It is a trouble to know whether Asquith is denied the big story by his masters, or is by his own nature powerless to find it.

I think, myself, that like many other brilliant young men of his training and generation, he is a damned sight too remote from ordinary things to discover it easily. It is not enough to recognize bigness by its classical reference (for this Asquith can do on his head); it must be recognized, without reference at all, out of one's own most private sense of importance, if there is to be power of revelation. I cannot tell you what the secret is, but it should be plain on the face of it that there are more powerful spirits to be called from the deep than you are likely to get from stories of this sort.

(Everyman, 31 December 1931)

Hitchcock and Asquith are an amusing pair to think of together. They are opposites. Hitchcock has all the Training-in-the-School-of-Life background which Asquith lacks. He has the gusto Asquith lacks. But Asquith has the academic schooling, the little knowledge of this and that in music and painting and aesthetic, which Hitchcock has had to grab on the side. He has more taste, in the old rather empty sense of the word. He knows more in his head and less in his solar plexus. D. H. Lawrence used to talk a great deal about the two brains of mankind. He was right enough in principle, but located number two quite inaccurately. Number two is the one Asquith is short of. . . .

Asquith, however, is reaching out for a manner and method which will mature presently into something definite and individual and of great worth. Since *Le Million* came along the studios have been calling for an English René Clair, which is their way of saying that they want a director of fantastic and intellectual comedy. Cecil Lewis is mentioned by B.I.P. for the rôle, and is being schooled for it. Asquith, who is also with B.I.P., seems to have slipped their minds.

The fact, of course, is that Asquith, with or without knowing it, is going to match René Clair quite easily in a couple of years. He has all the qualities of observation and humour. He has a sense of movement. He has at least equal intelligence. His sense of fun is not so much less as different. But it is the negative side of him that will drive him into *Le Million* method. He has no feeling for people except as they can be observed from the outside. He is born and bred a spectator, capable of treating people only as puppets. That is to the good. Puppeteering is as great a trade as any if you take it seriously for the satire, fantasy and poetry that is in it.

The trouble with Asquith is that he was also born a Liberal. A Liberal is one who has a conscience about suffering humanity without knowing anything about it. Asquith, accordingly, has been kicking himself into a dramatic genre he has no power to master. He has been trying to compete with the directors who know people and the things they do, and feel them. When he learns to be himself and the puppeteer he was meant for, I promise you tricks.

(*The Clarion*, January 1932)

This is as good a time as any to review our English films. These are days of do or die, and national responsibilities are upon them. Could they not bring us fame again in the world? Could they not—far more importantly—give us some plain sense of the things that are in us and fire our imaginations again? Art, as it took Trotsky to demonstrate, is not only a mirror to life but a hammer to fashion life. We need fashioning. Cinema, by reason of its contact with millions, is the supreme fashioner of democracy.

I have in mind five films which are now doing their rounds: *The Ghost Train*, *The Outsider*, *The Skin Game*, *The Calendar*, *Chance of a Night Time*. They are good popular films: they are successes and they are English. Indeed, there is no doubt that we are witnessing the very blessed spectacle of a renaissance in English studio work.

Technically, we are striding along with seven-league boots. Hitchcock's production of the Galsworthy play is as neat and good a job as you could wish to see. His *Skin Game* is far more skilled and delicate than the original stage version. You may think the Galsworthy drama itself too pretentious; you may refuse to believe that this fight between an industrial landlord and an old-time landed landlord touches on any real issue in our body politic; you may, in fact, think Galsworthy an old woman and regret that Hitchcock remained so very, very faithful to him, but the power of Hitchcock and the film world in presenting the story cannot be questioned.

There is the same skill in Hayes Hunter's *Calendar*. Racing is meaningless to me, and our world of gentlemen gamblers cannot, I feel, be the sort of English world we should talk very loudly about; but the film will hold you for the bravery with which it is done. All the tricks of the trade are there, good acting, and a dash of very special English humour in the person of Gordon Harker. He is not the Cockney comedian of the ancient persuasion: he does not, by innuendo, cringe and whine in every wisecrack. He is your proletarian, independent before his masters and, in a curious fashion, superior to them. Well he might be. There could be nothing in the cheap and futile racing world about him to phase the old soldier that

he is. Edgar Wallace, Hayes Hunter, Gordon Harker himself, who-
ever was responsible, has supplied *The Calendar* with its own criticism. English character goes a trifle deeper than the scenes and
settings which so generally represent it.

Chance of a Night Time and *The Ghost Train* both play the silly-ass
theme, with Ralph Lynn as one ass and Jack Hulbert the other.
Hulbert has the justification that silly-assdom is necessary to his
rôle as a detective and essential to his annihilation of the bad, bad
Bolsheviks who are running arms into England. Lynn is the plain
straightforward silly-ass, and this on the whole, without the bad
Bolsheviks, is preferable.

The best of the bunch in every way is Lachman's *Outsider*, the
story of a quack doctor who cures a girl in face of all the mandarins
of the medical profession. The story is sentimental, but I found
more strength tucked away in the handling of it than I can remember
seeing in an English film before.

The film, it may be, had a devious passage before I saw it, for its
cutting was in many spots both rough and raw. It gave the impression of a film that had been made bigger and at some point or other
had been surgically reduced to something less than the director intended. It was not so fine a job as, say, *The Calendar* and *The Skin
Game*. But it did do something the others failed to do. It took courage
in its hands and went up in the air. On a sentimental issue it even beat
its way into sentiment. The building up of the night of crisis, which
was not, I suppose, in the script the main passage at all, is worth
examining. It potters naïvely in short cross-cuts, between one scene
and another, but it does build up into something sizeably imaginative. Lachman should be proud of it.

And this I think is the main thing to be said about English films
at the moment. We have all the skill we need to make a name in the
world, yet we do not often build either to size or imagination. All the
critics are hammering on one theme just now: that we need the open
air, and the events of the open air, and some physical achievement in
our films. That is one way of putting it. We do need the breath of
reality in our films, and of our own reality, if the imaginations of our
directors are to be properly engaged. We need something better to
build with than racing scandals and the campaigns of silly asses
against impossible Bolsheviks. We even need something more real
and present than a fight between landlords who, in fact of history,
went into partnership three or four generations ago.

The Outsider is saved by its underlying issue between orthodoxy
and unorthodoxy, between the old and the new, between men certain
in tradition and a man certain in himself. It may be sentimental and

even silly to present such an issue in the world of medicine, but at the bottom the issue is one that belongs to the world we know. It is not, therefore, just a question of choosing outdoor themes—of industry or commerce or colonial achievement—though these themes would indeed give our films the breath of life they require. Even indoors, even in the studios, if they make play with issues of character and give their heroes some meaning we can recognise, they can help us to a national quickening.

(Everyman, 5 November 1931)

In a week of cosmic disaster, with the Indian Conference, Chaplin's publicity, and the pound sterling all breaking up together, let this column break out on a note of optimism. The English film which is 'as good as Hollywood' has actually appeared. You have heard of that film so long, and rubbed your nose over it so often, that this also may sound incredible. If, however, you look for a little modest film called *Rynox*, you will see it in the very body. No one has proclaimed it: it has, in fact, just appeared at the Empire as a second feature, without even the grace of a credit list in the house programme. But there never was an English film so well made. The director's name is Michael Powell.

I do not mean that *Rynox* is a masterpiece of art or insight. The story tells how the big boss director of Rynox died for the old firm. It is, in other words, on the naïve side, and, if you look into it, even on the morally naïve side. For the boss director commits suicide and stages it as murder so that his insurance money will see the company through. You cannot, of course, ennoble a swindle even when the victim is a plutocratic insurance company.

But never mind the story. My point is that here is a film which in beautific settings, in superb photography, in dressing, in angle, in movement, in direction generally, achieves all the neatness and finish one has come to regard as the exclusive possession of Americans. English films tend to tumble their way through a story, even when they are good. The only possible exception recently was *The Calendar*. *Rynox* is a slicker job than *The Calendar*.

(Everyman, 10 December 1931)

The Star Reporter is an English film, done by Michael Powell. Powell is a young director who promises to stand up presently in the publicity line with Asquith and Hitchcock. I threw him a bouquet recently on your behalf for his film *Rynox* and here he has again demonstrated the same solid ability and (more important still) the same solid certainty of himself. The story is by Philip MacDonald, the detective writer, and by Ralph Smart, the B.I.F. graduate who last year made the very excellent Sunlight Soap film. Powell not only makes a slick businesslike job of it, but gets a very considerable size into his presentation of one or two of the sequences. This is going some for a film produced at speed.

The passage showing the arrival of the *Berengaria* demonstrates a unique power of observation which promises much. His angles are strong, his continuity, shot by shot, direct and definite. Powell can certainly see things. One only waits now for evidence of his powers to recognize ideas. *Rynox* was the story of an insurance swindle; *Star Reporter* is the story of a stolen diamond with a Fleet Street reporter marrying into Mayfair. This sort of thing may be all right to practise on but it obviously cannot be taken seriously. Powell must step presently into something more sensible.

(*Everyman*, 11 February 1932)

How better begin than with *Cavalcade*, our only cinema comment on the state of Britain? It is old news now for it has been running fourteen weeks at the Tivoli, but on that consideration its public importance only begins. Presently it will be showing to millions of people in the country and providing them with the first articulate history of their lifetime. It will sketch for them the history of England from the Boer War to the Great War, and from the Great War till today: commenting gravely on the evils and the disasters of the period, isolating the honours, presenting its version of the realities. It will, in effect, give or help to give each of its many million spectators a philosophy for his time. It will determine or help to determine in each, not only his attitude to the past, but also his attitude to the future. It will affect, as probably no film before has affected, his loyalties. Political change is determined by the capture of loyalties.

Seeing *Cavalcade* again I find it an even more curious and contemptible performance than it seemed at first visit. With earliest recollections in the celebration fires of the Boer War I cover the period exactly, and in all the parade there is nothing I recognize of the people I know or of any country I would live for. It tells us of two wars, of the sinking of the *Titanic*; it concludes in the pessimisms and perversions of the years after the War. On its personal side, it records the superior affection of a rich mother for her children, and makes sad ado of the changing attitudes of the people below stairs to the people above. The central figures of the drama are stupid and useless people. They think of nothing, they fight for nothing save blindly, they create nothing. They fight in the Great War as they fought in the Boer War, without question. They subscribe to every second-rate patriotism and every complacent ceremonial. They are at the greatest pains to behave properly: their avoidance of social criticism being the measure of their propriety. And the tragedy of the era and of the play and of the film is that these good rich people, significant presumably of the spirit of England, have been tragically done by. They have lost their sons; they have no England of the future as brave as the England of their youth to look forward to.

It will be a pity if the millions, carried away by the acting of Diana Wynward and Clive Brook, and by the tragic fate of the two sons, subscribe to defeatism so silly. It will be a greater pity if, in sentimental regret for the personal fate of the old lady and gentleman, they stir themselves to further defence of the disastrous regime they stand for. With every step of the disintegration recorded, there has been, in fact, the suggestion of a new integration—of new hopes, new plans, new organizations for giving effect to them; new attitudes to war, new attitudes to labour, new attitudes to women and children and slums: and a liquidation of many things in the offing. That is half the story of any generation, ours or another; and no public accountant with tuppence worth of insight would have lost sight of them. Coward does. For all his creative skill he is an uninspired young man at bottom, seeing no further and feeling no deeper than the limited sector of society for which he performs.

(New Britain, 24 May 1933)

Our national story takes a new turn this week: passing with peal of merry bells from the pessimistic half-truths of Mr Coward to optimistic back thumpings from the Messrs Priestley and Asquith. Here are the medicine men for your blues, national, personal, and any other: trading Ted Lewis's blazing old formula:

> When you're down-hearted what do I do,
> I bring a smile . . . AH HA . . .
> When life makes YOU sick, my MUSIC
> Will make everything seem worthwhile . . .
> No, I don't give any pills for your fever and chills
> With my musical thrills . . . I amuse,
> Yes, Sir, I'm that old medicine man for your blues. . . .

Take your choice, little ones, between *The Good Companions* and *The Lucky Number*. They represent the same happy quackery. *The Good Companions* bids you throw your job to the winds, take the high road to any old where, and gipsy in ecstasy to every dream come true. *The Lucky Number* tells you fervently to achieve a similar end by shutting your eyes and wishing for it.

A lot of people (is it three millions?) will be glad to know this. No need for Bill Perkins to queue up for his fifteen bob per week or worry about the Means Test. 'Shut your eyes and wish for happiness', Bill: Anthony Asquith says so. 'Jump on a truck and go anywhere', Bill: your philosopher friend J. B. Priestley advises it. Being the pauper you are, Bill, you will answer in the manner of your kind, but no matter.

Putting these first things first, I have to add that *The Good Companions* and *The Lucky Number* are very efficient performances. I would not be worried about them if they weren't. *The Good Companions* is excellently played, and its gipsery made as romantic as any silly inhibited heart could wish. If you know the story, you will appreciate the feat, from a film point of view, of bringing the various characters smoothly from all over England to their appointed centre: the schoolmaster from his shepherd's pie and prunes, the Yorkshire joiner from his crabbed wife, the lady from her manor, and the wandering minstrel from his four times round the world. Add to this the problem of keeping the concert troupe on its staccato path from one local hippodrome to another. I give you the job as a triumph of scenario work (maestro: MacPhail) more effective in its path and pace than the novel itself. The beastly issue of the story (so strangely contrary with its emphasis on starlit success to the gipsying with which the story began) I leave to your sense of humour. I noticed with personal delight that the film was accompanied on the stage by a male voice choir in scarlet hunting costume, singing that celebrated English hunting anthem 'Ole Man River'.

Asquith, too, has done well with his *Lucky Number*. This, on Asquith's personal account it is a particular pleasure to record; for as a new found professor of the box office he will be able to pick up his own stories. Asquith has more directorial taste and intelligence than any other director in England and only subject matter has prevented him doing remarkable things. Here the subject matter is no great shakes either, but he has built on his tale of lost lottery tickets a vast amount of good character and good fun.

His story takes you to football matches, to the dogs, to side shows, to a pub, to a pawnshop, and to Paris. As that classic writer Roundey, of Madison, Wis., used to remark, what more could be fairer? The sketches Asquith makes in each are as nearly and richly observed as we are likely to get from our film studios. The highest compliment I can pay the picture is that his pub (with Gordon Harker publican) is the best English pub to date; and how many dim wits have tried!

The story struggles somewhat between the call of straight romance and the call of comic fantasy, with Asquith leaning heavily on the side of fantasy. A trifle heavier leaning, and Asquith would have turned a prettier picture still. His case is very similar to that of Clair. His capacity to turn a straightforward episode into a riot and shake a crowd into its essential components of rogues and rustics is too rich for the pauses of sentiment. The use of musical and sound background for commentary on the action is particularly remarkable in this film. Freed from the agonies of love and lotteries it may yet be more.

(New Britain, 31 May 1933)

Vessel of Wrath is the Somerset Maugham story of the beachcomber in the South Seas who in drunkenness and debauch defies the reforming zeal of a couple of English missionaries and finishes off by marrying the female member of the godly pair and keeping a pub in Sussex. Charles Laughton makes it a study of comic misbehaviour. There is great skill in his insolence and a nicely calculated vulgarity which is very near that gusto we have been missing so much in British films. Viewed as a comment, not on missionaries, but on those wretched Women's Leagues of America who have been taking the corpuscles out of American films, Laughton's performance has a certain importance. A little more of this sort of thing and the British cinema will be able to challenge the American on the simple ground of sophistication. No one will be more sensible of the challenge than the Hollywood producer.

Like any first film from a new production unit, *Vessel of Wrath* is a problem child, and just because it is important one has to say so. *Henry VIII*, the epic of the Royal bedsheets, produced no heirs male. This one may if its errors are realized and the Mayflower unit's arrangements tightened up accordingly.

For one thing the film does not drive through to its ending. The last third is no resolution of the first two and the film fails in narrative power. I think I know why. Hunt Stromberg once pointed to the fundamental necessity of having someone decide the mould of a film and see to it that all the participants fit their contribution into the mould. Here the mould has not dictated the part of the actors. They have spilled their business on and over and round about, with great generosity but a minimum of discipline.

In the first place, for reasons of economy, Erich Pommer has acted as both producer and director — a silly thing to do as Pommer should know, better than anyone. Where the cold-blooded eye of the producer was wanted, the warm appraising eye of the director has taken command. Director and actor have produced a similar undisciplined situation. Because presumably Laughton was partner in this new venture he has been given more than his due, and I know of no more fearful spectacle under the sun than an actor footloose. I do not blame Laughton but Pommer. After all it is in the nature of a good actor to be the worst of critics. Especially when he is good, no one will ever convince him that a medium which, like the film, can do so much of his acting for him, is not stealing his personal thunder.

I like Laughton very much, for he is a brilliant fellow, but I like the future of British films even more. He will not mind, therefore, if I suggest an elementary lesson in the categories. The trouble with Laughton is that he is good at several very different things. He has skill in tragedy and has an ambition to play King Lear. He speaks rhetoric with a flair almost unique among modern actors, and though there may be mannerism in the way he slides across a full stop, no one will forget his reading of the Bible in *Rembrandt*. He is, moreover, a dangerously good and upsetting showman in his capacity for lagging on a cue and exaggerating an acting trifle behind the back of his director. No scrum half ever played the blind side of a referee more knowingly. Add to these talents the equally various ones of being good at comedy and quite brilliant at slapstick and you have a deadly mixture of virtues.

In any single film you can't possibly have the lot. Lear cannot possibly at the same time act the Fool, and Macbeth take his place among the porters. That precisely is what Laughton is forever doing. He does not understand economy, and by the mere process of being everything in starts and nothing long, is the greatest saboteur a film could have. It may all come from his anxious desire to add everything of himself to the value of the film. But the damage is certain. Laughton one at a time would be the wonder of the day. Five at a time he is a producer's headache.

I have quarrelled a great deal with people over *Vessel of Wrath*. But I soon found we were quarrelling over very different things. I viewed it as principally slapstick and was prepared to forgive the odd departures into drama and sentiment. My arguers had viewed it as drama and were bewildered by the fact that it was mostly slapstick. See the film as, nearly, in the category of Laurel and Hardy, and you will see *Vessel of Wrath* at its best. But this does not absolve Pommer and Laughton from making up their minds more decisively next time. Knowing Laughton a little, I think he should come through. A strategic retreat from his own talents is what is called for.

(*World Film News*, April 1938)

A Yank at Oxford has been presented as an important picture. It has been presented with the full benefit of what they call a 'diplomatic première', and the dignitaries of London, with that blind appetite for free shows that so amuses the foreigners, turned out in full force. If *A Yank at Oxford* had been a call to national unity in Westminster Hall, it could not have been so handsomely received. One's first reaction is to wonder how so trifling a work can command the great, for it is like catching the Cabinet with its feet up, deep in the adventures of Augustus D'Arcy of the *Green 'Un*. But perhaps there is more to this than meets the eye. I heard someone not without responsibility say he thought *A Yank at Oxford* a huge contribution to Anglo-American friendship, and, at the present time, a vital one. That, of course, would explain anything.

I cannot pretend I did not like the film. The Yank who goes to Oxford, thinking he will show the old place a step or two, is caught in the toils of Oxford's traditions, and a measure of English diffidence is added to his American vitality to make him something, if not all, of an English gentleman. That is the story, and it runs easily and warmly, and one forgets that the alcohol going to one's head is strictly synthetic. On examination it is, of course, the old ackamarackus with a vengeance, and remembering it in colder blood, I never saw in all my born life such a funny University or such a footling lot of students. Everyone is so desperately serious about winning things, and not being cads, and shaking hands as between white men, and cutting you dead, and, in the last resort, giving up all for one's friend, that I would not be surprised at all if America mistook Oxford for a host of golden daffodils.

On the other hand, and in spite of this spurious schoolboy nonsense, the film goes with a lick, the dialogue is witty and good, and the acting has streaks of real excellence. This is particularly the case with C. V. France's playing of an old and somewhat dithery don, and Vivien Leigh's account of a vamp in a bookshop. Robert Taylor is so much better than his publicity men allow that he ought to sue them for damages. With a whale of a part, he takes it like his own 440, flying. He not only outruns, outrows, out-wisecracks and out-sacrifices his lesser brethren of England, but he also — and it makes me a trifle suspicious about Anglo-American friendship — is given every opportunity to out-act them.

M.G.M. has been very skilful about the whole affair. To give Robert Taylor the associated value of winning the Oxford–Cambridge 440, stroking the Oxford boat to victory, and then licking the limeys in everything else, is nice work in star building.

With all this in my mind, I begin to doubt if *A Yank at Oxford* is such terrific propaganda for England after all. There were moments in the film when the leaves of England stirred, and the sun came out, and Oxford's bells and Magdalen's choristers sounded very sweet, and time stood still a little in the fields of England. On each occasion, old and hardened and suspect of original sin as I am, I sat up in my seat, and waited for the English film we were promised to happen. I thought perhaps that where so much age and so much youth were mingled, M.G.M. could not fail to achieve an occasional thin wisp of poetry. But the gaudy chariot of stardom rolled on relentlessly, throwing out its tinkling pennies of action and wisecrack, and a win for Robert Taylor every minute. In spite of all the promise, it is like the rest of them. The damned thing has no roots, and what is the use of saying otherwise? Will those who see it remember the glimpses of reality, or the slabs of fiction: the choristers, or the wisecracks? Is there enough of England in the glimpses to stir the heart, or is it just the same old story of the magnificent young man and the magnificent young woman, with Oxford providing a decorative background? If so rootless, will the Anglo-American friendship it brings mean any-thing in a twelvemonth?

But you need not trouble to answer. The cinema does not live on nice distinctions, and M.G.M. or any other film company would not bother, anyway. The real answer I got from a big exhibitor. 'I know it's good', he said, 'but the worst of it is that Sam Eckman, the sales-man, also knows it is good, and what with the diplomatic première, he won't take less than fifty per cent.' If that price were ever justi-fiable, I would say, on balance, that M.G.M. had deserved it. The film is a good rollicking piece of filmcraft, and does no one any harm. If it pretends so much to be an epic of England, God save us, who are we to debag it? Oxford has been staring us in the face all the days of movies, and we have not had the wit to use it so well, much less better. I say *floreant* to Ben Goetz, Sam Eckman and Louis B. Mayer. They will make a packet, and Robert Taylor is a greater gold mine than ever.

(*World Film News*, May–June 1938)

At this time of the year the film critics are all busy at their little game of placing the best films; and it is surprising with what unanimity across the world the first twenty or thirty are selected. But *World Film News*, with that nice variety of method which distinguishes it, has gone beyond the critics and asked experts in other fields to help in the adjudication. There is James Bridie, the dramatist; Sir Hugh Walpole, the novelist; David Low, the cartoonist; A. J. Cummings, the political writer; Sir Archibald Sinclair, the Liberal leader; McKnight Kauffer from art and Herbert Read from the higher criticism. It is a noble company and there must surely be a special word of wisdom among them.

Set their judgement against the official list of firsts issued by the National Board of Review in New York. Here is the American order of merit: (1) *Night Must Fall.* (2) *The Life of Emile Zola.* (3) *Black Legion.* (4) *Camille.* (5) *Make Way for Tomorrow.* (6) *The Good Earth.* (7) *They Won't Forget.* (8) *Captains Courageous.* (9) *A Star is Born.* (10) *Stage Door.* Except for *Zola, The Good Earth* and *Captains Courageous* — brave and spacious films all of them — our British experts have very different views. They make their selections from a wider world: from Germany, France, Russia — even from Britain. The American list, in comparison, is self-centred and rather parochial.

For me the special significance of the British choice is that British films are included with affection, and that they are the simpler films like *Edge of the World, Farewell Again, Storm in a Teacup* and *Today We Live.* The thunder of those expensive masterworks which, two years ago, were to conquer the world, has died down; and the small voice of the simple things well done is being heard at last. Our British film world has, like the Prodigal Son, been journeying in far countries and wasting its substance in riotous living. There is even a certain sweet accuracy in the ancient description that 'when he had spent all, there arose a mighty famine in that land, and he began to be in want . . . and no man gave unto him.' No man gives unto him today.

It has been true all along that the best interest of British films, as of any films, must lie in honest and patient work. Brilliance of showmanship may bring its great successes but the basis is good story telling, good acting and good craftsmanship. Unfortunately, we have had the whole business of cinema wrong way about. We have permitted it to think fancifully of fortunes instead of making a simple return on its money. We have allowed it to serve the vanity of a few egotists instead of creating a picture-making community working in coordinated teams.

There is nothing on earth to stand in the way of an immediate development of the British cinema. All that is wanted is some honesty, a little humility and an interest in the work for its own sake. I believe that any producer who appreciates the simple and essential values of a good story well told, knows how to keep to the mark of his money, and is strong enough to keep dreams of fortune out of his head, can wade in now and make an honourable contribution to the future. The larger themes and the more spectacular achievements will come not by extravagant and melodramatic assault, but as by-products of a quieter process.

The question in my mind is whether our lead is good enough. Will the men who control the distribution machines appreciate the good sense of a long-term constructive policy, or must they continue to fall for the confident accents of the faker? Will capital, which has been deceived so much, come to its senses about films and film people? Will it give honesty a trial for a change or must it, too, be wooed with idiot's promises? Will the writers and artists realize that the big money is here today and gone tomorrow and that simpler salaries may mean longer and more solid returns? There is no great mystery about the future of British films, only the mystery of really wanting it, really working for it, and trusting those who sensibly do both.

And so I am glad to see in the list of films for the year the honourable mention of films like *Edge of the World*, *Farewell Again*, *Elephant Boy*, *Storm in a Teacup* and *Today We Live*. They may not be smash hits but every one of us knows how, in each case, sincerity and good workmanship went to their making. It is just possible that they represent together a turning point in the history of British films. May their tribe increase!

(*World Film News*, January 1938)

10 · From France and Germany

We had, it seems only recently, René Clair's brilliant *Sous les Toits de Paris*. It has remained in the West End ever since and other French films come tripping along to take the limelight it created, and it still goes on after that. Considering the very alien nature of the language and the provinciality of the town, this may be considered Success.

Le Million, Clair's later work, is now in process of digging itself in. I like it better, though it misses in its music the sentimental appeal which binds the other to the box office. Its humour is more mature; its farce is certainly more footloose.

Sous les Toits was, if you remember, always on the verge of the picaresque. There was a tendency to make pocket-picking rather a happy pursuit. *Le Million* dives straight into the world of pocket-picking and makes a good fairy out of the chief pick-pocket. This is something fresh and new, so far as I am concerned. I did not realize that Lazarillo de Tormes and Colonel Jack were so near to fairy-tale. Now I am told it is clear as can be that the super fairy-tale is one beyond Good and Evil, and that the ogre and angel business is a drab Teutonic invention we should have been rid of long ago.

The story has some concern with the fate of a lottery ticket. It wins and disappears, and the film spends its time chasing it from the studios of Montparnasse to the haunt of the Most Principal Apache, to a comic gendarmerie, to the stage of the Opéra and back again. I found myself engaged not so much by the ticket as by the Most Principal Apache. When Apaches parade like policemen in a Gilbert and Sullivan and a gendarmerie holds fourteen identifiable comedians of the first order, and when a scramble in the coulisses of the opera turns to a rugby game with crowd noises and referee's whistles complete, and a burglar disturbs a lady to ask her '*Aimez-vous le piano?*' the world is as wild as I want it.

Clair's genius for picking out faces and poses and gestures of character stands as it did. His building of a chorus construction with the human detail of an entire tenement is not only a good talkie trick but brings the tenement itself to articulate life. And there is a continuous rhythmic basis to the film, now of chorus, now of action, now of one merging madly into the other, which will convert any Old Believer in the silents who may yet survive. Clair in his own merry line is pretty big. Yes, he is bigger than Lubitsch. He has fairy-tale.

(*The Clarion*, June 1931)

Two convicts consider the bleakness of their lot and very rightly decide to be done with it. They file to work of a morning; they sit down by numbers; they manufacture wooden horses for far-off Christmasses under a warder's eye which is an arithmetic table in itself; they consume their daily soup in militarized swallowings. But only one does actually—and very rightly—escape, and he starts a gramophone shop. In half a dozen dissolves it has progressed at least one step further in rationalization than the Victor plant in New Jersey. Its workers file in of a morning, sit down by numbers, manufacture little gramophones under a guardian eye that is an arithmetic table in itself, and eat in militarized rows from a travelling band. There is not a lick of difference between this home of modern freedom and the convict prison. Our escaped criminal is the director of all the directors; alias the governor.

With this bright contribution to social commentary René Clair wades into his new film *A Nous la Liberté*. It is an event in the film world as it could not fail to be. Only half a dozen directors make a personal contribution to their work which is recognizable and unique. Clair is one. He may not be as solid a performer as Pudovkin or as slick a one as Lubitsch, but for his power to do something new and fine and entirely his own he stands as high as any of them. He has power of fantasy and fairy-tale; he can jumble sound and sight together and make a crazy quilt of good sense; and he is, above all, French.

I saw his film after a couple of hours in the Exhibition of French painting. The continuity was as it should have been. The same humour, the same even temper in all things—even in making fun of all things. Nobody except Cézanne (who was a Nordic in disguise) to break through with self-inflicted agonies of effort! But there was this also in continuity: the Frenchman's strange capacity for breaking loose into sentimentality. I regard him, myself, as the only European who has any claim to call himself a civilized mortal, but I would run a mile before I would witness again a French funeral or a French parade or a French celebration of victory or a Frenchman attending on his mother or his mistress. I have seen the freest and best satire in the world at the *Deux Anes* and the *Dix Heures* in Paris suddenly slip into some depth of *pour la patrie* slop which would shame a village idiot in any other country.

Here René Clair is also French. The foil to his convict-director is, of course, the brother convict. He drops in later when the great gramophone company is in full blast, to remind his opposite number of the liberty he has lost. There is embarrassing reference to flowers in spring, green fields, twittering birds—and a back-lit maiden who seems in some way to belong to the same menage. I tried hard to think that Clair was being funny about all of them, but I have to bring you the sad conclusion that he was not. He was back with Papa Rousseau (the papa of all French sentimentalism) to the nutty brotherhood of the bees and the birds and the beasties.

So for one-half of the film and bits after, we have all the good things we expect from Clair. Thereafter Liberty inclines (as it must on this sentimental interpretation) to tedium. You will bear very ill the repetitious moonings under the moon. You will certainly curse to find that our picaresque convicts do not go off at the end to more comic adventures in social commentary. They fade out on the old bewhiskered road of sentimental journeys, ragged and happy and singing for sous.

The emphasis must remain, however, on the fun you get before that: in the idiot pretention of big business, in the idiot subservience of its sycophants, in the comic luxury of its ceremonials. Clair will prove to you past all doubting that the one insaner thing in the world than the paranoia ward at Colney Hatch is a dinner party in Park Lane. When the convict-director snaps out of the nonsense and comes to, he shies a bottle of Bols through his own full-length portrait. It stabs his monkey suit to the midriff.

The technique is not quite so firm as in *Le Million*. The orchestration of sight and sound which was the most remarkable thing in that masterpiece is not quite so considered. This is possible because Clair used for *Liberté* the slow and not very exciting music of M. Auric. I understand that Auric has a reputation in the musical world. He sounds like it. He has still to make intimate acquaintance with the visual side of cinema, and allow the images to play their proper part in the score. The music here is almost entirely background music.

What an amateur handler of crowds Clair still is! If he has them in militarized line he is excellent, but whenever the script calls for general whoopee—I am gravely afraid they just straggle. A couple of correspondence lessons from D. W. Griffith would turn the trick.

(Everyman, 18 February 1932)

Le Rosier de Madame Husson deals as faithfully with its de Maupassant story as any enthusiast for French humour will require of it. It describes admirably the pass to which Madame Husson was put in the search for her annual virgin, and how, all due analyses and stocktakings made, the coronet of purity had to be placed perforce on the head of one Isidore, the village idiot. Of what befell thereafter and of the dance that was danced with another Madame in celebration thereof, I leave you to find out for yourselves. I believe there was some fear at first that the film was too French for English consumption; but the Film Society showing soon proved the civilizing influence of the Entente Cordiale on the more savage English mind. Now the graceless Isidore is breaking records, and only two trade unionists (female) have complained to the management about blacklegs. In the field of morals I have therefore to report progress.

(*New Britain*, 31 May 1933)

Poil de Carrotte is well acted and beautifully made and is one of the special film pleasures of the moment. I cannot, however, follow the film's more fervent admirers in their belief that it deals sensibly or seriously with childhood. The story of a boy, consistently, designedly, and malevolently ill-treated by his mother, is plainly the story of a freak case, and outside the realms of either significant psychology or significant drama; and the attempted suicide to which the film rises is proportionately unreal and fantastic. How much better the self-affectionated, self melodramatized suicide of everyone's childhood, would have been!

But forget this side of the matter and look how the director Duvivier has packed behind his action images which help out the moods through which the boy passes: how pigs and cows and horses and ducks are cut into his festive wedding march across the fields; how scenes of happier childhood are slipped into the background of his furious drive home; how nobly rolling are the clouds and hedges when it is all over and he has found his father again. That is great stuff and will remind you how little we have made of the wide world background which the cinema has given to drama. How very little we make—imagistically or otherwise—of the perspectives cinema allows us. There—in the *background*—is a new dimension for the screen, as plain as that Aeschylean axiom called 'narratage', and more important. I must think of a fancy word and get a pie-faced financier to say a piece about it. No doubt the studios will then take notice.

(*New Britain*, 8 November 1933)

The Blue Angel is undoubtedly a very able production. It is the first German talkie to be shown in this country and marks the return of a prodigal Jannings to Ufa and Pommer. Von Sternberg, the young American Jew who made *The Salvation Hunters* and

The Exquisite Sinner and some box-office successes after that, is the director.

I wish the story of *The Blue Angel* were more solid, because what there is of it is very well told. It is the somewhat bewhiskered story of the honest bourgeois who takes suddenly to women and concludes in the gutter, and it is probably the best version of that particular fairy-tale since *Vaudeville*. I am not sure why, but I do feel the innards of such a story are a trifle feeble. Destruction by woman is an old-fashioned subject, not because your female destroyer is any less adept, but because there are so many deaths one dies nowadays which are more impressive. And, another reason, the myth cannot quite survive our continuing capers with the moral law.

If a middle-aged weakling cares to slobber himself to the gutter in sudden sex-relief, he is by all our modern standards a figure for comedy, for he is making a grotesque to-do of what reasonable people do easily and cannot take seriously. To make him a figure of tragedy is impossible, I should say, by thirty years. By such short temporal yardsticks may one plumb the much advertised depths of the human heart.

The story telling of *The Blue Angel*, however, I must very particularly recommend to you, for much of it is excellent. On that count, and possibly on all, you may rank the film with any of the masterworks of the late Thomas Hardy, O.M. It is as superlatively sentimental and as masterfully and massively maudlin. The cloud of doom appears on the horizon (no bigger than a man's hand) and grows and grows and grows, smoothly and imperceptibly, till old Jannings is in consequent doomstorm blown to smithereens. That is good work in any film. There is perhaps one jump in the logic of events, somewhere about the middle, but if you will follow the directorial sheep ahead of you, you will find the magnificence of a really stalwart ending to balance it. The sound technique is much more intelligent than usual, but I shall reserve comment on that till I can compare it with Hitchcock's *Murder* and discuss sound technique separately.

(*The Clarion*, September 1930)

War is Hell is the best propaganda film for Peace ever made. It is not in the grand manner like *All Quiet on the Western Front*, but most simple in its story and spectacle. 'Not even the longer word explains it,' said F. H. Bradley of the 'subconscious'. In the larger effects, the real tragedy of war has often been lost.

War is Hell was made in Germany by Victor Trivas and appeared as *No Man's Land*. It is a story of No Man's Land. Five soldiers—

a Frenchman, a German, an Englishman, a Negro and a Jew—are isolated in a shell-hole: the common victims of a common Enemy. We saw them at home, with their different domesticities in odd parts of the world, but most similar in their friendly preoccupations. In the isolation of their shell-hole the impersonal interventions of war are well lost. They talk together, sing together, cook together, and help together.

In quite symbolic emphasis of the issue, the smoke of the camp fire starts a new and strange offensive. The smoke is spotted by French and German guns alike; and in equal symbolism the men join together to build up an earthwork against the forces of destruction. They work feverishly, passing sandbags from one to the other; and driven out at last, they advance in a single line—French bayonet fixed by German bayonet fixed—as a last gesture against the Enemy.

This description cannot possibly give the colour of the film. Imagine the whole story done with a minimum of the sets, actors and crowd effects which producers hold so dear. The Peace invaded is an account of quiet seascape and idyllic landscape, of a birth and a marriage and a boy with toys. The outbreak of war is a simple affair of flags and drilling soldiers. The war is done with half a dozen explosions and—No Man's Land. After all, No Man's Land is the essence of the business: of the desolation and the blind destruction. Its idiocy is pointed in the shell-shocked gibbering of the dumb Jew and in the ironical dependence of everyone on the Negro. He was a vaudeville dancer in peace time and travelled the capitals. He is the only one who knows all the languages and can bring their minds together.

Symbolism I ordinarily detest as a crude and priggish method of explanation. It reminds one too much of the pulpits of one's youth. Here you will endure it gladly for the great humanity of the central figures. One might very easily in a film like this have produced a stage Frenchman, a stage German and a stage Englishman; but they are all finely done. The dumb Jew is poignant.

If I have any complaint, it is not against the workmanship but against the argument itself, which is properly the concern of the editorial department. The League of Nations argument (and the film is League of Nations to the root) is too simple and sentimental. War is not terrible because it interrupts domesticities and makes kind men kill each other. It is terrible only when domesticities are invaded for no decent purpose. Kindness is not so ultimate that it should be extended to the Devil. And there is Devil enough in the Universe to make the very best case for dynamite and sudden death. Some wars are hell. There are others from which the people rise on the third day to resurrection.

(The Clarion, April 1932)

Mädchen in Uniform is coming to the Film Society. Those of you who have access to the sacred ceremonials of that assembly should very definitely see it. Its subject, which I ask you not to find forbidding till you see the film, is the sentimental attraction between one female and another in a girls' school.

In this account the school is a heavily militarized establishment for officers' daughters in Prussia. The rigmarole of its discipline is brilliantly translated by Leontine Sagan, the woman who directed. It is translated in straightforward logical terms which accuse every male director of fuss and extravagance. And the acting is superb from end to end: I can only think that Frau Sagan was as tough and uncompromising a disciplinarian as the old devil of a schoolmistress.

Not a man in the whole film: only girls and their mistresses, toeing the line and, like Enobarbus, dreaming dreams when not! It might easily have been an unhealthy film with its emphasis on the dreams they dream, but I found it powerfully not. I may be excused for liking the notion of females coming to a sense of themselves and (possibly) excused for liking its demonstration in the film. I like all squawkings for spring. As for the relation between girl and mistress, an affair most beautifully played and most strangely (for a German picture) saved from slop and sentimentality: this is a matter for the specialist criticism of women. In this case I plead my country origin.

(Everyman, 25 February 1932)

Mädchen in Uniform is at the Academy, and a very fine film it is. Its lovely and delicate account of young girls growing up at school is the sort of thing which shames the trivial and mechanized 'human interest' of the ordinary films: they are so seldom either human or interesting. The story is of a girls' school and of a girl who breaks down under its discipline. You may or may not, as you care, worry about the issue between the stern unbending old dame of a schoolmistress and the affectionate young teacher who takes the girl's part. If you see a note (intentionally or otherwise) of something more than affection on the part of the young teacher, you need not worry about that either. The achievement of the film—and how rare it is—is to take a mass of people and make the spirit of life bubble out of it. When it bubbles from youth and catches the rapture of youth, the embarrassments, the excitements, one feels the same sort of gratitude for it as for mavises in woods after rain. That is about the only real sort of compliment a critic can pay.

(*Everyman*, 12 May 1932)

Hunted People will remind you very forcibly of the good things which cinema has, in recent years, forgotten. It is a German film, by one Feyer, and in the great tradition of *Caligari* and *The Student of Prague*. I did not see it from the beginning. I found what, at first, I took to be an amateur documentary of a Mediterranean port, with a wobbly camera swirling inconsequently round streets and docks and railway viaducts; but the film tumbled presently to more solid dimensions. An hour and a half later I saluted it for a very respectable experience.

A village joiner is taking a wife for the second time. He has done well, his bride is the daughter of the mayor himself, his fellow villagers wish him well. At the height of the festivities a photograph is published, and the police are reminded that he is a convict who escaped ten years before. They proceed to hunt him down. The film is the story of the hunt.

It is, I suppose, an ordinary story except that the hero of it is prosperous and fat and only a village joiner. But the analysis of his terror and the description of the hunt assume proportions which swell finally into something like full-blown tragedy. Nothing that the joiner does is important in itself, but the manner of his doing it is. He escapes with his son Boubou (a brilliant little actor) in a coffin. He jumps a train. He wanders bewildered through the narrow streets of Marseilles. He begs a disguise in a pawn-shop and sleeps on the beach with the hobos of the town. He conceals himself in a Chamber of Horrors and the legless lady turns out to be the murderer he himself is supposed to be. All this is straightforward melodramatic material and might, in a less powerful rendering, be dull enough. But the film sits up over the sequence of event and takes life to itself. The distinction is in the acting: in a manner of presentation which makes a more than personal agony of every reaction and every suspense.

The acting tradition in cinema is all too personal. It is naturalistic in the sense that it is, nearabouts, appropriate to the occasion. The theatrical manner is avoided; exaggerations are avoided; the movie actor does his best to act as though the circumstance was a real circumstance and he, the person, a genuine particular in it. Only in a slim sense does he try to interpret. He is Tom, Dick or Harry hunted; he acts accordingly, with a consciousness of the terror which Tom, Dick or Harry might properly feel. The terror thus described is all too seldom of more than passing importance. Cinema does not often give us terror which is a study of terror, which, transcending the particular, plumbs the depths of individual reaction, and takes the full measure of human emotion.

The secret of success in this case, as in previous German examples, is very near the Shakespearean secret of poetry. By its strangely profound reference, the ordinary in Shakespeare is transmuted to tragedy. Mortal or fool, poetic buskins added, become abstracted significant figures, standing against the sky. The cinema has its own manner of abstraction. Caligari moved against distorted landscapes. He moved in ballet fashion, shaping natural movements to a significant pattern in space and time. Again in *The Stone Rider* and *The Grey House* and *Waxworks* and *The Golem* and *Destiny* and *The Student of Prague*, we saw something of this style; and the atmospheres and the occasions seemed the greater for the pedantic tempos and the weird dance-steps into which action and reaction fell. This style was Germany's greatest contribution to cinema. Nothing of its kind, if you except the occasional balletesque qualities of Chaplin, was ever attempted elsewhere. It has unfortunately been swamped in the fussy and fuddled naturals of the boys and girls from Hollywood.

Hunted People is important, if only because it reminds you of this forgotten tradition. Ten years ago we thought the future of the studio film was with *Caligari*. We saw a future opening up before us, not of *Jack's the Boy* and the like, but of great ballets in which pantomime commanded wider and wider horizons. Hollywood by suddenly buying up Murnau and Freund and Pommer and Lubitsch broke the back of the German school and destroyed this possibility. It may be that we shall never have true cinema again till we have recaptured the lost manner and begin where *Caligari* left off.

(*New Britain*, 18 October 1933)

Dovjenko's *Earth* is one of the very finest films ever made, and an experience so powerful that I cannot remember more than a dozen films that have given me the like. The curious thing is that it is a very simple film indeed. It has none of the complex structural work of a big Hollywood film or of a Pudovkin film. Peasants and kulaks wrangle in the Ukraine; the peasants of the collective farms fetch a tractor and plough across the land of a kulak; a young peasant is shot by the kulak; he is buried by his fellow-workers, who sing hymns to the future: that is the whole story. And yet, so deeply established in the earth is this story, that every little circumstance of it has a power or a significance far beyond itself. Not necessarily a Socialist one. There is some ancient skill in Dovjenko that gives an air of finality to the Bolshevik idea, which puts it outside the realm of politics. The peasant boy, as it seems, dies not for a doctrine, but for the fruit of the orchards and the harvests to come.

There is a timelessness about it all which is itself finality. An old man and his friends talk among the apple trees of the sixty-odd years he has laboured in the field, and talk familiarly about death as peasants do. And dead, his old friend comes to his grave to talk to him, again with that air of easy familiarity in the presence of death which those only have lost who have lost contact with the soil and the continuing cycle of growth and decay which is the soil. I cannot think how Dovjenko makes it plausible—as he does—if it is not by performing the really great miracle of bringing the mind back through the complex fol-di-rols of modern life, to earth again. His apples, his sunflowers, his wind in the corn, his young people, the gaiety of the women as they tie up the stooks, the gaiety of the men as they drive the tractor, and by the devious if stalwart methods of the peasant replenish its exhausted radiator, the quiet of the peasant men with women and women with men, and a man dancing down the road from the village after the day's work: these are the gestures of his magic. There is not an element of them all that those who know the villages—here or anywhere—will not recognize as a simple and ancient truth is recognized: with a somewhat strangling recollection of beauty.

Perhaps I am sorry that this film was not made for England, but I cannot very well see how it could have been. We have forgotten the

Land in the sense of believing in it. We could hardly show the young men singing a hymn to the future of the English soil, for there is no longer any faith in its future. As the industrial nation we are, we had better perhaps concentrate on the factory and discover a hymn of the future for that.

(*Artwork*, Winter 1930)

With Dziga Vertov's *Man with the Movie Camera* we are at last initiated into the philosophy of the Kino Eye. Some of us have been hearing a great deal about the Kino Eye over the past couple of years, and it has worried us considerably. Only the younger highbrows seemed to know anything about it. They have dashed back from their Continental rambles with hair more rumpled, neck more open, and tie more non-existent for gazing on it. But on the whole articulation has failed them, and it has been difficult to gather from their wild young words what mesmeric virtue this Kino Eye possessed.

Now that Vertov has turned up in the original, it is easier to see why intelligent students of cinema were betrayed into their extremity. The Vertov method of film-making is based on a supremely sound idea, and one which must be a preliminary to any movie method at all. He has observed that there are things of the everyday which achieve a new value, leap to a more vigorous life, the moment they get into a movie camera or an intimately cut sequence. It is at that point we all begin; and, backing our eye with the world, we try to pick the leapers. The secret may be an angle, or an arrangement of light, or an arrangement of movement, but there is hardly one of us but gets more out of the camera than we ever thought of putting into it. In that sense there is a Kino Eye. In that sense, too, the Kino Eye is more likely to discover things in the wide-world-of-all-possible-arrangements which exists outside the studios.

Vertov, however, has pushed the argument to a point at which it becomes ridiculous. The camera observes in its own bright way and he is prepared to give it his head. The man is with the camera, not the camera with the man. Organization of things observed, brain control, imagination or fancy control of things observed: these other rather necessary activities in the making of art are forgotten. *The Man with the Movie Camera* is in consequence not a film at all: it is a snap-shot album. There is no story, no dramatic structure, and no special revelation of the Moscow it has chosen for a subject. It just dithers about on the surface of life picking up shots here, there and everywhere, slinging them together as the Dadaists used to sling together their verses, with an emphasis on the particular which is out of all relation to a rational existence. Many of the shots are fine and vital; some of the camera tricks, if not very new, are at least interesting; but exhibitionism or, if you prefer it, virtuosity in a craftsman does not qualify him as a creator.

The Man with the Movie Camera will, however, bring a great deal of instruction to film students. The camera is a bright little blackbird, and there are rabbits to be taken out of the hat (or bin) of montage which are infinitely magical, but . . . articulacy is a virtue which will continue to have its say-so. Here by the *reductio ad absurdum* is proof for the schoolboys.

I have just now been watching an Atlantic liner putting to sea, from – I am happy to say – the liner's point of view. Shots have been cropping up for an hour that I would describe as sheer cinema. The patterns of men rolling up the cargo net, the curve of the rope shot in parabola to the tug, the sudden gliding movement-astern of the tug, the white plume on the *Mauretania* high up in the dry dock, the massed energy of the black smoke pouring in rolls from the funnel and set against the rhythmic curve of the ship against the sky – they have all, possibly, a visual virtue in themselves. But the dramatic truth, and therefore, finally, the cinematic truth too, is that the ship is putting to sea. She is in process and continuity of something or other. Say only that she is setting out to cross an ocean and has the guts for it; or say, by the Eastern European emigrants in the steerage, that a bunch of people are going with hope to a new world; say what you like, according to your sense of ultimate importances, the necessity is that you say something. The Kino Eye in that sense is only the waiter who serves the hash. No especial virtue in the waiting compensates for a lunatic cook.

In heavy contrast to the Vertox film is an English mining film, Hanmer's *Toilers*. Hanmer describes himself as a pitman producer, and he has indeed been associated with coal mining all his life. He has laboured as a pony boy, and at the face, and in later years has been in the thick of disasters as a rescue expert. He knows the pits inside out and the men who work in them, and along his single track of knowledge is the most enthusiastic and sincere man I have seen in Wardour Street for many a day.

Hanmer, I should say shortly, has not the Kino Eye, and his film would not excite the highbrows at all. And yet so clear is Hanmer about what he wants to say that the film is, on the whole, a better job than *The Man with the Movie Camera*. The movie camera in this case is not a very good camera, but the man behind it, by the weight of his authority and singleness of his purpose, does in a strange and surprising way leave you with a new insight into the industry. I have been down pits a few times and thought they made a pretty good show. Hanmer and his photography do not permit of any reaction so sophisticated nor, for that matter, so ineffective. It is the bowels of the earth or nothing with him, and that is the right point of view.

In his next production, however, he must take more out of the camera and more out of the cutting bench. If you know your stuff, as Hanmer knows it, the Kino Eye will flash up the story no end. That is its virtue. On consideration therefore, I nominate Vertov as cameraman for Hanmer. They would make a great team.

(*The Clarion*, February 1931)

I have never set eyes on a film that interested me more than Vertov's *Enthusiasm*, nor one that demanded more solid criticism. But I never saw a film that was so fundamentally un-Bolshevik in its excitements. If an amateur Bolshevik with a training in the studio leap-frog of Paris had made it, it would have been incomprehensible. It is all dazzle-dazzle and bits and pieces, whoopee for this, whoopee for that—like any masterwork of the close-up school. But body of thought or body of construction it has none.

Enthusiasm is a hymn of praise for the Five-Year Plan in the Don Basin; it praises the steel and stalwarts of the Don Basin. If the Five-Year Plan is no clearer in the head than the praise of *Enthusiasm*, heaven help the Russian workers. If the film is any guide, they will be doing in year five the job they already did in year two; they will repeat themselves endlessly. And they will have the darnedest job finishing at all. For a thousand feet *Enthusiasm* tried to bring itself to a conclusion. Uncertain of the success of its whoopee for steel, it tried a whoopee for the land. Uncertain of that, it tried steel again. So far as I am concerned it is still trying.

There was a story in the Don Basin. There was a story of the steel-workers laying a foundation of steel for the new Russia; that is to say, doing something good and definite as *Turksib* did. There was an alternative story: the story of Russian workers leaving the fake enthusiasms of the Christian church for the more decent enthusiasms of creative Socialism. The one story meant an epic of most definite achievement. The other meant the creation of a new poetry.

I think Vertov tried the second issue. He demolished the mysticisms of the ancient religion at the beginning of his film and tried to build up a new mysticism in the relation between the worker and his machine. It was a job worth trying, and he has brought all his great power over camera angles, and all his sense of percussive cutting, to help him. But he has failed. And he has failed because he was like any bourgeois highbrow, too clever by half. He has given us ten thousand clever effects—of split lenses and tilted cameras and angled details. He has missed, however, the simple things which are the root of all poetry and mysticism. He has given us everything of the mechanism and nothing of the people. He has described every beat in the industry of the Don Basin except the heart-beat.

At the same time I must indicate some of the amazing things there are in this film. It is so full of ingenuities that practitioners like myself will be feeding on its carcase years from now. Never were workmen so energized by a camera. It gets under and over them. It gyros to their movements with a growing intensity of movement which makes excitement of something most ordinary. Industrial happenings are generally so ponderous that it is the despair of a director to pace them. Vertov will show you how to under-emphasize and how to exaggerate. He will demonstrate how the most simple incidents (a girl with a pair of telephones or a couple of men on a two-handed hammer) can hold a whole sequence together. By sheer variety of observation—there never was such variety before—he turns a plain process into a fairy-tale of excited happening.

As I suggest, it all leads nowhere, but it certainly leads furiously. Much the same sort of thing can be said of the sound effects. You will find sound cut in beats to the beat of the images; you will find it syncopating with the images; you will find most excellent passings of mechanical sound into musical sound: you will hear it distorted till it screams, and you will find feeling in it.

You will, however, still be dissatisfied. Whatever the band of buglers at its head, a film must march somewhere. This film is all bugling and marching and marching and bugling. The banners fly and the troops give the salute; the citizens cheer along the line of march; the soldiers raise their voices in lusty chorus. There is Enthusiasm and no mistake. But I could not for the life of me tell you whether the enthusiasm is an empty one or a full one. Vertov has not told us.

(*The Clarion*, December 1931)

It is hard to discover what is happening in the Russian film world, and no major effort has come to us from the schools of Sovkino since Turin's *Turksib*. Pudovkin's last film was shelved by order, one understands, of the political censor in Moscow. Ermler's *Stump of an Empire* did not emerge from the Customs' theatre in Endell Street. Its propaganda was too local in its intention. Vertov's *Enthusiasm*, the last ambassador of the school, was too muddled in the head to carry on the great tradition. For two years, indeed, Russian cinema in this country has been living on its reputation, and there is no compensation for the loss.

I am not sure that Nikolai Ekk's *Road to Life* will make any great difference. It is an interesting film of vagabond children, and shapes its drama very skilfully out of the fights between the forces of order and disorder. The Commissars would make citizens of them, and the villains of the underworld would use them for their villainy. I found myself a little less than enthralled. The young actors are the film's chief distinction. They were themselves once vagabond children, according to the introduction by Professor Dewey of Columbia, and Ekk has certainly to be congratulated on his ability to bring them into genuine action. In sound, too, the film has points of great interest, especially in its use of background choruses and its use of sound for dramatic commentary. When, for example, the hero is brought back to the Collective for which he dies, it is the engine which brings him which expresses the sorrow of the people. The concluding blast of its exhaust, as it pulls up, has the effect of a colossal sigh. If, in spite of these effects, the film is less than enthralling, it is because of a certain disappointing spirit in the well-doers themselves. The committee in charge of the boys are too hearty by half in their work of uplifting, and just a little patronizing. The sudden joy of the youths in hygienic dormitories, all-in bathrooms, and honest work is admirable, but a little less than human. It is only among the lesser religions that conversion is swift. Bolshevism does itself no great credit by sharing their naïvety.

(*The Clarion*, May 1932)

Pudovkin's *Deserter* is a great film by a great director. If you follow my prejudice, you may even believe that Pudovkin is the only director with any claim to greatness, and that this is his greatest film; but I would not publicly insist on so fervent a judgement.

There was a last Pudovkin called *A Simple Case*, a dreadful little film with an ingenious use of slow motion, a host of lovely images, and no point. *Deserter* is Pudovkin on the rebound: more complex in his effects, surer in his technical hand, and even stronger in his theme than he was in *The End of St Petersburg*.

If you remember your Dostoievsky or your Joyce or your Melville you will know how leisurely the masterpieces may sometimes proceed: how, damning the audience, they may sometimes fly suddenly off the earth, or, by perversity, from off the earth back to terra firma again, without a by your leave: taking good pains to bore the lesser minds with inconsequent pondering on the guts of whales and the exact nature of disease and disaster. *Deserter* has something of this curious strength. If, in its hobbling from one odd chapter to another, as it freely does, the film extends your patience, you will respect it, as like as not, for the size it brings. Only the little fellows care what twiddling echoes go round your pipes and, sycophantically, measure the music to suit you. The big fellows call their own tune. You will certainly have time to consider this matter, for the film runs near a couple of hours: in innumerable acts and sub-divisions of acts: shifting from scene to scene in titles, and sometimes plain blackouts, as I cannot remember anything doing so variously since *Antony and Cleopatra*.

When you come to consider the continuing theme of the film you will be wise to look for none, but content yourself with the vast description it gives of the world today: of high-powered industry, of unemployment, of poverty, of the accumulating fire of public effort, of the stresses and storms between men and men which economic disaster has brought in its train. The net effect is of great tragedy, in which the beauties of blue sky and morning, ships and machinery, young faces and hopeful faces, are strangely stifled in the common disaster. For long passages there is argument: as of dictatorship, leadership, solution; and you will need to know Russian to know every turn of the dialectic. But you will regard even this as part of a necessary effect.

For my part, I shall only record that no film or novel or poem or drama has sketched so largely the essential story and the essential unhappiness of our time, or brought them so deeply to the mind.

(*New Britain*, 25 October 1933)

It is a waste of time to consider what Eisenstein would have done with *Thunder Over Mexico*, if he had been allowed to cut it. The fact is that he was not allowed, and alibis on the part of Upton Sinclair that the cutting was done 'in exact accord' with Eisenstein's script are merely silly. One might as well talk of writing a George Moore novel from George Moore's notes; for with Eisenstein, as with Moore, the style is nearly everything. He is not a poet like Pudovkin, whose conceptions are themselves emotional and uplifting, nor a finely descriptive writer like Flaherty, whose observations are of themselves intimate. His raw material is common documentary, and sometimes very common. It is his power of juxtaposition that counts, his amazing capacity for exploding two or three details into an idea. It is not how his actors act, nor yet how the camera looks at them, that is important in Eisenstein, for his acting is often bad and his camera work meretricious: it is the odd reference he adds to his actors' presence that gives meaning and tempo to their lives. Say this for brief, that Eisenstein is detailed and cold in his shooting, and that he warms his stuff to life only when he starts putting it together. It is his method of approach; and there could be no genuine Eisenstein film without it.

Thunder Over Mexico might have been a good film with Eisenstein, or it might not; without him it is pretty dull stuff, without style, without ideas, and without construction. What I hear was intended to be a vast description of the Mexican spirit turns out to be a niggardly slow-told tale of how a peasant girl was raped by a feudal lord and how her peasant lover rebelled and was executed.

There is a symbolic sequence at the beginning which is meant to describe the age-long suffering of the Mexican people. It is full of dissolves, super-impositions and wipes, in a manner never before associated with Eisenstein, and I cannot understand its presence. If Eisenstein intended it, he has certainly deviated from his own stalwart doctrine. He was always an enemy of such vague methods of mental association as are represented by the draping of symbolic figures across the landscape; and I remember how he raged at the symbolic example of *Joan of Arc* when I once put it to him. This sequence, if it is anything, is just bad *Joan of Arc*. The tale of rape follows, in a setting of heavily filtered clouds and foreground cactus. The clouds and the cactus will pass for great photography among the hicks, but they are, of course, easy meat for anyone with a decent set of filters. The lovely moulding of form, the brilliance of near and intimate observation, which you get in *Moana*, say, are a mile away and beyond. These are superficial qualities only. But, as I suggest, one never looked to Eisenstein for great photography or intimate observation, and one's only disappointment is that Hollywood has fallen for these clouds and things and let the film go to the devil for the sake of its glycerined scenic effects. The types on the other hand are superb, for no one holds a candle to Eisenstein when it comes to picking faces. The acting, too, is much better than we ever associated with Eisenstein in the past, though never as fine in its nuances of reaction as we get in Pudovkin.

But there you are and what of it? The significance that Eisenstein might have added to the tale is not there; and types, acting and glycerined clouds cannot turn a simple tale of village rape into the passion of a people. There were other things up Eisenstein's sleeve, or he is not the dialectician I have always taken him for. A brief sequence at the end, describing industrial Mexico, suggests as much, but it is too brief to enlarge the idea of the film, and give the peasant theme its fatalistic place in the story of a people. The industrial sequence is, in any case, wrongly interpreted by the nit-wits of Hollywood. Eisenstein could never have intended to show industrial democracy as the high heaven to which Mexico has reached since the Revolution. But so to the egregious Sinclair (after all these years of pretended dialectic on his own account) the issue appears.

Sinclair says in a foreword that he showed the picture to Chaplin and Fairbanks. Chaplin said, 'It is lovely; it is revealing; it is powerful.' Fairbanks, using 'very beautiful words', said: 'It unrolls itself with beauty, with charm, and with purpose.' What is wrong with Upton Sinclair might make an even better theme for criticism than the film, for he used to be better than that. Alas, you have a spectacle of the great Upton wheedling your sympathy and your pennies for a bastard article he should be kicked in the slats for. If you back an artist you have to go through with him even if he is difficult; for that is how it is with artists. Sinclair did not go through with Eisenstein, and now acts and talks and excuses himself like any beastly promoter. Eisenstein or no Eisenstein, an artist has a creative right in his own film. If we are to have films at all that principle must be upheld, and if the money grubbing factor makes it impossible let us have no slobbery about 'exact accord with the scenario', no lies (when it comes to the box office) that it is the genuine article, and no malicious hints about the wastage involved in shooting thirty-five miles of film.

(*New Britain*, 10 January 1934)

12 · Garbo, Dietrich, Mae West and Co.

In pursuit of my duty to you I have observed Miss Garbo in *The Rise of Helga*. No lesser duty would have made me do it. In this grave matter of Garbo, I am not of those who walk in the tradition of the Elders, but eat with Unwashen Hands. The celebrated charms, the worshipped mysteries of the great medicine woman pass over my innocent head. She leaves me — quite strictly — cold.

It is all very embarrassing. My friend Belfrage turns up in the *Express* with a whoopee for Garbo, which is not like his own sane self at all. He shatters an entire Sunday forenoon with his 'Garbo is back! . . . Garbo is back!!' kicking the ceiling between shouts. Sober young men whom I know to be good citizens and honest critics turn on me this week with a pitying gape they never dared before. A pitying, pendulous gape, or a flush of knightly defiance.

I produce scalpel and hatchet in the usual way. I say she is surely a frigid lady, this: making love with the enthusiasm of a codfish in the Arctic. But no, they are Garbans!

There is no weathering the fashion, and you will see *The Rise of Helga* in spite of me. It tells the sad and sadistic story of a young lady whom Time and Circumstance wronged from the first. Her mother hadn't a ring and died when she was born. Almost immediately Helga became dishwasher for relatives who hated her for her bastardy. And cruel relatives they were, just as we used to get them in the old melodramatic Metropole in Glasgow: whose every look was a lash and every gesture another smack in the eye.

She grew up in this way, poor Helga, and what should they do to her but try to marry her to a drunken brute. They always did. And Helga ran away and found Clark Gable, and then she hadn't a ring either. Clark, with a twinge of conscience, went off to get the fateful ring, and what do you imagine happened then, children? You are right. The cruel relatives came along, and there was the very separation established that sadistic directors lick their directorial lips over.

It was just hell on earth for poor Helga after that. For the circus manager got her, then somebody else and somebody else (*ad infinitum*, children!), till there was nobody left in the world but Clark Gable himself. And Clark, as you can guess, was very sad and sick about it when she got round to him. He gave poor Helga the worst smack in the eye of all. She chased after him desperately, but no, he was gone — and only a tough landlady to say she didn't know where. So more world wanderings for Helga and more, and poor Clark Gable going to the devil too, in the mad malarial swamps of somewhere or other, and drinking real bad, with three days' growth on his manly face. But Greta found him, and said she was good again, and Clark Gable punched her on the nose several times to fool the audience, and only changed his mind a minute before the close-out.

Personally, I have never seen so much understanding in one film; and if drama is the overcoming of obstacles, this is a hurdle jumper's nightmare. The first part, however, is very cleverly done with Jean Hersholt playing the cruel old relative superbly. There is a birth at the beginning (in a snowstorm, as it should be), and very lovely shadows on a curtain to show us Helga growing up. After that Garbo registers all the sadness and sorrow (and mental deficiency) the script calls for, from the bedraggled humidity of the storm in which she escapes, to the bedraggled humidity of the dive in which at last she finds her Gable.

The finer touches I must leave to the enthusiasts. My experience, however, is that they will not take you far. They will gabble the name of the Divinity over and over most reverently and, like other men of religion, breathe noisily through their teeth. They will probably tell you then that they cannot analyse these Higher Things. I am sure they would be very foolish to try.

In direct contrast to the manufactured misery of Helga, is the Fairbanks manufacture of merriment in *Round the World in Eighty Minutes*. This is Fairbanks's own story of his recent journey to the Far East, and a very fine feat of story telling it is. There is nothing new in the material, and ten thousand travelogues have been better photographed. The secret is in Fairbanks himself. He turns the old descriptive dross into a valley of diamonds.

On his magical map he takes a run from Tibet to the coast of China, and leaps into the Philippines. He plays a chip shot from Japan to effect a landing in Hong Kong. He brings in Mickey Mouse to illustrate the sacred dances of Siam. His magic carpet used once upon a time in *The Thief of Baghdad* brings him back swiftly from Bombay, across the columns of ancient Rome and the skyscrapers of modern New York to Hollywood.

Fairbanks, by such novelty of presentation and by the unquenchable gusto he brings to every single thing he says or does, makes a fantasy from what might otherwise have been a very superficial globe trot indeed. He sees the usual things, the street scenes and palaces and ruins; he meets the usual camera-gazing potentates; but no one ever enjoyed them half so much or conveyed his enjoyment so heartily.

Robert Benchley, the best and funniest commentator in the world, is the reputed author of the wisecracks, but to hear Fairbanks you would not believe it. He does not repeat a wisecrack; he exudes it.

This film will make a great change in all travelogues hereafter. You must see it for that reason alone. Its maps are exciting; its leaps in space and time are the feats of fantasy they should be; and the world is made once again the magical old play bill the imagination of youth would have it. The film was made as a jest. It is almost a fairy-tale.

(*Everyman*, 28 January 1932)

There is good light entertainment in the double-barrelled Barrymore version of *Arsène Lupin*. The brothers, John and Lionel, team up for the first time. John is Arsène himself, the ace of Parisian crooks: Lionel is the arch enemy Guerchard (*né* Ganimard), the ace of Parisian detectives. But *plus ça change plus c'est le même* Barrymore.

Michael Arlen once remarked that he might not be a great writer but he was certainly a born one. The distinction applies very prettily to Barrymore the younger. I hold him for the biggest ham that ever strutted out of *Hamlet* into Hollywood; yet every mediocre thing he does is done with such faith, such self-possession, and such gusto, that I never miss an item. Fredric March sketched him to the innards in *The Royal Family of Broadway*: as the perpetual actor off stage and on. It was a satiric sketch with John inventing preposterous hoops to jump through at every turn; but March made you like him. As Salieri argued to Mozart, there is a pride of craft which is sometimes more honourable than genius.

I have seen Barrymore play Hamlet and Hyde and Captain Ahab and Don Juan. He played every one as a character in a penny dreadful, without, I am sure, the faintest notion that they represented anything else. On that level, however, he is superb. He plays them with delight, as one who knows everything a penny-dreadful character should be. I class him with Buck Jones, Emil Jannings, and the old time Bill Hart. He is one of the very respectable company of enthusiastic single-trackers.

Lionel is a different proposition. There is an intensity about the man which varies in nature from picture to picture, and this, I take it, is the sign of a greater actor. Once in Gloria Swanson's film of Maugham's *Sadie Thompson* (*né Rain*) he rose to greater heights. There he played the preacher whose evangelism turns suddenly and disastrously to rape. I saw *Rain* in its heyday on Broadway, when Jeanne Eagels had already held America in thrall for a couple of years. Lionel lifted the play higher still to the larger and subtler intensities of a lunatic asylum. He has always been popularly regarded as a good, reliable workman, with John as the flashy member of the family and the lad of genius.

Except for the great personal interest of the Barrymores comparing themselves in public, *Arsène Lupin* is a slight film: no better and no worse than, say, *Bulldog Drummond*. Take a comfortable three-and-sixpenny seat and relax, and you will have nothing to grumble about. I have a sentimental memory of the feud between Lupin and Ganimard. It was a merry romantic affair, with the wit and humour and sleight-of-hand magic of one outsmarting the dour doggedness of the other. Lionel has managed the dourness of Ganimard, but the wit and humour is sadly lacking in the Lupin of John. Of course, he had no sense of humour to put into the job: he never had. Perhaps he makes up for it in the romantic passages. He bears down on his female with a single eye and a steady profile.

A better film by far, I think, is *High Pressure*. Nothing makes me so certain of the greatness of America as its capacity for kicking itself in its own slats. Babbitt is a queer fellow. He turns into a most intelligent and toughminded fellow the moment he pushes the curtains of a Pullman smoker: the moment, for that matter, he descends from the small-town respectability of his front-room to the moister mysteries of his basement. You may laugh at America's hundred-percenting, but it takes a hundred-per-cent American like Ring Lardner, or Donald Stewart or Robert Benchley or Will Rogers or Raymond Griffith to be funny about it.

High Pressure is funny about American salesmanship; it debunks it; it shoots it to pieces with a rollicking cynicism no one in this country would dare to apply to a national institution. Not even Bernard Shaw. You will find yourself not so much concerned with the story as with the incidentals of it: the professional president, the 'front' money, the rigmarole of big business premises with nothing to do the business on, the 'pep' speeches, the exploitation of 'nuisance values', the convention choruses. The queer aspect of the film is that it is a straight account of the picture business as most of us know it. We sell films before they exist. We boost them to the skies and deceive the world without seeing them. We make reputations out of nonentities and believe them ourselves.

Powell is the master of ceremonies; Evelyn Brent accompanies, and tucked away are a dozen first-rate faces.

(Everyman, 10 March 1932)

Marie Dressler is at the Empire and Gloria Swanson is at the Tivoli, and the news of both ladies is pretty bad. I used to like Swanson before she got Sarah Bernhardt ideas into her noddle. She was as dashing a blade as slapstick and the old go-as-you-please tradition ever turned out: and the very best slavey I ever saw in films. But then Bernhardt.

I met Swanson twice in the States: once being intelligent about *Potemkin*, before most people were intelligent about *Potemkin*; and another time when she near-hove me from the Uptown Studio in New York. An able, attractive woman, but always too bad a director to be the great actress she might have been. Paramount gave her a false sense of reputation. They got it into her head that she was the screen's greatest gown purveyor. Gradually the dressy tradition of drama muscled in on the redoubtable slavey, and when slapstick went out of the window, almost everything that was Gloria went after it. I walked out of *Tonight or Never*, after bearing what I could. Wag my ageing beard as I may, I cannot be consoled. These yere days Gloria ain't what she was.

And Dressler. They call her the pride and joy of the screen, meaning that she is the pride and joy of every tinkling till in the business. Laugh and weep with Dressler, they tell you. When you see *Emma*, you will be inclined to weep with her, and wonder if you haven't made her the pride and joy of everybody but herself. This particular vehicle carries the heaviest load of hokum since D. W. Griffith was at his darndest. Frances Marion picked it and loaded it.

The old family servant—nursing, charing, managing for thirty years—married at last to the master—left a widow as soon as married—turned down by the children she has sacrificed her life for—accused of swinging the will and murdering the old master—her only faithful stepson killed while flying to help her—acquitted—starting all over again at sixty-five. Do your best with it. I give it up, Dressler and all.

(*Everyman*, 3 March 1932)

The Greeks had a Name for Them is a bright, sophisticated affair of gold-digging blondes. It is just a little more than a sophisticated comedy, and you may enjoy the distinction. The ordinary specimen of that very continuing genre may be depended on for smart answers and crackerjack acting. But one of its plain limits is that underneath the fuss and the foam it is as sentimental as the ordinary romance. Its silken undies are all done up with the usual pink and blue baby linen. The cross-talk done, the mental superiority of the salons duly recorded, your ladies and gents step like their lowlier brethren under the moon. Wilde to Lonsdale, it is much the same.

These gold-digging Greek girls are slightly superior in their adventures. For one thing, their gold-digging gives them a purpose in life, and like all purposes great in drama, it is proof against the tweedle-dum and tweedledee of sentimental attachment. The result is something that passes clean beyond sophisticated comedy to the higher heights of the picaresque.

Picaresque, of course, is the world of lighthearted highwaymen; and its single essential is that the highwaymen neither apologize for their villainies, nor are they apologized for by their author. The gold-diggers come up to scratch. They live on their wits, and live merrily, and no reason is suggested for their not even continuing to do so. There are so many ways, after all, in which the Ninons give you your money's worth. Let the duller dames rage as they may!

Ina Claire is the central figure in this case, and what a brilliant person she always is! Joan Blondell, who helps her along, is better than I have seen her before, and is now to be taken almost seriously as an actress, but the nuances of the Claire woman are not yet in her. Having raised the banner of picaresque, I have possibly promised you too much. Drunk, sober, affectionate, catty, whooping up a party, or vamping a victim, or snoring over a symphony, Ina Claire will balance the account.

(Everyman, 30 June 1932)

I am not sure what to say about *Storm at Daybreak* at the Empire. I thought the film was well made and worth seeing both for the presence of Walter Huston and for its many smooth and rhythmic sequences. The story on the other hand may easily alienate you. In this, the ten millionth triangular example, the husband is the Serbian mayor of a Hungarian border town, the wife is a patriotic Serb hating Hungarians, the dashing young blade who comes between them is a Hungarian officer, and there is a certain bother about Austro-Serbian political relationships in the offing; otherwise the mixture is as before. The agony of the lady torn between loyalty to a kind husband and love for a more promising bed-fellow is bound by this time to have worn a trifle threadbare. And no consideration, on the lovers' part, of loyalty to a best friend makes the issue any more new and sensational.

In the background the Austrian Archduke is being murdered at Sarajevo and the Great War is murdering fifteen million people, but only echoes of the more important matter reach us. The story, blessing its blinkers, passes as thousands have done before us to a finale in which the husband splendidly suicides to give his wife and his friend biological gangway. He could from the beginning so much more easily, and with even greater generosity, have put them up together in one of the wings of his castle. It would have saved everybody a great deal of bother.

I don't know why one should object to all this, for the film is well intended and almost disarms criticism by its bewildering insistence on purity. One objects, possibly, to the fact that the fifty million people who see *Storm at Daybreak* should be deceived for an hour and a half of their lives into believing that this issue between marital bread tickets and biological urges is a dignified one, and that the upshot of grand sacrifices adds a cubit to human stature. That, please you, is the implication. You will ask, as I do, if there is justification for taking a small matter of body choice so seriously when, ordinarily, there are ten thousand and one chores to do and no one has time to be so stupid.

But another notion occurs to me. Perhaps Hollywood means in the goodness of its heart to give us warning by its repetition of these triangle stories; and it would be fairer to regard them as propaganda pictures. Obviously we must watch our wives like lynxes and keep a sharp eye on these best friends of ours (snakes in the grass that they are!). But let the propaganda be done quickly.

Boeislavsky directed, Walter Huston is the mayor, and Kay Francis, singing Tzigane, is the wife.

(*New Britain*, 16 August 1933)

Any short word of four to six letters will describe *Dinner at Eight* at the Palace. You cannot escape hearing that it is the film of the week, the month, and the year; though the whys and wherefores are lost in the smother of advertisement. It is one of these shows where the stars move down on you in massed formation, and Barrymores are as thick as jackdaws in Haverfordwest. And yet—the remark may or may not be appropriate—I never knew a greater pother about nothing. *Dinner at Eight* has its own curious comment that in the length and breadth of it there is no dinner.

The original idea is fair enough. A society hostess summons a bunch of guests to a banquet. Who are they, ask the authors Kaufman and Ferber; what personal particulars have these forked radishes who are incidentally business men and professional men and racketeers and actors and movie stars? In principle, the question was worth asking, for the manners and motives of the bourgeois deserve at the moment considerable research. What a piebald gang of rogues and thieves a writer like Swift would have found in them.

The Kaufman–Ferber answer is softer; so soft indeed that you may feel it is no answer at all. It turns out that the celebrated movie star was really a ham actor after all, that the society doctor is a seducer of women, that the financier is a crook, that his dolled-up wife is a guttersnipe, that the daughter of the house is the movie star's mistress, and so on and so forth. The answers you observe are fairly easy, and amount in the mass to nothing. It is amusing to think that people accumulated round a dinner table are not all that they pretend, or all that they seem. But the detached particulars of each personal lie are, as in this case, only gossip. The *News of the World* will do as much for you, for tuppence.

Creatively handled, the little personal lies might be built into one grand accumulate lie, commanding men's horror or anger or laughter, or only their pity. *Dinner at Eight* does not give you anything of the sort, and, to do it justice, does not try to. You are left, in default, with the easier honours of charade: a competition in thespian mannerism which could just as sensibly have been staged as a vaudeville turn.

If the film has any virtue it is in the freedom of the competition. The direction is so naïve that you have every opportunity of seeing the stars (Beery, Dressler, Harlow, Lowe, the Barrymores, etc.) in their own original conception of their native best. Wallace Beery's remark on Cukor the director was: 'That young man! Why he was no trouble to us at all.' He certainly was no trouble. They are just as Beery and Barrymore as they please. My chief delight was to find that Jean Harlow, deprived of directorial brassiere, is a far more bouncing baby than she ever was. I see Ernest Betts is calling her orchidaceous: she is as orchidaceous in this as the wife of Bath.

(*New Britain*, 13 September 1933)

'Just a rough diamond in a platinum setting—in tights, tiaras, tea-gowns—singing songs that will make the town gasp . . .' As a tired business man myself, I felt the invitation to the Carlton was a personal one. Then I saw strange things indeed. Beside me were two benevolent grey-haired old ladies. They chortled and chuckled and dug each other in the ribs at every wisecrack. A couple of rubber-tyred spinsters behind me raved. Young women in scattered singles stood off from their swains in sudden access of sophistication. Mae West was plainly not the dame for dithering men I expected of her, but something quite opposite. She was the woman who fulfilled not the first desires of males, but the last desires of females: who showed her weaker sisters how to 'find them, fool them and forget them'. The vicious streak in that curious cocktail was obviously going to the sisters' heads.

And why not? The character Mae West has created is the darling of every mill girl's and every duchess's dreams. She gets her men and plenty of them and plays the lot for the suckers they undoubtedly are. She demonstrates what every woman knows and only lacks the courage and coolness to exploit to the maximum: the fact that the muzzier moments of the male are pretty muzzy. What matter if she is old and fat if she can hold them! Is it not part of this exquisite female romanticism that she holds them despite both age and fattery? No need indeed to fiddle and fuss, no need to belly crawl with a hundred and one abdominal titivations and facial falsifications, if a steady eye on the muzzier moments and a cool grip on the emotional occasions can out-countenance the victim. And if, in the upshot, one need not give even the last indignity away, so very much the better.

I imagine women feel as proud of Mae West as men feel of Tom Mix. She is the two-handed gunman of the parlours and the bold bad bandit of the bedrooms: as heroically unashamed as the other is heroically unafraid. I submit the feat to your attention as worth considerable applause. Mae has succeeded where D. H. Lawrence, in a lifetime of hard writing, failed miserably. If D. H. had known his subject half as well as he professed, he would have left it to the honky tonk girls from the start.

Apart from these deeper considerations you will get a great deal of fun out of *I'm No Angel*: in Mae, in the original wisecracks of Mae, and in the equally original movements of Mae. She is a thoroughly bad actress in a thoroughly bad story but, as a turn, she is worth the hour and a half she devotes to herself. On any ordinary ruling the Censor should have stopped her innuendoes in her throat. On a Rabelaisian ruling they pass with honours. 'It isn't the men in my life I am worried about: it's the life in my men,' says Mae—and very justly. I only wonder what the family trade will say about her. Will the ladies stir with pride and possibilities like the Carlton lot, and let danger be damned; or will the sickly look of recognition in their attendant males warn them to let sleeping dogs lie. Maybe it were better. Mae may find 'em and fool 'em, and so do they all in their fashion. But the wiser course is not to crow about it. The only weakness of Mae West's set up is that she crows her head off. In so doing, she gives more than the game away: and no doubt women, on further thought, will spot the weakness. The female she presents is female enough; the manner of presentation, with its rip-roaring exhibitionism and self-certainty, is male. The thought may give house to her female admirers, and I expect it presently will. Mae is in for a short life and—bless her—a merry one. In the meantime, may her every hip wriggle be priced in gold, her every shoulder shimmy above rubies. What honky tonk queen should cost less?

(*New Britain*, 6 December 1933)

'For a temporary paradise you are prepared to kick a helpless girl into a permanent hell?' asks Baron von Weissnichtwer. The sculptorman seizes this heaven-sent argument as an excuse for getting out of his responsibilities. Millions have done it before him: serving morality, bad philosophy and tarara-boom-de-ay in one fell gesture. He abandons the little Dietrich to the more plutocratic embraces of the Baron himself. The Baron even marries the Dietrich, old as he is, and teaches her to play the piano and sing Schumann's very lovely 'Roslein'. But, alas, the Dietrich heart is sick for the sculptorman and desperately sore at his perfidy; and the cheek bones tighten to say so. And when he turns up to claim her, what more natural than that she should slip from the embraces of the Baron and the sculptorman both, to the embraces of the Baron's factor. In other words, she does Dietrich. With these simple exercises in promiscuity she becomes the full blown courtesan you expected from the beginning.

Peasant girl, sculptor's model, countess, courtesan: 'everything passes' somebody says, '*everything!*' For a moment we thought the Dietrich was as good as done for. We reckoned without the sculptorman. Weary and footsore he marched the highways and byways till he found her beat. And, fetching her back to the studio in which love was first born, he forgave her little peccadilloes and she forgave his, and together they reached out their arms to the moon. 'We'll climb again and find the sky, perhaps,' says the sculptorman: adding the 'perhaps' to complete the pentameter.

I find it difficult to say anything more serious about *The Song of Songs*. It was directed by Rouben Mamoulian whom we had come to associate with good things; but he must be a cheap skate to have anything to do with servant-girl nonsense of this kind. And pretentious nonsense it is at times, and unclean nonsense even more often. The theme on which the tale is carried is taken from the Bible, no less:

> By night on my bed I sought him whom my soul loveth:
> I sought him, but I found him not.
> I will rise now and go about the city in the streets and in the
> broad ways I will seek him whom my soul loveth.

That is the original: all, as you see, about sculptors' models and lecherous old barons. You may like Dietrich's repetition of the lines or, again, you may find it impertinent and, by implication, in the lousiest of taste. It is that sort of film.

Only among the nudities of the sculptor's studio is the film really at home. There it plays whoopee and plenty. They tell a story of a

Hollywood producer who on seeing the waist nudities of the natives in *Moana* commanded a director to 'fill the screen with 'em'. They were to be the great new 'angle'. A hundred Hollywood girls were tested to the waist to 'fill the screen with 'em', but the picture never matured except in the testing studio. Now Mamoulian has done what was there intended, and got away with it.

Was there ever a better dodge for disrobing a lady on the screen than by making a statue of her? You can have your nude in long-shots, close-ups, closer-and-closer close-ups; and not a censor to stop you. You can converse lecherously with background of nudes. You can even have your conversers fondle and fumble as they lecherously converse. And who, theory of art being what it is, is to deny you use of the most photographically realistic nudes imaginable? For my part I would punish the whole censor's department for passing *The Song of Songs*. It is an abominable breach of duty on their part to permit its deliberate indecencies to get through.

This Day and Age is the new Cecil DeMille film and 'the first spectacle of modern times'. It follows *M* so closely that the wicked may charge it with plagiarism. Even the recurring whistle is there, and the lynch trial in the local brickyard. The theme is slightly different. In this case the figure who is hunted is the local Al Capone and the lynchers, who have taken the law into their own hands, are the local schoolboys.

M was more than a spectacle. It tried to probe the mind of the man who was hunted. It made him a figure of tragedy when his captors tortured him. DeMille knows nothing about such distinctions. He is perfectly happy to build up the hunt and refine the tortures. The first gives him spectacle, the other gives him his own peculiar DeMille species of satisfaction. He can achieve both splendidly.

All it gives him in the end is just one great big boy's story with the very greenest of covers, but maybe you like boy stories. Otherwise you may feel perturbed at the anarchy it so viciously recommends. The police and the courts are brought into contempt and a species of trial is excused in which the captives are lowered into rat pits and confessions are wrung by torture. There was one film the censor refused to pass because it was a 'blue print for revolution'. This is a blue print for mob action, which no youngster who sees it is likely to forget.

How desperate the situation must be when direct action can be so glibly extolled. And how derelict the situation must be if mob law by children can be seriously represented as an aid to good government. *This Day and Age* performs its cheap and impossible miracle as Gabriel did before it. Other things having failed, who knows what dictatorial president calling on the Lord, or dictatorial youth calling on any messy species of idealism, will not turn the trick? One silly solution is as good as another so long as DeMille and his fellow hicks can deafen their mind in drum taps. Who knows: when the lesson has been driven home even more (to lynch and march, and march and lynch, and wear uniforms and sing songs and in general go Nazi) the boys and girls who hike and bicycle to nowhere will presently be lowering us all into rat pits: just as blindly, childishly, perversely and viciously: with just as little sense of the realities to follow as the boys and girls in the film.

(New Britain, 4 October 1933)

In last week's description of *This Day and Age* and *The Song of Songs* I had in mind to discourse on the psychology of the unendurable. I found them maddeningly difficult to sit through. I now find it difficult to understand why I not only sat through Ronald Colman's *Masquerader,* but even comfortably did so. The psychology of the unendurable may indeed be an even more interesting study than the other, and the disarming of criticism the most diabolical of arts. Certain sure I am that *The Masquerader,* for all its simple wiles, is nothing much to write about.

I have noted before this quality in Colman. He does nothing much: just decently smokes, decently drinks, decently enters into female juxtaposition, and decently solves the decent and ordinary problems of life. Nothing much, but that very consistently, continuously and without bother. I wonder if this may not be so unusual in the atmosphere of films that one is secretly grateful for it.

I noticed with great interest at the Tatler last week the different methods of attack adopted by the films in the programme. *The Gaumont Mirror* had a flashy and even brilliant account of rubber-tyre manufacture. It did not waste a split second in the swift career of its camera among the various processes. But I could not remember after it was done how rubber tyres were made, nor felt certain if I knew any more about the people who made them than I did at the beginning. I had a similar feeling about the *Mickey Mouse.* It was just a speedy fuss of episode on episode, dance on dance, storming the attention but never claiming it. Perhaps it was afraid, as the *Mirror* certainly was, of claiming attention. It did not seem to be sure enough of its inspiration to command patience.

Once I had a letter on the subject from Catherine Carswell. You are all in a hurry, she said in effect: cinema is in a hurry, and cannot be art till it ceases to be. In the Tatler programme, as if to demonstrate her case, was Basil Wright's *Windmill in Barbados.* It is a leisurely film with a leisurely theme. The windmills of old Barbados turn; the life they represent is as slow and quiet and complacent and patient as themselves; into this Eden comes machinery, speeding up the life about it, bringing steam engines, cranes, factories, hurry and impatience. Wright's film is long, and too long. It smacks esoteric lips over fine photography, slow pans, repetitions of revolving sails; and makes the audience wait till Wright and his windmills have enjoyed themselves. But it sinks in. You would not easily forget the Barbados atmosphere it conveys. I do not defend its length or its measure: I merely note it as representing a manner of approach which is strange, and even alien, to the present spirit of cinema.

Colman has this lost quality. His bearing is unhurried; his gestures are understated; his stories, romantic as they are, studiously avoid sensation. In *The Masquerader (John Chilcote, M.P.)*, he impersonates a Member of Parliament (playing both parts), takes his place in the House and Party, falls in love with his wife, and makes only a quiet affair of this headline scandal. Even the delirium tremens of his other rôle is done quietly, with only the vaguest suggestion of the pink rats and sea-green creepers a more vivid interpretation of the situation would have insisted on. A harmless tale, and not important, with a speech in Parliament which must be the most idiotic piece of political nonsense ever penned or spoken: but none the less very endurable. Accustomed as the cinema makes me to spectacular scenes and sensational embarrassments, I was glad to find that one single quiet presence, consistently despectacled and de-sensationalized, the obvious occasions for both. I almost wish we might have a cycle of dull and decent films for a change. It may even be that dullness and decency are the breath of art, for the greater quietness and the more patient observation they imply.

(New Britain, 11 October 1933)

In *Turn Back the Clock* Lee Tracy is his tough, wisecracking, unmodulated self, and this is good measure at any time: but his new story has an originality of its own. It switches him from life as a meagre post-War counter clerk to the life he thinks he should have lived.

The trick is old, but it has the additional interest this time of making the hero re-live the War and re-live it with the knowledge of what is to come. In the result, Tracy is an odd mixture of go-getting and prophecy, and not nearly so exciting a figure as he might have been. It may be fitting for the counter-clerk figure he really is that his dream should concern itself so much with the petty personal triumphs which are represented in invitations to Washington and the salting away of 'Grands'; but there is no special point in drawing cosmic (creative) attention to the fact. Only the shape of the story is original: the conclusions are not. With such an opportunity Tracy could be made any sort of prophet, yet I doubt if in this case he is half so significant a figure as he was in the conscientious objection of *Private Jones*. There is some slight indication of the fact that others think him crazy. With knowledge of the future, what a splendid lunatic he might have been made.

In all such stories there is a moral. The moral in this one is that Tracy could not have done better than pursue his meagre life as a counter-clerk and marry a good little girl of his original choice. And why? Because he found in his dream that flashy wives are unfaithful and that big money is doomed to disappear in the financial crash. With these insignificant arguments the film concludes. Ben Hecht, who wrote the scenario, was once one of the most promising writers in America. His *Thousand and One Nights in Chicago*, as they came out in the *Chicago Daily News*, were probably the finest flashes of human description that ever appeared in a newspaper. Nothing then seemed too high for Hecht to reach. Then he went to Hollywood, and this is it. His scenario is smart and able and goes trippingly on the brain — but what of it?

You may have noticed recently in this connection a great spate of alibis from the number-one picture people. DeMille had an article in the *Daily Herald* saying: 'If I were to turn out a film which would appeal only to a small community, and which could be hung with all kinds of esoteric 'arty' phrases, you may be sure it would be labelled an 'artistic'. But for a film to appeal to all classes and grades: to doctors, mechanics, storekeepers, policemen, statesmen — *that is true art*. . . . the day of the million-dollar spectacle film has arrived. . . . the public are the ultimate arbiters of the question. . . .' And B. P. Schulberg is even cheekier in the *Daily Film Renter*, for he blatantly denies the description of art to anything but the beastly box-office successes he stands for. And our own Victor Saville, who knows better, joins the gladsome circle on the occasion of his new contract, and lets himself in for the same implication. The end of the cinema is to be financially successful and loyalty to the shareholders is the crown of directorial wisdom: the *corona sapentiae* which used to be, in the old days, so much something else.

As they say, cinema is an entertainment business: and no one will complain if they make their entertainment snappy and hot, and sell it for all they can get. Nor even, if following Ford and Woolworth, they go for that highest common factor, or lowest common multiple, or whatever mean of dramatic want it is that turns sentimentoromanticism into a blithering success. Let them follow their trade as good showmen and good business men if they like. All that is wrong is their tendency to confuse their pay-rôle with aesthetic leadership. They are two very different birds; and, if you follow the authority of Leonardo, you will believe that even the air they fly in is different.

Let us be thankful on occasion for the 'pallid youths and esoteric phrases', for the 'claptrap jargon of montage and rhythmic tempo' which, according to DeMille, 'miss the whole point of cinema'. They only miss the point of DeMille cinema; for, to my certain knowledge, they are not looking for it. A great deal of half-baked rubbish is talked in the name of montage. God knows: but, in the last analysis, these esoteric phrases represent another world of discourse: in which the cinema is expected to be visually beautiful in the same high sense that a Cézanne is visually beautiful. If Cézanne is not to be measured by the size of his public (and who would suggest it?) why should this other cinema of which the young men so esoterically dream? DeMille may save his curses. The only moment of contact between his million-dollar spectacle and the critics in question is the moment in which they refuse it their own particular brand of importance. What, on Cézanne levels, does DeMille ever want to give them? His right to define true 'art' — and the right of all time-serving producers, authors, directors, and critics, however able and however successful — is to be determined accordingly. It is business success they are talking about, not art: let there be no confusion about *that*. In the meantime, blessed are the pallid youths and esoteric phrases. If they do not sufficiently describe the higher aspects of visual beauty, they at least have the urge toward that beauty.

(*New Britain*, 27 September 1933)

13 · From Para Handy to Picasso

Para Handy is, of course, one of the great Scottish folk tales—with that little puffer, the *Vital Spark*, and her alcoholic Highland crew belting their way up and down the Clyde, and all the way to Ullapool and Ireland itself, you remember—you have a sort of Odyssey of the little men, with Para Handy as Odysseus: an Odyssey of the common man with all his prides and all his humours, wandering through the little places and getting a terrific bash out of life wherever he goes. That hard bitten crew know every trick of survival.

Where its appeal lies—and especially today—is that it is the epic of the non-metropolitan, and a reminder that life is life and the same life wherever it is, and that you don't have to go to London—no, nor even Edinburgh—to get the excitement. It's a tale that crops up a lot in the Scottish mind and, of course, in Scottish writing. You get it with Linklater in *Laxdale Hall*. You get it with Compton Mackenzie in *Whisky Galore!* And one of the interesting things to me is that it is so basic in its appeal to our Scottish minds that we get to thinking that all the stories in the tradition belong to us personally. I am quite possessive about them. I went to see *Whisky Galore!* with my brother and I'm blessed if we didn't quarrel furiously afterwards as to who had invented it. We forgot all about Mackenzie. We thought it was us. When I produced *Laxdale Hall* there was the same curious illusion. I had, of course, to show it to Linklater but I found myself wondering what the devil he was doing there.

That to me is a kind of clue to the television version of Para Handy. It is a belonging to all of us. Some people have been saying they are a bit disappointed and I know what they mean; but here is the first show in a series and a long way to go—and happily, more time for the actors to get into their parts, more time to take over the *Vital Spark* properly and get the feeling of belting it out in the Western Seas, more time to take to that merry and dishevelled and wandering life of the MacFarlanes and the McPhails, not to mention the McLauchlans. For if Para Handy is as basic as I think it is, then it's like whisky. It can be good—it can be not so good—but it can't be bad.

First of all, I liked Duncan Ross's script very much indeed. The odd thing to say is that the actors didn't seem—didn't seem yet—to be quite up to it. I remember watching Chaplin get into his baggy trousers and shuffle around for an hour or more till he got into his part again. This lot didn't seem to have shuffled enough. And I think I know the reason. They hadn't nearly enough time to rehearse. So what did we get? We got a bunch of skilled actors using their trained dramatic tricks, but not yet out and away from the theatre and the theatricals, out and away to the miracle world of Para Handy where you have only to drop a hook or nose the bow into a Highland pier and everything happens to you. You get a sense of the actors actually stifling the script. There's nothing much to worry about. It'll come, but it will need a lot of work. The only thing I'm afraid of is the influence of London. There's always the fear that being very intimately Scots, we speak ourselves out of the English theatre; and we know, of course, the sad experiences of James Bridie and Tommy Lorne, and of Duncan Macrae himself on one occasion. But against that you have the fact that the more the French have been French in their films the more universal their appeal has been. Rossellini was explaining this to me only last week. In other words, do not compromise with London or the *Vital Spark* will be out and the smartest craft in the trade sunk without trace.

Finally, about the actors. I think Roddy McMillan is going to make a perfect Dougie. Sunny Jim, which is a difficult part, is most promising with Angus Lennie, and I liked Douglas Murchie as Archie, or is it Erchie? What bothered me was that Duncan Macrae has the biggest job of all to do if he is going to get into his part. He's a grand person and in my view one of the great Scots comedians of my time; but he has built an image of himself which — whatever it is — just isn't Para Handy. I had a sense that he was talking in three accents and it was a bit troubling to have him come off the boat speaking, I will swear, in pure Kelvinside. Above all, Para Handy has to be a very lovable character and not high hat at all. I confess the prospect of Duncan Macrae playing perpetually Duncan Macrae's very false image of Duncan Macrae isn't anything I look forward to. I wish he'd stop being the big actor. I wish he'd follow his own God-given genius and get back to the much subtler art of just giving us the fun of life. In fact, the whole point about Para Handy is that its one great thesis is — not being big but maybe a lot of nonsense, and the pride of the little people is in making a splendid affair of being little.

(*Arts Review*, B.B.C. Scotland, 17 December 1959)

I must declare my interests on this film, *Rockets Galore!* It is yet again the old Scottish joke about how the little people of the Highlands bewitch and bewilder the Englishmen who come amongst them and try to control them for one reason or another. There was *Whisky Galore!* to begin with. This time they got a lot of whisky and the English Customs men tried to get it. In *The Maggie* it was an American who tried to exploit the crew of the never to be forgotten *Para Handy*. In *Laxdale Hall* it was a commission from Whitehall trying to put down a revolt of the good people of Applecross because they wouldn't pay their taxes. Now I produced that one and I think it was very funny but, so to speak, I know the script by heart.

It's the same script in every case and the same joke. Be sure the islanders will be very cunning. Be sure the Englishmen will be very sentimental. Be sure there will be a Highland school teacher or something, very beautiful, whom the English gent will fall for and give you your love interest. Be sure there will be the moment when some excellent actor from the West End of London will say: 'I never knew it before but, you know, the peace of the Islands—I've come to love Toddy'—and he's away into a clinch with the usual redhead. My one, the best of the beauties, was Katie O'Brien who could out-drink the entire cast of *Whisky Galore!* at a sitting.

Rockets Galore! is about *Whisky Galore!*, about *The Maggie*, about *Laxdale Hall* and about the island of Toddy or Barra doing the English Sassenach in the eye. It is by our old Highland chieftain, that hard-working old monarch of the glen, Compton Mackenzie. He is concerned with the rocket range that was threatened to Barra. He says, like they said at Verdun: the Sassenach shall not pass. And they don't. They paint the sea-gulls pink and all the bird-watchers of the world—English, Russian and Armenian, Krushchev and Dulles —join together with the Highlanders to preserve their island, not for the sake of humanity or anything silly like that, but for the sake of pink sea-gulls.

I liked the film very much, and if Sir Compton will permit me, I think it is a lot better than his book. It has a script by Danischewsky, who is a central European with the comic genius of Sholem Aleichem behind him, and if you add Jewish humour to Highland humour it improves it immensely. The Jews at least know what it is to be a down-trodden people. The Highlanders and Compton Mackenzie only talk about it.

Now I'm not going to say which is the best of the lot, though I half suspect it was *Laxdale Hall*, because Roddy McMillan was terrific in it, without saying a word, as the inarticulate, half-daft undertaker whose hearse broke down at the right places. I follow my brother in these matters. We went to see *Whisky Galore!* together, and he was very silent at the end. He said: 'This is personal, let's get rid of our women and go have a drink.' And we did. And he said: 'You know you and I wrote this story long ago and you let Compton Mackenzie get away with it.' And it was true in an odd way, because I brought the *Idomeneus* into Vatersay Bay in the First World War and the Navy was tight for a couple of weeks. Then when *The Maggie* came along he stormed into my place and said: 'You call yourself a film producer and you didn't make *The Maggie*.' He was very angry and again because he thought it was our joke together—and so it was, from our youth in the Western Highlands. So I had to make *Laxdale Hall*, just to keep my place in the family.

Now there's this one. It's like a Western to me. I know all the conventions. I know it is unreal and out of this world. I know everyone will say it is outlandish and exaggerated and whatnot. But I loved the whole thing as ever—because of the mad thought in it that the meek can inherit the earth. I don't think the Highlander could fight for toffee, except in his own most material interests, but I like the dream, so dear to Scotsmen, that he might.

Frankly, I don't think the Englishmen are so poor this time as they were with Ronald Squire and Raymond Huntly. But all the usual Scotsmen are on deck, including Jameson Clark and Duncan Macrae, and they have played the part so often it's like *The Covered Wagon*. But the star of the picture, to me, is Danischewsky of *Passport to Pimlico*. He has improved on Mackenzie and again made a wonderful sport of making asses of the Englishmen.

My rating now is: 1. *Whisky Galore!* 2. *The Maggie*. 3. *Rockets Galore!*, but I still think Eric Linklater's *Laxdale Hall*, with Roddy McMillan, is fit for the company.

(*Arts Review*, B.B.C. Scotland, 6 November 1958)

If there are any fans of John Buchan's still surviving I hope I won't disturb them in their Bath chairs by saying that in *The 39 Steps* there is nothing of the old boy left—except the title. In fact, the new film seems to have followed that odd weird procedure established by Alfred Hitchcock when he made the last version. He confessed cheerfully that he hadn't even read the book.

Now that is a great pity. The original story was pretty naïve in its way—a sort of comic strip of the thriller. It was wild with impossible coincidence: it was sometimes so simpleton in its devices and difficulties that you would think there wasn't a telephone in the country. Any small boy today brought up on the comic strips would have solved half of Richard Hannay's difficulties on his ear. But it did move along at a fast clip—and it used short words very attractively, and surprisingly too because Buchan was a big-word type in everything else he did. But that wasn't all. It had atmosphere—the atmosphere of the impending First World War with Germany and of the desperate efforts of desperate men to get the dispositions of the British Fleet on mobilization. In the background was a big affair and a sense of it. It was big and sinister as in *The Riddle of the Sands*, which I think is still the best of them all. This, of course, was very important from a story-telling point of view. Even Richard Hannay at his silliest was touched by the grandeur of the big affair in the offing. The new film has none of this sense of impending world event and the result is a lightweight lark in spying and counter-spying which is often on the edge of farce — at times a very happy farce, but never likely to put you into a cold sweat.

I see no great harm in the picture as a piece of light entertainment; but I don't think anyone is going to nominate it as a masterpiece of the year. You roll along lightheartedly with the lighthearted Kenneth More, never quite taking his murders and his conspiracies very seriously. Even his sensational escape from the moving train on the Forth Bridge doesn't make you gasp, because you are no more seriously engaged than he is. I don't think it is a failure of casting, but a failure in laying down the necessary premises for a big thriller. This lighthearted approach — if that is what you want — is very richly aided by Brenda de Banzie as a sex-mad old crystal gazer running a small Highland hotel. She is, of course, excellent stuff, and so is Reginald Beckwith as her poor cuckold husband. I never saw him better. And when you have a good-looking young woman called Taina Elg attached to More by handcuffs and having to spend the night with him — on a bed (because he is tired forsooth) — the alien menace to our island home is well forgotten in the arch and gamey innuendoes of the situation.

As I say, it is a lightweight: it is a gay, happy-go-lucky frolic and everybody but the Buchan fans will enjoy it up to a point; but, save in odd spots, it lacks intensity of interest. It fails mostly to conjure up the unique power of the cinema to give intensity, and it just isn't a great spy film.

(*Arts Review*, B.B.C. Scotland, 25 March 1959)

The Old Man and the Sea is, of course, the long delayed Hemingway novel, turned into a colour film by John Sturgess. A lot of production trouble about it somewhere. It is about an old fisherman who catches the great fish of his dreams and fights it for three days and three nights. Yes, he kills the great Marlin but the sharks come and rob him in the end. It is a parable, just as *Moby Dick* was a parable. The great fish this time isn't the spirit of evil as Moby Dick was. It is, I think, the symbol of man's everlasting search for manhood: the old man is old and, if he just makes it, it is a sort of last sad effort. So really in the end it is about old age weakening and lonely—what Hemingway thinks is the tragedy of no longer being young and violent and sexual and strong.

That's to say, it is Hemingway romantic as ever, trying to proclaim that a man is a man is a man; and, of course, that is fine too, just as you find it among the Zulus and the Maoris and the American Westerns—and the cartoons of Superman. Julian Grenfell once made a good poem about it. 'He is dead who will not fight; and who dies fighting has increase.' It is a fine healthy viewpoint, but also primitive: a bit too muscular and, though I think Hemingway writes like a prince and a hunk of walnut, not very deep. 'I hate you and I love you,' says the old man to the fish. It can even get sentimental.

Now the critical thing about this film is that it isn't about the Zulus and it isn't a Western. It hasn't the scale. It is about one old man in one small boat, muttering away to himself Hemingway's romantic philosophy of life—and he mutters for a long time—and there are no horses to bring on, no rides to the rescue. Nothing visually splendid to liven up the theme and stack it against the sky. In fact, it is a somewhat monotonous and certainly disappointing film, because it just doesn't transfer to the screen the honours and nobilities of fighting manhood which Hemingway certainly can bring alive with his words.

I find the visual side of the film not even good for a travelogue. It concentrates on the mere action of a man catching a fish. It isn't enough to give lift to a theme essentially poetic.

Then again the film very rightly makes much of the small boy growing up who reveres the old man. It should have helped greatly to emphasize the theme of weakening lonely old age, adding to the wistfulness, showing that youth like nature itself will go on and on, completing with hope the circle of Hemingway's thought. But the boy is so badly conceived and so badly directed that he is just a horrible little boy who lifts up your heart nowhere.

This picture was made at great cost, I think foolish cost, with the thought that it was a big box-office proposition. It ought to have been made by a poet who didn't care a damn about the box office and who believed that the sun and the wind and the sky and the old man and the sea were everything. It wasn't. The ironic thing is it isn't going to make much money after all.

(*Arts Review*, B.B.C. Scotland, 28 August 1958)

I think this *Titanic* film, *A Night to Remember*, is the most ambitious production we've had from England since Alex. Korda and Gabby

Pascal were around. It's full of what the pros like to call production value. Huge and splendid sets of the great luxury liner going to her doom, inside and out. Hundreds of good actors: it's like a roster of the rep. players of the West End and Dublin and Belfast, and I even saw our own Andrew Keir bashing about in the engine room awash. Yes, and all the models of the great ship in the wilderness of sea and ice and the terrible irony of the star-lit sky above. But the models are not so good—stilted and lifeless. Compensation, however, again by remarkable excursions into what went on below deck when the dear dashing unsinkable started diving by the head and the furniture of the impossibly rich and the crockery went crashing and everything that could come unshipped came loose and bashed their own little worlds of security to smithereens. A survivor said that 'A steady roar thundered across the water.' Earl St John should be proud of his production, as a technical production. So let us pay this initial tribute to the size and wealth of the spectacle as a spectacle.

The trouble with the *Titanic* is that however you slice it up for an epic it is basically a foul story—one of the foulest in the history of the sea: a foul story like, say, Passchendale, where the incompetence, the stupidities, were so enormous as not to be glossed over or forgiven even now. A foul story because a hundred honours came unstuck; bravery and sacrifice ceased to be qualities you had, the illusion went with the privileges of position and power and wealth. On the *Titanic* the upper class of that period demonstrated that it was by and large rotten. In the surviving boats, in the presence of so much death, they bickered and they fought abominably, and only one boat, No. 14 under 5th Officer Lowe, had the guts to go back to answer the cries of 1,600 drowning men and women. Oh, yes, there were heroes and the Straus's and the Guggenheims of the *Titanic*, they will always be remembered with honour.

But what was the real story? Women of the First Class, only 4 were lost and 3 of them by choice, out of 143. Second Class, 15 lost out of 93. Steerage—and this is it: 81 women were lost out of 179. Children, all First and Second Class saved. Steerage, only 23 were saved out of 76, with the chairman of the White Star Line Ismay and a hundred other bums in the boats. For all you hear about the courage in the boats and all this film so soothingly says, here is the truth. Except for No. 14 they stood off and refused to go back. The boats were 65-passenger jobs. No. 5 had 40. No. 2 had 60 per cent full. No. 6, capacity 65, had 28 and so on. Of 1,600 people who went down—that is to say, when the *Titanic* dived—only 13 were picked up by the half empty boats moving around. And the sailors aboard couldn't sail, or in many cases couldn't even row.

Now an English film, such is the established tradition of English films, couldn't possibly tell this dreadful tale. I don't know why. Perhaps the cinema of Eisenstein could—I don't know. What the writer Eric Ambler, working closely to Walter Lord's book, and the director Roy Baker have done, and done very well, is to make a spectacular best of the bad, bad job in human crisis but noting, as they honestly have, this ignominity of the story, they have shied away from it and have not penetrated it. Straus and Guggenheim shine splendidly, so does Andrews who built the ship and was a man of quality. But Captain Smith, who dismissed six ice warnings and lost control of the port side, is idealized. I think too they could have done better by the unsinkable Mrs Brown in boat No. 6. She too was a millionaire, but by her own hands and character out of the prospecting West; but when it came to the pinch the old powers and the language too broke loose again. The film tends to make her a bit of a trollop from Brooklyn. She just wasn't. And when she died a few years ago she was still the Queen of Denver and messages came in from all over the world. I sent one myself.

On the other hand the film is excellent on old Dr O'Loughlin who repaired to his pantry at the last as the only place an old drinking Doctor could decently die in. That's Joe Tomelty—a wonderful piece of casting. And the film is quite brilliant with Joughin, the miraculous baker who filled himself up with liquor, worked like a madman doing all the odd things the officers had forgotten, tanked himself up again, walked off the final disappearing stern into the ice-cold water and lived through the night, believe it or not, happily hanging on to an upturned collapsible, as the French say, *tout à fait impermeable*. He is honoured remarkably by the playing of David Rose. There is so much good stuff in this film and the bit playing so good generally that poor Kenneth More can't be much of a star as the Second Mate Lightoller. Perhaps as well. The only star in the Atlantic that night was probably Captain Rostron of the *Carpathia*. For sheer efficiency and inspired seamanship he stands out for a wonder in contrast and I wish the film had followed his side to the rescue more powerfully than it did.

But of course the real dramatic issue was the social one, the one the film-makers have noted but have not dared to penetrate. The upper classes to the boats, the poor down below forbidden to join their betters even in death. In one blinding episode the world witnessed the other dirty side of the Edwardian illusion with its arrogance of wealth and its horrible conspicuous waste. That other side, like the symbolic iceberg which destroyed it—one-ninth above and eight-ninths below, which in fact ripped the ship to pieces. It was a night to remember all right for, thank God, England never felt the same again about its so-called betters, not ever again. The rockets that went up unanswered by the *Californian* went up unanswered for a class system that was on its way out. The forgotten underworld of the iceberg did its symbolic part.

But I sometimes think the sleeping unanswering figure of Captain Lord in his bunk below in the *Californian* was the most symbolic figure of them all—a sort of sleeping clergyman—in that anything but Greek tragedy, not Greek because in the essence there was nothing noble to weep over.

(*Arts Review*, B.B.C. Scotland, 10 August 1958)

I found it one of the great privileges of my life to be present with Picasso drawing and painting *ad infinitum*. To see a great master at work—to see his mind move—is surely a compensation for all the mediocrity of life, and one's own in particular.

I have been lucky. I watched old Bernard Shaw once for an afternoon. He wasn't at his more youthful best. He was very arrogant and said he could talk about anything under the sun—which he certainly could. I told him to talk about the microphone in front of him and so he did, brilliantly. I had to say to him at one point, because I was directing the film, 'Mr Shaw, I hope you don't mind, but if you mind your business, I'll mind mine.' 'Quite right, young man,' said old Shaw—but he was old and incontinent and a fuss-pot—and brilliant.

I once got a telephone call from another old man—another great old man whom I worship still this side of idolatry. He was H. G. Wells. He said he was bored and unhappy and would I come along immediately to cheer him up. When I got there the old boy in his squeaky voice said: 'I can't get an angle, I can't get an angle. I've been walking this room for hours and I can't get an angle.' And I thought, by golly if it's difficult for H.G. to get an angle, how much more must we all walk, poor devils. And that's the way I think it is.

I used to know a man in a pub in Paris—we talked painting and everything else. One day he asked me what was my name and I said 'Grierson' in my best voluble bad French and he said: 'Moi, je suis Derain' and if I remember I fell off the stool.

It is great to meet great artists and that is all there is to this film of meeting Picasso [*The Picasso Mystery*]. You meet one of the greatest artists of all time. He draws for you and even now, old and past as he is, it is wonderful to see. He is over seventy. He isn't what he was, and who could be, except wicked old miracles like Father Karamazov and Titian. You are seeing an old man like Shaw, incontinent in his skill and memory of skills. The description of maturity isn't there.

He is terribly good when he is abstract but, in nine examples out of ten, he is better at the beginning than he is at the end. That is what happens I suppose in old age. I think in this film we have a complete revelation of what may always be great in Picasso—and also what was always weak.

I think myself he is the greatest line drawer since Leonardo and Cranach. He is delicate exceedingly with values unbelievable in line alone. But I don't think he was ever very good dramatically and that is surprising in a Spaniard. He keeps on thinking of bull fights but finishes up inevitably in the chill coldness of a skeleton. He keeps on thinking of Don Quixote and Sancho Panza and Rosinante and Dulcinea del Toboso and never falls in love with any of them.

Picasso is a cold man, the finest, coldest, most classical man in painting we have had in our time. A sort of Bertrand Russell of a painter. What a privilege it is to have seen him work—what a privilege it is to have seen him so intimately as this film allows! He is old certainly and the light is going out—but to have seen the great even in the glimpses of a thunderstorm is to see something you fear you will never see again.

This isn't a film. It's no good as a film. It is an experience.

(*Arts Review*, B.B.C. Scotland, 21 May 1958)

14 · Robert Flaherty

I first met Robert Flaherty around 1925. He had just come back from British Samoa with *Moana*, and he was having the difficulties he was always to have in the last stages of production. In this case it was Paramount that did not see it his way. There was talk of a grass-skirted dancing troupe at the Rialto on Broadway and a marquee offering of The Love Life of a South Sea Siren.

I was doing an extra column at the time for the New York *Sun*, in which I was supposed to be a bit more highbrow than Cohen, the ranking film editor, and the sort of odd body who looked after the lost causes, including, as I remember, most of the people who happened to be good. I took Flaherty's case like a sort of critical attorney. Off and on, and not without the strains and stresses that go with such a relationship, I have been his critical attorney ever since.

He was at times as difficult with his admirers as he was with his commercial collaborators. Yet I will say in the end that, not in spite of but because of all difficulty, he was a great man to know. His troubles came out of a man's relationship with his art: out of his deep inner revolt against all the conditions which modern life was imposing on the artist — not least so in the complicated and expensive world of film-making. He, so to speak, carried with him always the burden of the individual and personal artist in a world — and a medium — growing ever more impersonal. He hankered after, and often bulldozed his way to getting, a species of freedom — with art, with money — that only the anarchists any more allowed for in their theories. In all, and never frivolously, he was born to be troubled.

Yet the crazy thing about Flaherty was that he could never see the logic of his rôle or why it should always be painful. He was a conservative who deplored the implication of being actually a revolutionary. It was a pity that inevitably, on this paradox, he could never meet his brethren; for he was an enormously friendly man and you might almost say built in physique and heart for friendship. He was big, wide-shouldered, and handsome, with the sort of face and forehead you carve a hundred feet high on rocks. He had the blue, clear eyes of the sailor and the explorer. With it all went a sort of boyish innocence of expression, and enjoyment that invested his hospitality with a spontaneity and his conversation with an inquiring eagerness which made him one of the richest men to knock around with in a generation. It is curious now to think that while his films reflected all his innate grace and gentleness of taste, not one of them ever reflected his uproarious power of drinking joyfully into the night, or his quite unusual command over narrative on these more ebullient occasions. For he was a story teller in a million.

The fact was that Flaherty had not been brought up in the metropolitan world in which he was finally compelled to operate. He was born in Michigan of an Irish father and a German mother, but went to school and grew up in Canada. By and large, the best part of his life was spent so close to the far frontiers of Britain's Empire that he absorbed unconsciously, not the technological traditions of the United States, but the Victorian, or at the latest Edwardian, traditions of a nation and a period in which the highly personal command over far places and the paternal privilege over distant peoples went with a precise sense of the graces that wealth could bring to the personal life.

It was a world in which, at the least, no one ever grew sick for the lack of leisure or of understanding how to use it. Indeed, Flaherty was a lost soul in the United States, save perhaps in the near English atmosphere of the Coffee House Club; and he was never more comfortable in London than in the red-plush, marble-tabled Café Royal, which the exquisites of the mauve decade had left behind.

How deeply and how often I had come up against the problems he created in our very different midst; for one came to adopt an almost passionate care in preserving this lost child of the arts in his once fashionable illusions. This exponent of real life had, it seemed, to be preserved from even the proximity of reality; and no one could be more damnably hurt by the different viewpoint which brought in for him a world he could not accept and could not live in.

I think it was true to say that Flaherty lived for two years in Samoa in genuine illusion that he was near to the earthly paradise; yet six months after he left a commission from New Zealand was sent to clear up a situation in the islands that was, to say the least, not exactly salubrious. Similarly, the Men of Aran turned out to be not just simple innocents against the sea, but tough and even sophisticated characters—alongside Flaherty—with an excellent sense of their worth and in one or two cases an intimate working knowledge of his own America which he would never learn in a lifetime. When he made *Industrial Britain* with me, his flair for the old crafts and the old craftsmen was superb, and there will never be shooting of that kind to compare with it; but he could not simply bend to the conception of those other species of craftsmanship which go with modern industry and modern organization.

Yet, in one film he did face up to the modern facts of life, but only, I think, after the hard schooling of six years with us in England. He returned in 1939 to America to make *The Land* with Pare Lorentz. The spirit of F.D.R. was over the nation but, more particularly, there was in the White House a regime of personal patronage of the arts, the flavour — strange and finally distasteful in America — of the Medici. Even at a distance, Flaherty had found a squirearchic environment to which he was attuned. I never knew a man more excited; from all over the continent and at all hours he would telephone to tell an old radical like myself how — and you would think it was for the first time on earth — he had discovered this poverty and that. The little Negro boy shelling peas in his sleep was a moment in Flaherty's education like the bursting of a bomb; and with it went the first fine careless rapture — surely unique for an American in 1939 — of discovering the efficiency of the machine. Among other things, it was his quite personal discovery that it could do away with poverty.

I personally regard Robert Flaherty as one of the five great innovators in the history of film. I think that with him go Méliès, the first of the movie magicians; D. W. Griffith, for developing the strictly movie terms in which a drama could be unfolded; Sennett, for transferring comedy from the limited space and conventional props of circus and vaudeville to the infinite variety of the world about; and Eisenstein for his study of organized mass and movement and his great sense of film's potential in both physical and mental impact. Flaherty, great personal story teller as he was, did not especially think of film as a way of telling a story, developing a drama and creating an impact, either physical or mental. For him, the camera was veritably a wonder eye, to see with more remarkably than one ordinarily saw.

It never occurred to him that a shot should be foreseen, and when we came later, because of the expense of the thing, to work out everything beforehand as best we could, there was something in Flaherty that instinctively revolted. Some have said it was indolence, or disorder, or even a will to waste in him, but I will say it was nothing of the kind. For Flaherty, it wasn't what he thought or saw which was important, but what the camera revealed to him.

Whence the infinite and infinitely patient experiments with movement; whence, incidentally, his pioneering work — not nearly sufficiently recognized — with panchromatic film, with filters, with telescopic lenses, with keys in black and white to make a graciousness of the greys, with shooting at hours of the day, and under conditions of light, that the orthodox discarded. No one ever, or so significantly, studied his rushes so closely. Rushes were not the result for Flaherty, but the beginning: the moment of revelation. Expensive? Yes, it was. But the reason for it was as I have said, not otherwise. If paper had been as expensive as film, they would have said the same of Flaubert.

On one level the camera was for Flaherty an extraordinarily convenient way of recording one's reminiscences; and reminiscences meant for him what they once meant for Boswell: the test of a man's penetration and of his capacity for life. It meant, moreover, an extension of horizons for everyone, the backwall of the proscenium cut out and a window on the world. He loved to emphasize the mobility of the camera, and he was, to the end, a man impatient and even angry with the great heavy contraptions which not only needed a team of men to handle them but put half a dozen other pairs of eyes between Flaherty and the object.

It was with a hand camera, the Newman Sinclair, that all his work was associated. With this lightweight affair, one had the notion of a camera as a highly personal instrument, like a pen or a brush; and in nothing did Flaherty depart so considerably and perhaps importantly from the studio conception. Take this personal contact away, for whatever purpose and by whatever means, and Flaherty was lost, as he was on *Elephant Boy*, *Tabu* and *White Shadows*. 'My God,' he would say of *White Shadows*, 'you should have seen them on their knees, in the South Sea Islands, trying to tune in the Coconut Grove.'

It may not seem so on what I have said but, behind the explorative and modest and near-mystical belief in the camera's power of sight, there was, of course, a basic pattern in his observation. His long early years in the Far North had given him a special affection for primitive peoples and an intimacy with nature and man in his relationship with nature which showed always in his clear blue eyes, and, in the pinches of more complex argument, never left him.

His first instinctive revolt against movies—and I think nearly all movies—was that the story was imposed on the background and did not come from within. He was shocked when Hollywood, following up *Nanook*, made a film on the Arctic with a phoney Eskimo girl and a love story which had nothing to do with the Eskimo's normal and very proper appreciation of polygamy. Flaherty was no theorist and tended, like so many, to fit the theories afterward to the facts. He faked a bit like all of us, and a little more so after they whipped him in Hollywood with the charge that he had no sense of box office, but he had a genuine passion for the genuine.

When he talked of the difference between a hunter throwing a spear and John Barrymore impaling a rubber shark with his profile, he had something which the camera, if no one else, understood with him. When he discoursed, after reading my piece on the subject, on the 'movement of craftsmen and priests that time had worn smooth', be sure it was not I that had done the shooting to deserve the theory but Bob himself who was the only begetter. He was too dramatically precise for his day when Nanook didn't make any fuss at all as he came out of the blizzard and found the shelter of his igloo, or when anyone, more or less, had a pleasant Polynesian Sunday afternoon flaying poor Moana in the big tattoo. He stayed where people were, and if he did not impose greatly upon them, except to gentle everything he saw of them, it was again, as with the camera, in the modesty that forever the Almighty was a considerable artist and that you had only to look on His works, under and under, and you couldn't miss.

It is a point of view shared by Wordsworth in some of the best, as well as in some of the most naïve, of his works. It is a point of view shared at the present time by many of the younger colonial peoples, and you could pick it up easily in Canada, for example. It is not exactly fashionable these days among European artists and metropolitans generally, but this is to be said for it. Flaherty returned us to the origins of all observation: where the seasons are, where flowers not only grow but are worn in the hair; where people take, or fight for, the fruits of the earth, and dine well and pour a ceremonial libation on the ground to the gods and dance in thanksgiving; where the difference between a man and an animal of the wild is only one of degree; where storms come and go and are merely a great spectacle in their passing, and children are forever the assurance that time is timeless, and the horizon, finally, without too much pain.

Perhaps he was over in love with the merely decorative, and nothing on earth, for example, would keep him from putting his most staggering shots at the opening of his films. He made it possible for the less sympathetic to say of them that it was all packed away at the beginning, with nothing thereafter deeply to emerge. But something there always was, even if it did not come in the classical cathartic terms. He thought, for instance, that the opening of a flower was a sufficiently dramatic sequence in itself; but he was in fact better than that. The day fulfilled itself to the last shadow; people rested after the burden of the day; there was always a nice sense of the world tucking its head under its wing for an inevitable sunrise.

The child motif was constant. The boys in *Moana*, *Aran*, *Elephant Boy* and *Louisiana Story*, the bullfighting boy whom Orson Welles took over, and the Hudson Bay and coal-mining boys he never made represented an essential to him. Some chose to say it was the boy Flaherty that never grew up, the admiring son of a remarkable father, or again that it was the son Flaherty never had. I choose to think that this child forever growing up, affectionate but always a little detached from his elders, finding his own solitary contact with birds, beasts and trees, fishing from cliffs, capturing alligators, taming racoons, riding elephants, and paddling canoes, gave Flaherty a path to expressing a detachment from the world and a sense of innocence among the tumbling facts of life which he personally craved.

On one occasion he talked of 'the poignancy of the horizon', and perhaps it was the same thought in him. It was after *Aran*. He had felt bitterly the implied criticism of his friends that he had idealized this tough world of tough men and lost the reality of a landlord-ridden poverty to decorative horizons and artificial issues with basking — and very harmless — sharks. 'Isn't the horizon a larger reality?' he protested. And 'Why do they always want to make things shabby with their poverty, poverty, poverty?' Like Wilde, he hated the grotesque and deformed, objected to the thundering noise of *March of Time*; and I suspect that the Russian films — Dovjenko's *Earth* always excepted — troubled him more than he confessed. But this means only that he was a faithful disciple of Rousseau or, better still, that he was a Pre-Raphaelite beyond his time. He sought beauty as passionately as any, but it was not of his origin, his nature, or his habit to find it in the gutter. There the critical world split with Flaherty and not without a certain sadness; for it was those who denied him most who had learned most from him and were the first to acknowledge it.

Picture, however, the forces that were impinging on film-making in the 1920s. It was by and large a liberal world, with democracy everywhere on the move. Here was Flaherty pointing a way to the extended observation of mankind: proposing, in effect, an art which could match in its sweep not only the speeding inter-relations of peoples but man's conscience in regard to them. Here too were other voices — from Russia, Germany, and England especially — saying with equal validity: 'Beware the ends of the earth and the exotic; the drama is on your doorstep wherever the slums are, wherever there is malnutrition, wherever there is exploitation and cruelty.' 'You keep your savages in the far places, Bob; we are going after the savages of Birmingham,' I think I said to him pretty early on. And we did.

In doing so we aligned ourselves in many ways more closely with the Russian method than to Flaherty's. We borrowed from him his emphasis on the spontaneous; and something of his affection for seeing for seeing's sake crept into much of our work. But the Trotsky theory that art is 'not a mirror held up to nature, but a hammer shaping it', and John Stuart Mill's injunction that it is 'in the hands of the artist that the truth becomes a living principle of action' drove us to a certain deliberation of effort which Flaherty natively deplored. We were propagandists, not just discovering the dramatic patterns of 'actuality' in a vacuum, but of deliberation, bringing the working man to the screen, revealing the social relationships inevitable in a technological society, demonstrating the follies of · poverty in a world of plenty, and so on and so on.

Inevitably we were taken up by governments and powers and became one of the instruments of public education, public management, and — in the days of greater crises — of public persuasion, exhortation and command. Flaherty watched it all with a sense of bewilderment and no wonder; for, in fact, this other documentary school had correctly estimated its relationship with up-and-coming social democracy and was riding in on the tide. Sir Stafford Cripps put it generously — but it may be with a modicum of justice — when he said later that nothing made the new social-reform Government so certain in Britain as the work of the documentary film people in making the patterns of social justice patent to everyone.

For myself, I think the bombings helped not a little; but the point to make is that we had taken Flaherty's documentary film away from its mere contemplative origins. 'I don't like this business of looking at people as though they were in a goldfish bowl,' said one early exponent of the different view. So he went down to the East End slums of London, got to know the people pretty intimately, set up his camera and his microphone, and invited the people to 'take over the screen: it's yours'. The result was the remarkable *Housing Problems*, which revolutionized film approaches. Its maker, incidentally, was Flaherty's own pet pupil, John Taylor.

Flaherty made a handful of lovely films, all with enormous difficulty both in finance and collaboration. The documentary people who went the other way got financed by the million, established educational and propaganda services for governments all over the world, and made themselves films by the thousand. And yet and yet . . . I look at it all today and think with the gentler half of my head that Flaherty's path was right and the other wrong.

The new way became as easy and complacent as Flaherty's grew more difficult and finally distressing. In the ardent pursuit of good works, there has been overmuch accommodation to expediency. The film people have learned to be diplomats, politicians, administrators,

fixers. They have got so over-involved with technique and technicians that you would hardly know the glossy, chromium-plated,
overweighted contraptions of a documentary unit today from the
Hollywood set-up from which Flaherty revolted. Till recently, a
great number have been all too comfortable in the secure jobs and
the inevitably repetitious formulas which safety breeds. One might
almost say that the heads got fat.

Be sure something has been lost in the process. I miss the poetry,
as I miss the personal fervour of the original inspiration. I shall say
it in short by saying that I miss Flaherty. I figured it more practically
than he did, but have little comfort in the world I figured with so
much, as they barrenly put it, 'political correctness'.

I would not today take issue with Flaherty so hopefully and con-
fidently as once I did. The old boy was like a lighthouse; not much to
do with the comings and goings of the people on land, but much to do
with the more abstruse journeys of sailors. There is a fundamental in
art which is greatly concerned with such. Perhaps Flaherty's 'poignancy of the horizon', like Leopardi's 'Ode to the Moon', comes as
close as anything to expressing what most we are missing in the sick
and close-eyed days which now attend us.

(*The Reporter*, 16 October 1951)

15 · Sergei Eisenstein

I believe Eisenstein to have been the greatest master of public spectacle in the history of the cinema, and I am forgetting neither D. W. Griffith nor Cecil B. DeMille. He was a superb exponent of that tradition of collective art which is represented by the pageants of ancient Egypt, by the circuses in Rome, by the surroundings of the Roman Catholic Church, and by all the many and varied collective manifestations of faith. That he has also come to represent novelties in film technique is less important for me than his membership of an ancient theatrical tradition that was to be found once again in the work of Leni Riefenstahl, or in the Duke of Norfolk's presentation of the Coronation, or in the colossal resources of the Army, Navy and Air Force at the funeral of Winston Churchill. It was Eisenstein who could attack the Winter Palace with several hundred of the citizens of Leningrad, who could fire the first shot of the Revolution from the *Aurora* herself, who in *Battleship Potemkin* could use the Black Sea Fleet.

This was the very centre of his achievement. But he was also very much a man who reacted to all the forces of his time, and especially to the great new world of industry and technology; and in his art he sought to mirror the colossal power and resources of this world. He wanted the cinema, by its power over movement, to reflect the great industrial masses of the age, to turn film into what he called 'a demonstration of mass man'. To some extent he achieved this at the expense of human relationships, and a fault which I have more modestly shared with him is a lack of interest in people for their own sake. In Eisenstein's case he was much influenced by a phrase of his own master in the theatre, Meyerhold, who once referred to certain theatrical pieces that were all about 'worthless soul junk', and they both tried to flee from this 'junk' into what they saw as a much bigger world where simple statements were made for the masses of the people. Eisenstein proceeded to do this not only in terms of the Army, the Navy and the citizenry, but by using imaginatively the most colossal resource ever to be made available to the cinema: which is Industry itself.

Ultimately we in Britain were to deploy the smoke and sweat of industrial machinery far more than the Russians ever did, and yet Eisenstein's first influence on British art was quite unconnected with our own documentary movement. The first screening in London of *Potemkin* was to Ministers and officials from Whitehall who gathered under my auspices at the Imperial Institute, and were exposed to *Potemkin, Berlin, Earth* and all the other pictures we thought might guide them in the use of the cinema for propaganda or public information. But when these gentlemen saw *Potemkin* they were much less impressed by the documentary relationship than by the spectacle relationship, and the first man to make a practical suggestion about it was Rudyard Kipling. 'These Russians', he said, 'are doing all over again what we do so splendidly in our own country. They are making tattoos, and what we ought to be doing ourselves is making tattoos in film form.' It was Kipling who antedated my comparison with Eisenstein with the Duke of Norfolk and the Coronation by seeing him as an off-shoot of a Wembley Tattoo, and the immediate effect of *Potemkin* in Britain was not the documentary movement but a tattoo called *One Family*. It died the death of a dog, the pageantry side of *Potemkin* was forgotten and I came on to the scene very much as a substitute. But someone, in forgetting the pageantry of *Potemkin*, had remembered the battleship's thrilling engines. These engines at last came into their own, and the consequence was a little film called *Drifters*.

Now that we were in business ourselves we became aware in a very practical way of Eisenstein's genius at film editing. He was very concerned with the impact of one image on another and he expressed his attitude by arguing that 'two particulars make a concept.' Put one image together with another image and you get an idea. Take, for example, the image of some detail from a statue of the Czar outside the Winter Palace and then make an explosion from the gun of the *Aurora*. You get the boom of the gun, the smashing of the statue, and therefore the idea of the collapse of a whole regime. Eisenstein, moreover, used his images to create an explosive impact on the physical self of the spectator rather than to produce a linkage in narrative. He has to be called the master of hysteria, and I remember H. G. Wells accusing him of having an 'epileptic technique'.

He also knew, though he spoke of it less frequently, that when you put two images together you can create much more than a 'concept': you can create poetry. For me, the most moving scene in all Eisenstein's work is the sequence in *Old and New* where the peasant woman, Martha (surely the most beautiful face in film history), gets a milk separator to work. In that marvellous passage Eisenstein uses the art of montage, and the assembling of images, to express untold joy; and his achievement is pure poetry.

We were all influenced by Eisenstein's montage, but by its poetic possibilities rather than its intellectual ambition. For myself, for example, I made a mast, and I made a bird fly over the mast, and the mast seemed higher and more lonely because of the bird flying over it. If you want to know where the courage of poetry in *Song of Ceylon* came from, or the courage of poetry in *Night Mail*, then you must go for your answer to *Old and New* or to *Romance Sentimentale*. We were more deeply influenced by those later films than by the violent montage of *Potemkin* or *October*.

I've never been fond of intellectual theorizing, and we all know how a philosophy can be the product of necessity. We all know that the real reason why Eisenstein developed his films in movements, like a symphony, was that in most Russian cinemas there was only one projector, and the reels had to be changed every ten or twelve minutes. We had the same problem ourselves when we began to build up non-theatrical distribution in Britain. We felt that the existence of a single projector justified our approach to the film in terms of a series of 'movements', and later on there were schools of students who wrote in learned journals to say how clever we were.

It is equally true that one reason why Eisenstein developed the art of 'short cutting' — which was part of his 'shock' technique — was the physical shortage of film in the U.S.S.R. They were using what we call 'short ends', and they made a virtue out of necessity. Again we had a similar problem in Britain: I once found myself trying to make a masterwork out of 1,500 feet. It was all I had and I felt compelled to use every bit and piece of it, even those frames that were just blurs in the sky. The necessity comes first, then the art, and later still the theories about the art.

This practical problem of the shortage of film gradually left us all, and I personally believe that Eisenstein was most glorious, most truly himself, in his last picture, *Ivan the Terrible*. I know that it's been regarded as an artificial film with cardboard figures and pasteboard spectacle, but it remains in my memory as something not only visually memorable but vastly quiet; and when a great artist who is so full of energy — a Michelangelo, for instance — can be so quiet, he is a great artist indeed.

But it is never reasonable to discuss an artist's work without considering him in his own right as a human being, trying to relate the quality of humanity to the quality of the work. In Eisenstein this relationship has always struck me as strangely inconsistent. Superficially he was invariably good to meet, and on public occasions behaved extremely well. But he was also a man who carried within himself some deep hurt, and therefore an inability to take life's slings and arrows as easily as most of us. This capacity to be hurt, which may have had its origins in his early dependence on his beloved mother, seemed to fill his working life with a constant sequence of frustrations, and not all of them can be explained by the theory that he was an idealist who worked in a cynical society. No doubt there were terrible frustrations in his own country — disputes over *October*, the banning of *Bezhin Meadow* and the second part of *Ivan the Terrible* — but there were also frustrations nearly everywhere else. *Potemkin* was not shown in Britain until four years after completion, and there were his failures in Hollywood and Mexico.

This catalogue of personal 'hurts', both true in itself and yet in a sense somehow a deeper part of the man called Eisenstein, had two significant results. The first was that he gradually withdrew into what I would describe as a false illusion of academic intellectualism. It showed itself partly in his theorizing, the way in which he made up for his lack of popularity by producing numerous theories about all kinds of minute and unimportant aspects of his own work; and it showed itself in his curious habit of guarding all his notes, all his photographs, every drawing and every diagram, preserving and creating his reputation as ferociously as he ever made his films.

The second consequence of this sense of hurt came oddly from a citizen of the Soviet Union. He introduced something of the cult of personality which had previously been associated with the most monstrous manifestations of the moguls of Hollywood. I often suspect that when he went there himself he harboured the odd thought that he was really the biggest mogul of them all: that when he met a man who called himself 'Von' Stroheim, and another who changed from Stern or Sternberg to 'Von' Sternberg, Eisenstein wished that he also had the nerve to assume a 'von'. In those days I was helping to make documentaries, on no promises whatever, without reputation or money, working on a shoe-string, and with nothing but the hard sea-biscuits of looking from the outside at all the good things of 'show business'. It was quite a shock to find that Eisenstein, the maker of *Potemkin*, in no way shared our own disciplined outlook. I had the odd feeling that I was the puritan and he was not.

This, of course, is of a piece with my belief that his genius lay in his command of mass-spectacle rather than in any revolutionary discoveries in montage or in the theory of the cinema. I remember hearing him speak about his own techniques and noting that he didn't say much about the art of film-making — which was what most of us expected of him: instead he bragged about the enormous power he had over the movements of armies and navies and of vast crowds of people in the street. In saying this I am neither complaining nor criticizing, for the Eisenstein who spoke in that way was the Eisenstein who truly belongs to the history of art as a whole rather than to the brief history of the cinema. For the history of art is bound, sooner or later, to call back the glorious tradition of the public spectacle, and in the long story of public spectacle Eisenstein was indisputably a master.

(A statement recorded in 1970 for a B.B.C. *Omnibus* film on Eisenstein, produced by Norman Swallow)

16 · Charles Chaplin

The simple facts of Charles Chaplin's life, his *curriculum vitae*, are easily stated. He was born in the same year (1889) in which the Englishman William Friese-Greene, and Thomas Edison, the American, invented the motion-picture camera. His lifetime is exactly the lifetime of the cinema and it is just possible that he has, in fact, seen it come and go as the great instrument of universal entertainment and universal persuasion it promised to be. He might today be Louis XIV the *roi soleil* of the cinema saying '*Après moi le déluge!*'

I cannot pretend to speak with accuracy of his origins; the accounts are various and have not been helped by, shall we say, a certain diffidence on the part of Chaplin himself as regards his origins. He has said that he was born in Fontainebleau near Paris, but the generally accepted version is that he was out of the meaner streets of Kennington in South London. Incidentally, it is recorded by one of his biographers that there is no record at Somerset House in London of his birth being registered under the name of 'Charles Spencer Chaplin'. Both of his parents were strolling players of the music-hall type. His mother, Spanish and Irish, they say, was a mimic of great quality. His father, partly of French and Jewish origin, they say, was a baritone and a sort of 'Gentleman Johnny' of the halls. The father died an alcoholic. The mother died, after a long tragic life wrapped up in the irrational.

I cannot, as I say, swear to these facts, but they have been published often and it has been part of Chaplin's pride, part of his sensitivity, to leave the whole thing very confused. We begin to understand much from this simple fact. It means, of course, a desperately unhappy and desperately derelict childhood of a hungry boy in the gutters of London, of orphanages, and the condescension and the indignity that went with such a condition in the horribly divided life of London in the so-called Golden Age of Queen Victoria and Edward the Seventh. There was much of the dreadful world of Dickens to match the glittering wealth of the new industrial empire —enough certainty to create a mental image for all time in a sensitive mind and, in his own young self, as desperate and outraged a little victim of it as any in the land. He was a 'beat generation' rolled into one, from the start—and what an image he has made of it!

We all wonder about the public behaviour of Chaplin sometimes. He has called himself a social anarchist—the phrase is his—and he has certainly found it difficult at times to be the balanced figure we naïvely expect from the rich and the powerful. His private life has seemed odd at times to the outside observer. His public tantrums on the greatest public occasions have often seemed perverse. But it is interesting to note that they were never more perverse than when, at the height of his great fame, he visited his own native land. Jim Tulley—who was, like so many others, unfortunately, once a great friend of Chaplin's—said this of him: 'If Chaplin pitied the poor in the parlours of the rich it was often hurt self-interest.' Hurt self-interest instead of compassion. But think of it yourselves and with your own sense of compassion. With an image of childhood so hurt as his you must expect strange, inarticulate, unwarranted acts that reflect the doubts, the insecurity, the defensiveness, the lack of confidence in others, the ultimate disbelief even when the great people whom he never hoped to meet were at his feet. He said of his visit to Bernard Shaw that when he rang the bell he was suddenly frightened, and ran away.

Now I have read somewhere that Chaplin when he was young was a great student of Schopenhauer, and from the beginning something of a philosopher in pessimism. It makes fine reading these days for a man who came in his great days to meet Barrie and Shaw and Wells and Einstein and to refer in a public speech to his 'friend' Winston Churchill. But I think we should be much nearer the mark if we say that his formal education was scrappy and even nondescript. And I for one say that this, in the light of what he did so greatly master, was not important. He has been from the first, and because of his origin, a great, intensive bundle of sympathies for, sympathies against, and it is out of that, and that alone, that he has forged his genius. He is the greatest clown of our time and, it may be, of all time.

When I say sympathies for and sympathies against, I am saying that you mustn't think he's a warm little figure. How could he be? There's not only that youth behind him, but even when he became greatly known there was always the fight with the financiers to get what he thought he merited. At Keystone, at Essanay, at Mutual, at First National—always the haggling for his fair share. Even when he was master at United Artists he had to put out *City Lights* independently. They didn't believe in it.

Chaplin's personal experiences did not make him an easy man, and I do not wonder. And it is all reflected in the tragicomic figure whom he called 'Charlie', in the French 'Charlot', and Escarlino, and Carlos, and Carlitos. I once sat in on a conversation between Chaplin and Donald Ogden Stewart. We were talking about the logic of comedy and the exact nature of the Charlie figure. Stewart was talking about Groucho Marx and how he represented a sort of superman attitude to comedy—the superior spirit in man, not to be impressed by anything on earth. Why, he said, even in the presence of the Niagara Falls, Groucho wouldn't be impressed. He'd pull out the tie of the guide. Chaplin went on to say that that was the very opposite of his own conception of comedy; he imagined his Charlot figure to be based on the Christian conception of humility before the Lord, of the utter worth of the simple man, of the permanence of the thought that the weak would be protected and the poor would be comforted and the meek would inherit the earth.

But Chaplin was not quite right about his Charlot. He is something a lot more various and complicated than the humble little man. With his cane and moustache he aspires to *class*, as with his hat, a size too small, and the still daring of his shoulders, the desperately still daring of his shoulders, he aspires to survival and to dignity. But he is not altogether the wanderer on the face of the earth he sometimes pretends to be. He has a sharp eye for the fast buck. And even for the fast million. He may be respectability in straits, suburbia in tatters, a *petit bourgeois* Ulysses against the horizon; he may be at times the complete romantic, the dreamer, the tramp caught up in the toils of unsympathetic reality. But watch out! He is not from the gutter for nothing. He has the same blackbird cleverness of the street urchin that Cantinflas has. And you just cannot complete the image of Charlot without noting the occasional streak of envy and malice and cruelty in his make-up. You may even ponder the thought that when Chaplin made *Monsieur Verdoux* he did not abandon Charlot as much as he thought and said he did: he merely developed the angry streak in him.

Now, all this is not to diminish the figure of Charlie but to enrich it; and a very rich clown image it is—as I think, the richest in our time. It has been so powerful in its impact, it has been so universal in its appeal, it has been so much appreciated and honoured by commoner and intellectual alike, that we may well think about it a little. Certainly, if we mean to honour Chaplin, it is not because of anything he has said or directly communicated to our philosophy, and it is certainly not because of any of his odd excursions into political analysis and political sympathies; it is totally and entirely for the clown-image which he has given to our mind and imagination so richly, so warmly—and so to our experience and to our life. It is as an artist—an artist, first and last, who has only ever been able to communicate effectively and greatly in terms of art. And it is as an artist who has raised the mad world of the cinema from a mere article of commerce to an observation post on the comedy of man.

I confess I have myself always been devoted to clowns, as I have been always devoted to puppets and dolls. They simplify, but by simplifying they may go deep to the heart of human experience. I think I've seen most of the great clowns of my time, and they've all had something in common. They've all expressed something which was common to human experience. I used to admire Fridolin, the French-Canadian clown, very much and only regret I've not seen him in years. Chaplin was much interested in Fridolin, and I once took some shots of him, of one or two of his acts, simply for Chaplin to see what Fridolin looked like. The Fridolin I saw and remember was the young man just growing up, very simple but not as simple as his elders supposed, just as we all were and probably are today, and he carried as the warning image of his power the sling of David. Because you expected nothing from a simpleton so simple, his seemingly innocent comments were quite savage in their impact.

His innocence in politics was quite beautiful to behold, and not least when he talked about the Dominion of Canada. A lesson in Canadian geography from him was more brutal in its impact, as I remember it, than anything I ever read in a French-Canadian editorial. One day he slipped away from his growing-boy image. He was an advocate from St Hyacinthe or somewhere like that. He was dead, and he was speaking to God. And he was explaining why he hadn't been the great poet he was written in the book to be, like Dante and Ariosto. He was telling God, no less, just what it was like to be a provincial boy in the Province of Quebec, in the Dominion of Canada. Fridolin, as I saw him, was a true clown, speaking the accents of innocence but saying much that affected us all; and not only in Quebec, because the snobberies of provincialism are universal; even in Paris, France, and London, England.

I saw another couple of clowns in Montreal—clowns, again, in whom Chaplin was greatly interested. I asked him what was the greatest clown-act he knew. Once he said Cantinflas of Mexico City, but this time he said the Arnaut Brothers. They were white clowns. They were totally white, which, of course, is the colour of innocence and also of death; and in spite of all that whiteness the detergent people recommend to you, it is a very terrifying colour when carried to excess. The white clown was the original Pierrot, the fellow who was mocked by Harlequin, the fellow that never gets Columbine.

Poor stupid Pierrot!

Au clair de la lune,
Mon ami Pierrot;
Prête moi ta plume,
Pour écrire un mot.

With the years Pierrot grew up a bit; perhaps he never got Columbine, but he ceased to be stupid. He became a witty fellow who laughed at his misfortunes. He began to combine his tragic frustration with the idea of being smarter than the lot, and so you got the tragicomic clown, the great Deburau and Grimaldi and Dan Leno and finally Chaplin. I suppose Harry Langdon and Buster Keaton were other whites. I hope you will remember Langdon in that one phase of his, childlike in its simplicity, facing the world with his little twisted smile. Buster Keaton, with that deadpan of his, was the whole lot of us, you know, full of forbearance, suffering all things, until of course in the last act he broke loose and in the wild frenzy of the imagination commanded the world. But Harry Langdon was the simple child in all of us, the Christian Innocent.

You have it, in another mixture, in those remarkable characters Laurel and Hardy. They are not so innocent as Langdon because Langdon is never angry; he doesn't know how to be. Laurel and Hardy are very annoyed with each other, and most of the time they too are the poor incompetents, like all of us universally, who can't do anything right. Nothing on earth would please them more than a great permanence in all things, preferably in suburbia — the garden gate, the water-butt, and the window smooth on its roller, are their symbols of ease. But not a chance! There's a hiccup in the night, and the hiccup wakes the dog, and the dog wakes the landlord, and hell breaks loose, and before you know it peace and suburbia are in tatters.

And against all these white clowns, the innocents, the incompetents, the tragicomics of the world, there are their opposites. The braggadocios, the supermen, who storm their way through the world, or chisel their way through it; the bluffers, the grafters, the beyond-good-and-evil comics who like W. C. Fields will put a foot rudely on the face of a baby, on innocence itself. And that, too, is a universal image because the paradox of human nature is that it will join the one in this knowledge of innocence and incompetence and the hope of salvation, and with equal zest join the other in the defiance of either order or salvation. And mirth goes with both, because neither side of this is true without the other. We are not as innocent as Harry Langdon, though we can imagine ourselves so, and the absurdity of our being so. And we are not as bold in setting

the world on its ear as W. C. Fields, though again it is a part of ourselves taken apart, and a joy to behold in absurdity what a part of
ourselves, taken apart, could do to the peace of the community. It is
dream-life, dream-life conjured out of our nature and as dear to the
life of the imagination as anything in poetry or painting, or any
other art.

And where the Chaplin image is so rich is that he touches this life
of the fancy at more points than most, probably more than anyone.
I mentioned his origin, and how the image of the waif and the stray
grew, with a certain bitterness, from his own experience. That
touches us all, though some of course more than most. But think of
what an appeal this image of the down-and-out has meant in poorer
and more troubled days. And think again what it has meant to the
millions of poor people across the world, not yet emancipated or
with hope of emancipation. I've seen Chaplin films play to thousands
of Negroes in the African jungles, and how they took them to their
hearts! Oddly enough they had an even quicker perception of his
movements and of every development of a gag than I ever saw
evidenced by a white audience. As you know, Chaplin is such a
genius with a gag that he plays four or five or even six variations on
it, and these Negro audiences would howl their appreciation of each
move separately, exactly as the spectators in a bull-ring shout '*Olé!*'
to the separate passes of the matador.

But the waif and the stray, the poor man in a rich, cruel world, is
of course only a part of the image. Chaplin can be the strutting
millionaire too, and often is. He'll be the poor vagabond snitching a
drink from the passing waiter, but he can be as drunk as a lord, and
enjoy every split-second of it. He may pine for Columbine today, but
give him a chance and he is Lothario and Don Juan and Cassanova
and Benvenuto Cellini all rolled into one. He will solemnly take the
price of his meal from the tip left over under the plate, but just give
him the price of it and, as in *The Gold Rush*, he'll have not one fur
coat but two. Never make any mistake—ever since he skidded round
these corners with his hand holding on desperately to his hat, ever
since he learned to hook that cane around an ankle, he's left the
suspicion in all of us that he could at a pinch look after himself.
Indeed, it is Chaplin's greatest feat to have created an image of ourselves, our very own selves, that commands not only our sympathy
but our admiration. If he delights us more than others, it is in the
cunning thought he conveys of our own infinite capacity. And
behind that, of course, is his own uncanny, infinite skill as a
performer.

They said of Oliver Goldsmith that he wrote like an angel but talked like poor Paul. I think they'd better think of Chaplin in the selfsame way and forget all that odd and various business about his being a mastermind and a dangerous character. In my youth we had them all about us in Scotland—the men of infinite sympathy, the dreamers, the men who also called themselves social anarchists. They didn't believe in authority of any kind, they didn't believe in machines. Some of them didn't even believe in marriage. They especially didn't believe in Parliament, and they used to turn up at the elections with placards round their necks saying 'Abstain from voting'. Everyone has somebody like that tucked away in his family history, and they have wonderful mental relatives in people like William Blake and Prince Kropotkin and Count Tolstoy when he got old and decided the only thing on earth to do was to write parables. Certainly one of the most pleasant memories of my life has been the memory of the anarchists I have known. I even knew the man—he wasn't a social anarchist this one, he was a real one—the man who blew up the post office in Chicago in the First World War. He used to sell me gin straight from the bathtub, more or less, and he was as gentle and kind a man as I ever met. The best part of them is that they hark back hopefully to a state of innocence. They seek their Garden of Eden from which we were cast, and what is the Garden of Eden but the image in our heart and our subconscious of what we all before God might have been—an image we cannot somehow live without?

As I say, I don't take Chaplin seriously any more than I would seek out Picasso to tell me the true line of political development in France, or any more than I would have sought out Einstein to tell me the political equivalent or political implication of his world-shattering equation which, personally, I do not understand. But when it comes to Chaplin thinking with his hands, I beg you to consider that there may be a world of expression far beyond any of us, where things can be thought and said that we poor mortals cannot pretend to. There was an American clown once, called Bert Williams. I don't think the Americans ever knew how great he was. He was another suffering clown, forever tortured by the leader of the orchestra who didn't understand him. And in his moment of desperation he would get down on one knee and scream plaintively 'Oh, them bells' and 'Vive la France'. There is a point where you pass thus desperately from the world of the rational into the world of art.

Of that, Chaplin is the master. He is the greatest mime I ever saw. He says his mother taught him and in this he honours her tragic memory, but I've seen him, as so many have in private, tell stories without a word, sensational stories of when he was making *The Circus* and the great opera singer The Diva was faced with incontinent lions. And I've seen him show a film privately and invent a new character before the screen, and turn a heavy, romantic, Hollywood effort into farce. And in his films, always, not only the wonder of the mind, but the brilliance of the timing, that business of making more of a gag than anyone could think of, the infinite sense of dance in everything he did. Well, just remember for a moment that passage in *The Gold Rush* when he's so happy he bursts the pillows and he dances in a dream of eiderdown.

And all this is inspiration in action; the inspiration in action we do not have. Of course, as anyone should know, it is based on a schooling and a practice as intensive and as disciplined and as dedicated as anything we philosophical hacks and writing hacks and political hacks will ever know. See Chaplin as you would see Picasso. The one an actor, the other a painter. Supreme masters in their art. Picasso makes it look easy, as Chaplin makes it look easy. But think of all the paintings, all the pictures behind them over the years, each one an effort, each an experience, each an intensive reaching forward, vaguely, tentatively, and only sometimes triumphantly, to something vivid and just possibly lasting for the human eye. There was an odd moment in *Monsieur Verdoux*. He was counting the bank-notes. He counted them with a great flick of his right hand, you remember, and then just to show how easy it was he flicked them over even faster with his left, and you suddenly remembered that all his life Charlie had done everything superbly, whether he was a waiter or a dancer or a rollerskater or a tightrope walker, but behind the whole bag of innocent dramatic tricks there's all the trained skill of the music-hall, and the circus. When it came to his own practical trade: the mind and mastery of a surgeon. And no one has ever doubted his sharp and even diabolical powers of observation when it came to observing the foibles of his neighbours—rich and poor, he has ribbed them all, unto our bone sometimes, sadistic, delighted.

You hear wonderful things said about Chaplin by the great critics of our time. Shaw said he is the greatest genius the cinema has produced, and no film man will deny this. Mack Sennett said: 'Chaplin, he only happens to be the greatest actor that ever lived.' Robert Sherwood said: 'Chaplin is a great artist, an inspired tragedian, and everything else intellectuals say he is, but there can never be any doubt of the fact that he is fundamentally a clown. And it is when he is most broadly, vulgarly, crudely funny that he approaches true genius.' And Menken said, simply enough, when they were trying to burn him at the stake—remember?—that they were all morons and would never see his like again.

What I say is that this man Chaplin was made in odd and differing parts as so many of us are. His great and world-wide success has made the light of public observation, public opinion, bear down on him more intensively than a poor actor may easily sustain. He has tried honestly and honourably enough to be a public figure, but beyond his training and beyond his power to justify. And what would so easily be forgiven in most of us has not been forgiven in him because of the light that shone on him. We the public give ourselves omnipotent power to give but also to take away and we make unhappy the very idols we ourselves have created. We have done that with Chaplin.

For what is his fault? He has given us the greatest, the most universal, the most intimate image of our common humanity we have had in the mass media in our time. He has honoured the cinema as nothing else has honoured it. He has given us almost the only assurance that the cinema can be, apart from all that commercial falderal, a great spiritual medium. I talked last night with a man in a saloon, and I said I was going to say something about Chaplin today. I always listen to the Jewish fellows who know Shalom Aleichem because they have wisdom. He said, 'You can't be a genius in everything. So you're a genius! Who complains if you're a damn fool in something else. What's wrong?' He said, 'They don't have a sense of discrimination any more. Let's not be stupid.' I shall be very simple about it. I would sooner see a great Chaplin film than sit in on any committee at Geneva, and I have done both. I would learn more about the philosophy of human need, and it would certainly be funnier in the learning. I'd know that, in spite of everything, the life of art and the spirit is greater than all. The life of art and the spirit is greater than all, and so great that all is diminished before it, and that's a thing we all know whether we are looking at our men or our women or our children or our friends. I said Chaplin is politically naïve. Let me just read to you the speech he read in *The Great Dictator* when the little man with the little moustache took over from Hitler, that other little man with a little moustache, and think of the difference. Naïve it may be, but I cannot for the world think that you or I could ever deny what he is trying to say.

'I am sorry, but I don't want to be an emperor. That's not my business. I don't want to rule or to conquer anyone. I should like to help everyone if possible. Jew and Gentile, black, white, we should all work to help one another. Human beings are like that. We want to live by each other's happiness, not by each other's misery. We don't want to hate and despise one another. In this world there is room for everyone. And the good earth is rich and could provide for everyone. The way of life could be free and beautiful, but we have lost the way. Greed has poisoned men's souls, has barricaded the world with hate, it has goose-stepped us into misery and bloodshed. We have developed speed but we have shut ourselves in. Machinery that gives abundance has left us in want. Our knowledge has made us cynical. Our cleverness, hard and unkind. We *think* too much, and feel too little. More than machinery we need humanity. More than cleverness, we need kindness and gentleness. Without these qualities life would be violent, and all would be lost. Count your blessings. Count them one by one.'

And one is Chaplin.

(A talk in the 'Architects of Modern Thought' series for the Canadian Broadcasting Corporation, November 1958)

Index